Computer Science and Educational Software Design

Pierre Tchounikine

Computer Science and Educational Software Design

A Resource for Multidisciplinary Work in Technology Enhanced Learning

Springer

Pierre Tchounikine
University Grenoble 1
LIG
rue de la Houille Blanche 961
38402 Grenoble
France
Pierre.Tchounikine@imag.fr

ACM Codes: K.3, H.4

ISBN 978-3-642-20002-1   e-ISBN 978-3-642-20003-8
DOI 10.1007/978-3-642-20003-8
Springer Heidelberg Dordrecht London New York

Library of Congress Control Number: 2011932213

© Springer-Verlag Berlin Heidelberg 2011
This work is subject to copyright. All rights are reserved, whether the whole or part of the material is concerned, specifically the rights of translation, reprinting, reuse of illustrations, recitation, broadcasting, reproduction on microfilm or in any other way, and storage in data banks. Duplication of this publication or parts thereof is permitted only under the provisions of the German Copyright Law of September 9, 1965, in its current version, and permission for use must always be obtained from Springer. Violations are liable to prosecution under the German Copyright Law.
The use of general descriptive names, registered names, trademarks, etc. in this publication does not imply, even in the absence of a specific statement, that such names are exempt from the relevant protective laws and regulations and therefore free for general use.

Cover design: deblik

Printed on acid-free paper

Springer is part of Springer Science+Business Media (www.springer.com)

Preface

Object

This book is about *educational software*, i.e., software designed as a means to implement *computer-based pedagogical settings* and contribute to the addressing of some pedagogical objectives.

The focus is on the issues related to the design of software in reference to pedagogical settings. Design refers here to building new software and/or articulating software components (e.g., ICT-based educational software).

Audience

This book is for actors engaged in research or development projects that require inventing, designing, adapting, implementing or analyzing educational software and related issues.

The core audience comprises Masters students, Ph.D. students, researchers and engineers from Computer Science and Human and Social Sciences (e.g., education, psychology, pedagogy, philosophy, communication or sociology) interested in the issues raised by educational software design and analysis, and the variety of perspectives that may be adopted.

This book may also be of interest for teachers engaged in, for example, the development of ICT-based innovations.

Rationale

Considering computer-based pedagogical settings requires thinking, problematizing, representing, modeling, implementing or analyzing objectives, issues, models and/or software. This cannot be addressed by separating educational concerns on one side and Computer Science concerns on another: effective multidisciplinary work is required.

Such multidisciplinary work requires actors from different disciplines, but also with different matters of concern, to understand each others' perspectives and build shared constructions.

Technologists and computer scientists face the difficultly of understanding the particular issues and phenomena to be taken into account in educational software projects, and avoiding falling into a naïve techno-centered perspective. Actors whose background is in Human and Social Sciences, and teachers, face the difficulty of understanding software design issues and what must be considered when designing, adapting or analyzing software, and how computer scientists may engage in these tasks. All actors share the difficulty of understanding how to relate software dimensions and educational issues, in a context within which both technologies and learning theories evolve, and a field that is to a large extent an experimental field. As a consequence, many misunderstandings develop, and effective multidisciplinary work is an issue. Misunderstandings also develop within disciplines, in relation to the variety of perspectives or matters of concern that may develop.

The above-mentioned difficulties arise in both development projects (building a particular system for a particular context) and research projects. They are a central issue for knowledge capitalization, i.e., developing knowledge, providing bases for design, and avoiding that every new wave of technology leads to more or less to the same bunch of high expectations, disappointments and errors.

These difficulties cannot be solved by building a kind of "general theory" or "general engineering methodology" to be adopted by all actors for all projects: educational software projects may correspond to very different realities. They may be conducted within very different perspectives and with very different matters of concern. The issue of understanding each others' perspectives and elaborating some common ground must be considered in context, within the considered project or perspective.

Objective

This book addresses the objective of providing actors considering educational software issues (computer scientists and educationalists) with means for *thinking* the relationships between pedagogical settings and software and working together in a multidisciplinary way, in particular when constructing educational software.

This objective is addressed within the perspective of providing a substratum for actors to understand each other's perspectives and elaborate common ground. It is meant to provide a resource for conducting the context-dependent work of building, refining or confirming the adopted common ground, definitions, tools, strategies, etc.

Adopted Perspective

The adopted perspective is *software-design oriented*, *transdisciplinary*, *conceptual* and *pragmatic*:

1. It is *software-design oriented* in the sense that it focuses on the dimensions related to software design and software properties (which will be referred to as

educational software engineering), and not on general considerations related to software in education. In this book, Computer Science refers to software design issues (and not to mathematical foundations or to low-level technical considerations such as programming languages or technical frameworks).
2. It is *transdisciplinary* in the sense that it addresses educational software from the perspective of a given dimension (design) and not from a disciplinary perspective. This leads one to consider notions that appear useful when considering design or analysis issues in a way that transcends boundaries of conventional academic disciplines, as opposed to a projection of educational issues onto a technical plan. For instance, the notion of *computer-based pedagogical setting* is not addressed in general, but in a way that makes salient dimensions and issues related to software design, which leads one to consider specific correlated notions such as that of *software pedagogical rationale*.
3. It is *conceptual* in the sense that emphasis is on proposing means for thinking and problematizing, which may be used for conducting different types of work, and not on proposing a methodology or a set of guidelines. Similarly, implementation is addressed in terms of approaches, not going into technical considerations.
4. It is *pragmatic* in the sense that the underlying intention is to help with thinking, designing, constructing or analyzing systems in research and development projects.

The adopted perspective complements more general perspectives such as understanding how technology may be used in educational settings or how educational practices may be changed, and narrower perspectives such as studying how to build a particular type of system (e.g., Intelligent Tutoring Systems or networked learning environments) or how to best use some given technology (e.g., Artificial Intelligence or networks).

Content

Altogether, this book's content is:

1. A highlight of the fact that what is referred to by the "design of educational software" may be subject to very different perspectives, and the importance of making explicit matters of concern.
2. A general conceptualization that helps in disentangling issues and clarifying matters of concern.
3. A set of items that help in characterizing (a) the way the pedagogical setting is considered and (b) the software properties and construction processes.
4. A set of methodological considerations.
5. A perspective on the field anchored in an engineering approach, and propositions related to how to push the field forward.
6. Different examples illustrating issues and propositions.

Although this book addresses the field in a transversal way and does not describe a particular methodology, its content has heuristic value for conducting development projects.

Structure

In this book we introduce a design-oriented conceptualization, i.e., a set of notions and definitions making salient features of importance given design matters of concern. However, introducing definitions for core notions only makes sense within a general perspective, whose introduction requires reference to these notions. There is a bootstrap issue.

In order to deal with this issue, Chap. 1 introduces a general picture, which allows explanation of the rationale for the book's content and structure. The different elements addressed in this introductory chapter, and others, are further defined and explored in the following chapters.

A side effect of the adopted plan is that considerations introduced at some place may be better understood later on. While the book allows linear reading, deeper understanding of its content requires re-reading.

Acknowledgments

Considerations addressed in this book have been discussed with many persons (Masters students, Ph.D. students, researchers and engineers from different disciplines), in many contexts (research and development projects, theoretical work, European Networks for Excellence, international workshops and conferences), and over many years. Tracing all influences would be rather difficult. I would like to mention the colleagues who reviewed in detail previous versions of this text, which for some of them is indeed far from their comfort zone, and thank them for their help in completing and clarifying ideas and propositions: Chris Jones, Ton de Jong, André Tricot and Luc Trouche. Special thanks to Ton.

> *And the computer scientist said: "How is it possible that this guy doesn't understand how smart and pedagogically useful my system is?"*
> *And the educationalist said: "What a brilliant technical solution! Now, what's the problem?"*

April 2011   Pierre Tchounikine

Contents

1	**Introduction**	1
	1 General Picture	2
	1.1 Technology Enhanced Learning	2
	1.2 TEL and CS Technical Artifacts	3
	1.3 Educational Software	4
	1.4 Computer-Based Pedagogical Settings (CBPSs)	5
	1.5 Non-definitional Character of Software	7
	1.6 Summary	8
	2 Examples	8
	2.1 Examples of Computer-Based Pedagogical Settings (CBPSs)	8
	2.2 Examples of Educational Software	11
	3 Design of Educational Software: Different Realities	15
	3.1 Designing and Implementing New Software	15
	3.2 Articulating and/or Customizing Software Components	16
	3.3 Education and CS Interplays	17
	4 Addressing Educational Software Design	18
	4.1 Considering Software Properties	18
	4.2 Making Explicit Matters of Concern and Perspectives	19
	4.3 Importance of Explicitness	22
	4.4 Difficulty and Limits of Explicitness	23
	5 Content and Structure of the Book	25
	5.1 Objective	25
	5.2 Content Synthesis	26
	5.3 Rationale for the Organization	26
	5.4 General Comments	28
2	**A General Conceptualization for Educational Software**	31
	1 Reference Educational Notions	32
	1.1 Pedagogical Setting	32

	1.2 Teaching Setting	33
	1.3 Activity	35
	1.4 Pedagogical Objective	37
	1.5 Pedagogical Setting Design	39
2	Educational Software Notions	40
	2.1 Computer-Based Pedagogical Setting (CBPS)	40
	2.2 Educational Software	41
	2.3 Pedagogical-Setting Support Software	45
	2.4 Software Pedagogical Rationale (SPR)	45
	2.5 The Technology Enhanced Learning Field (TEL)	47
3	Important Dimensions and Issues Put to the Fore	48
	3.1 Disentangling Pedagogical Objectives	48
	3.2 Analyzing the SPR/CBPS Relationships	52
	3.3 Synthesis of the Introduced Dissociations	55

3 Understanding Differences in Perspectives ... 57

1	Notions and Definitions	57
	1.1 Examples	58
	1.2 Discussion	59
2	Nature of the Setting Analysis: An Example	60
	2.1 A General and a Domain-Specific Analysis	61
	2.2 Differences and Implications	62
	2.3 Conclusions	64
3	Acknowledgement of Influential Factors: Examples	65
	3.1 Impact of Software	65
	3.2 Software Usage and Socio-technical Dimensions of the Field	67
	3.3 Diagnosing Learners' Activity	69
4	Acknowledgement of Activity-Related Uncertainties	70
	4.1 Uncertainties Related to the Effectively Considered Task	71
	4.2 Uncertainties Related to the Effective Use of Technology	72
	4.3 Acknowledgement and Possible Implications for Design	74
	4.4 Conclusions	76
5	Disciplinary Dimensions	76
	5.1 Mono-disciplinary Work	77
	5.2 Clarifying the X-Disciplinary Dimensions of Projects	78
	5.3 Conclusions	79
6	Conclusions	79

4 Review of Prototypical Examples ... 83

1	*GeLMS*, the Generic Learning Management System	83
2	*Phys-edit*, the Physics Modeling Editor	86
3	*Argue-chat*, the Argumentation Chat Tool	87

	4	*Colab-edit*, the Collaborative Editor Environment	88
	5	*Bio-sim*, the Inquiry Setting Environment	90
	6	*JavIT*, the Java Programming Intelligent Tutoring System	91
	7	*Scen-play*, the Generic Scenario Player	93
	8	*Colab-solver*, the Collaborative Problem-Solving Environment	94
	9	*Geo-world*, the Mathematics Graphical Microworld	95
	10	Discussion	96

5 CS Perspectives and TEL 99
1 Roles of Computer Science in TEL 100
  1.1 Creating Novel Possibilities for Supporting
      Human Activities 100
  1.2 Elaborating Powerful Abstractions 101
  1.3 Implementing Specified Models and Processes
      on Computers 103
2 Engagement of Computer Scientists 103
  2.1 TEL as a Place for Clever CS Applications 104
  2.2 TEL as a Field Where Some CS Problems Arise 107
  2.3 TEL as a Proper Field 108
3 Conclusions 109

6 Educational Software Engineering 111
1 Engineering and Research 111
2 Educational Software Engineering as a Scientific Field 112
  2.1 Educational Software as Complex Artificial Objects 112
  2.2 Definition and Matters of Concern 113
  2.3 Transversal Efforts to Clarify Issues 114
  2.4 Specific Efforts to Build Engineering Methodologies 115
  2.5 Conducting Projects as Vectors for Knowledge
      Development 117
3 Reconsidering the CS-TEL Relationship 118
  3.1 Educational Software Engineering and Research 118
  3.2 Educational Software Engineering and CS Research 119
4 Conclusions 122

7 Characterizing the Design Context and the Software Artifact 123
1 Introduction 124
2 Characterizing the Design Context 126
  2.1 Research/Development Nature of the Work 126
  2.2 Theoretical Background 128
  2.3 Nature of the Targeted Outcome 130
  2.4 Rationale for Designing Software 132
  2.5 How Software Is Considered Within the CBPS 133
  2.6 Design Approach 135

		2.7 Actors Concerned	137
		2.8 Context and Historical Dimensions of the Project	138
	3	Characterizing the Software Artifact	139
		3.1 Level of Analysis of Software Properties	139
		3.2 Actions Considered at the Level of Software	139
		3.3 Reification of the Pedagogical Intention in Software	140
		3.4 Nature of the CS Treatments	141
		3.5 Level of Achievement	143
	4	Examples	143
		4.1 *GeLMS-4*, the Generic Learning Management System	144
		4.2 *JavIT*, the Java Programming Intelligent Tutoring System	146
	5	Conclusions	148
8	**Methodological Considerations**		151
	1	Clarifying Concerns	151
	2	Dealing with Complexity and Models	152
		2.1 Multiplicity of Models	152
		2.2 Foundations of Models	153
		2.3 Traceability of Models	154
	3	Making the SPR Explicit	155
	4	Considering Activity and Indirect Design	158
	5	Developing Knowledge	160
		5.1 Definition of Issues	160
		5.2 Definition of Results	162
		5.3 Evaluation of Results	163
9	**Conclusions**		165
	1	Educational Software Design and Evolution of Technologies	165
	2	Lack of Knowledge Capitalization	167
	3	Pushing Forward Educational Software Engineering	170
		3.1 Conditions for Capitalizing Knowledge	171
		3.2 Review of Possible Focuses	173
		3.3 Analysis of the Different Perspectives	176
		3.4 Conclusions	177
Index			179

List of Abbreviations

AI	Artificial Intelligence
CBPS	Computer Based Pedagogical Setting
CS	Computer Science
CSCL	Computer-Supported Collaborative Learning
HCI	Human-Computer Interface
ICT	Information and Communication Technologies
ITS	Intelligent Tutoring System
LMS	Learning Management System
SPR	Software Pedagogical Rationale
TEL	Technology Enhanced Learning

Chapter 1
Introduction

Abstract This chapter introduces an educational software oriented perspective of the Technology Enhanced Learning field, this book's motivations and objectives, and a first general overview of its content and structure.

This book is about educational software, i.e., software designed as a means to implement computer-based pedagogical settings and contribute to addressing some pedagogical objectives.

Design of educational software consists of imagining, thinking, elaborating and describing a computer-based system with respect to some pedagogical objectives and to the different educational constraints to be taken into account in relation to the setting within which the software will be used. The output is an understanding of the software to be implemented, i.e., what is to be made operational on the computer by programming. This programming technical phase may be conducted from scratch or build on existing software components.

Design of educational software may correspond to very different realities such as inventing and implementing new software or analyzing how to aggregate and/or adapt existing components according to objectives and constraints, as when using Information and Communication Technologies (ICT) to build ICT-based systems (see Sect. 3). It may be conducted in relation to different rationales, such as the implementation of a particular pedagogical setting (which consists of considering different issues from which software) or the elaboration of software whose existence will allow implementation of some given type of settings (e.g., software meant to support on-line collaborative problem solving). It may arise in different contexts such as a development project and/or a research project,[1] as a means for studying some research question or exploring some innovation. It may be based on

---

[1] We will use the term *development project* for projects whose only goal is to produce an outcome (a system, a software component) to be used in effective settings, by contrast to *research projects* which are projects seeking to produce research advances. As we will argue in Chap. 6, development and research projects are not mutually exclusive.

different entry points such as a learning theory or the specific features of an emergent technology.

In this book, we explore a transversal issue: providing computer scientists and educationalists with means to address together the relationships between pedagogical settings and software, in particular when considering the design or adaptation of software for some targeted pedagogical settings.

As a way to provide a background for understanding this book's rationale, content and organization (described in Sect. 5), this introductory chapter's structure is as follows. First, we propose a general picture of the Technology Enhanced Learning field or, more precisely, an educational software oriented perspective of this field. In particular, we introduce the core notions of educational software and computer-based pedagogical setting (Sect. 1) and illustrate them by examples (Sect. 2). We then highlight that designing software with respect to educational concerns may correspond to different realities and different education/Computer Science[2] interplays (Sect. 3). This puts to the fore a central issue, that of making explicit matters of concerns and perspectives (Sect. 4). The different elements addressed in these different sub-sections will be further defined and explored in the following chapters.

1 General Picture

1.1 Technology Enhanced Learning

Educational software concerns take place within a more general field that we will call Technology Enhanced Learning (TEL). Other terms convey similar meanings such as E-learning, Learning Technology, Computer Assisted Instruction, On-line Learning, Computer-Based Learning or Computer-Based Teaching. Using one or another of these terms may contextually denote a particular perspective such as when emphasizing the *on-line* or the *teaching* dimensions.

TEL is an arena where different disciplines such as Computer Science (CS), education, psychology, philosophy, communication or sociology intersect. We will refer to actors as *computer scientists* and (when unambiguous) *educationalists* as a generic term for Human and Social Sciences actors. An actor may act as both a computer scientist and an educationalist when competent in both areas.

Considering educational software design corresponds to a specific matter of concern in TEL, and not to a subfield. As a complex field within which different types of issues are to be considered, TEL is to be addressed within different

---

[2]In recent years, the term *Computer Science* has in some places been supplanted by the term *Informatics*, a term giving more importance to the human and social aspect of computer systems design, usage and evaluation. However, we will stick to the term Computer Science, which is widely accepted (the term Informatics is subject to different interpretations whose discussion is not a matter of concern in this book). In this book, Computer Science refers to software design and implementation issues, and not to mathematical foundations of computing.

perspectives. These perspectives are not only related to disciplinary issues and interplay of disciplines: they also lie in the adopted focus or matters of interest. For instance, how learning mechanisms may be enhanced by technology, how basic educational practices may be changed, or how to design educational software for some given pedagogical setting, correspond to different issues. They require consideration of different types of objects and features, but also lead to consideration of common objects addressed within different perspectives and different matters of concern (e.g., the notion of computer-based pedagogical setting or the analysis of software usage).

Considering notions such as *pedagogical setting* or *educational software* requires introducing precise definitions. However, definitions encompassing multiple perspectives are usually rather general. As a consequence, they provide little guidance and, more importantly, may create confusions or misunderstandings when one skips from a general discourse to precise considerations. In order to deal with this issue we will introduce working definitions, i.e., definitions making salient dimensions that are of interest given the considered topics and intentions. Such definitions introduce a conceptualization[3] of the field that is adapted to the considered matters of concern. It corresponds to just one view, to be complemented by others.

1.2 TEL and CS Technical Artifacts

With respect to computer-based technology, TEL systems may be based on software and/or hardware. As examples of hardware applications: gestural knowledge may be addressed with virtual reality systems embedding haptic devices; mobile technologies may be used for implementing in-the-wild learning settings; etc.

In this book, we consider software design issues. To a large extent, software and hardware raise similar design issues, and thus this book's content is also of interest when considering hardware. Hardware-specific issues, however, will not be addressed here.

Implementing software (we will also use the terms "computer-based systems" – systems for short – or "programs") is the technical task of making software operational. This is not to be confused with implementing a pedagogical setting, which consists of considering different issues (the context, the actors, the timing, etc.) from which software to use.

The use of software in TEL is strongly connected to both the evolution of technology and the evolution of learning and teaching theories. Seen from the point of view of the technology push, the advancement of CS continuously opens up new possibilities, providing ideas and means for innovative software and innovative pedagogical settings. The history of educational systems (and current trends) can be correlated to the history of CS concepts and techniques: algorithmic, hypertext and hypermedia, Artificial Intelligence, network and communication

---

[3]A *conceptualization* is a differential system of notions.

means or, more recently, mobile technologies. Seen from the point of view of learning sciences, the advancement of technology allows implementation of teaching or learning theories (and raises new questions). For instance inquiry learning, as such, has nothing to do with computers, and may be implemented in classrooms with no technology. However, the advance of CS technologies and the way they allow one to build simulations, to offer learners dedicated cognitive tools or to create means for collaboration allow changes in the way inquiry learning (on-line and in-presence) can be addressed.

1.3 Educational Software

Software used in TEL may be existing software incidentally used in a pedagogical context or software *designed for* educational purposes.

We will refer to software used in a pedagogical context whilst not having been designed according to any educational considerations as *basic software*. As examples: a basic chat tool may be used to allow a group of learners to engage in a collaborative task; a spreadsheet may allow implementation of a powerful simulation if its properties (symbolic formulas, automated calculus, graphical representations) appear pertinent for the considered pedagogical objectives; etc. "Basic" software may of course be complex, e.g., a virtual reality environment.

In contrast with basic software, we will define educational software as software *designed for* educational purposes (a more precise definition will be introduced in Chap. 2). The "design for" dimension puts to the fore the existence of relationships (intentions, expectations, hypotheses, etc.) between pedagogical objectives (and, more generally, pedagogical considerations), design decisions, software properties and ways learners use software.

Designing software for educational purposes leads to taking into account, at design time, educational considerations. This may consist in basing software design on specific educational conceptualizations or models. For instance, let us consider a piece of software meant to implement some given type of calculus that learners need to use while solving some type of problem: the way software is thought of and, in particular, the definition of the software role, may be addressed within a more general analysis of the setting and a model or theory of how learners develop knowledge when solving such problems. As a result, the software specification will be influenced by pedagogical considerations. In addition, software may also present specific educational-related functions or properties. For instance, software may embed knowledge related to the learning domain, implement teaching mechanisms or support learners in a way that is supposed to contribute to the addressing of pedagogical objectives.[4]

---

[4]To further examine the point that pedagogical principles may be embedded in software or only impact software design see Baker, M. (2000). The roles of models in Artificial Intelligence and Education research: a prospective view. *International Journal of Artificial Intelligence in Education*, 11(2), 122–143.

When considering the implementation of a given pedagogical setting or type of setting, if some more or less adequate basic software exists, designing educational software is just one option. When emphasis is on addressing the considered pedagogical objectives, whether the software used has been designed according to pedagogical considerations is not a matter of concern. Basic software may be appropriate to a given setting, or even if not particularly appropriate, may correspond to the most efficient solution for some other reasons such as its freeness, its availability or the fact learners are used to it.

Designing educational software is a requirement when no satisfactory basic software is available. This may be related to the fact specific functions (e.g., tutoring capabilities) or properties (e.g., the way a simulation may act as a cognitive tool or the way communication tools may support learners' collaboration) are required to allow the implementation of the considered pedagogical setting, are expected to increase learning outcomes and/or to allow the addressing of some other objectives.

The dichotomy basic/educational software is based on whether design takes into account some pedagogical dimensions, and thus puts to the fore the issues such a design may raise. It does not implicitly suggest basic software should not be used to implement pedagogical settings or that settings implemented with software designed according to educational concerns necessarily lead to better learning outcomes than if implemented with basic software (as will be discussed, software properties are just one dimension of why and how software is used).

1.4 Computer-Based Pedagogical Settings (CBPSs)

Nothing is "pedagogical" as such: almost any artifact may present some pedagogical interest and virtues in some given context, and software that has demonstrated virtues in some context may be completely inadequate in another one, or under different conditions. The core issue is not that of the software properties but what happens, i.e., the way settings unfold and, with respect to software, the way learners use it, and how this relates to the pedagogical objectives.

Design of educational software or analysis of educational/basic software pedagogical interests or impacts must therefore be addressed with respect to more or less precise settings or types of settings.

When designing educational software, the prototypical case is that of institutional settings taking place within some curriculum. Designing software for informal learning, however, also requires some definition of the type of setting considered (e.g., designing software that contextually helps users to draw connections between an experience they face in the context of their professional practice and some knowledge repository). Of course, the settings within which software is effectively used, and the way software is used, may differ from what it was defined for (and the implications of this may be part of the software specification, for instance targeting tailorable[5] software). However, design is never addressed without some anticipated uses and contexts of use in mind.

Considering educational software puts to the fore the notion of *Computer-Based Pedagogical Setting* (CBPS), which may be defined as a pedagogical setting involving some software that is meant to play a role in relation to the considered pedagogical objectives. When designing educational software, the scope to be considered is not restricted to that of the software but, more generally, the context within which the software is supposed to be used. The CBPS is an essential dimension of this context. In formal settings, another important dimension is the teaching setting, i.e., the different institutional, human and material features forming the context within which the CBPS takes place. More generally, different types of dimension may require consideration (e.g., sociological or cultural) and, of course, in some projects, actors' individual characteristics.

When designing or analyzing CBPSs matters of concern and, in particular, considered pedagogical objectives, may correspond to very different realities. Accordingly, software role may relate to very different features. As examples of the variety of possible concerns, software design may be addressed in relation to whether:

- Learners are provided with resources (e.g., content resources or communication means).
- Learners become familiar with an issue or a type of problem.
- Learners engage in some activity (e.g., problem solving or argumentation).
- Learners practice some domain-specific skills (e.g., addition of fractions) or meta-level competences (e.g., synthesis or learning-to-learn).
- Learners challenge their current knowledge.
- Learners acquire some target knowledge or develop some skills.
- Teachers[6] are supported (e.g., provision of automatic tutoring means that help teachers in supervising learners' actions).
- A setting can be organized in a way that fits with the institutional constraints.
- Etc.

This list (far from being exhaustive) illustrates that concerns may be very different, may relate to different notions and levels of granularity, and are generally intertwined. For instance, considering whether software provides access to content resources is different from considering whether learners will learn from these resources, although this is probably the rationale for providing this access. Considering whether learners *practice* some skills is different from considering whether they *develop* their skills, etc. We will come back on the importance of disentangling objectives in Chap. 2, Sect. 3.1, in particular for evaluation issues.

---

[5]A computer-based system is said to be *tailorable* if it provides its users with integrated support for modifying it in the context of its use. For an analysis of different tailoring techniques see for example: Morch, A. (1997). Three Levels of End-user Tailoring: Customization, Integration, and Extension. In: Kyng, M. & Mathiassen L. (Eds.) Computers and Design in Context (pp 51–76). Cambridge, the MIT Press.

[6]When unambiguous, the term *teacher* will be used in a generic way for *teacher, tutor, facilitator, pedagogical engineer*, etc.

1.5 Non-definitional Character of Software

Independently of whether software has been designed for a pedagogical setting, software is not *definitional* of this setting.

Pedagogical settings are socio-technical systems, they involve humans and artifacts (the setting as such, the more general institutional, human and material features within which this setting takes place, the resources offered to learners and teachers, etc.). Software may be meant to play (or appear to play) a more or less structuring role according to the setting and/or the type of considered software. However, software does not determine what will happen.

As an example, let us consider the way the role of (1) an Intelligent Tutoring System (ITS) and (2) a chat or a forum meant to be part of a set of basic tools offered in a network learning context may be thought of.

The basic principle of ITSs is to introduce a task to be addressed (e.g., a mathematics problem to be solved), a set of specific tools for achieving the task (e.g., an editor allowing learners to emphasize the different problem-solving steps and logical connections) and individualized tutoring based on the analysis and interpretation of learners' actions and output (correction, help, explanations, adaptation of the task to be addressed, etc.).

Networked learning settings are settings in which network technology is "... used to promote connections between one learner and other learners, between learners and tutors; between a learning community and its learning resources".[7] Such settings may for example be implemented with Learning Management Systems (LMSs), i.e., Web-based platforms offering general means such as generic communication tools (chat, forum) or file exchange zones.

When learners solve a problem with an ITS, the system makes salient some notions, imposes some actions, provides some hints, etc. The system plays a proactive role and, in some sense, orchestrates the setting. Its properties are designed to (and are likely to) have an important impact on what happens and how.

Differently, let us consider a group of on-line learners asked to collectively write a document via an LMS. The major definitional features are likely to be the task at hand and the way it is introduced by the teacher, the individuals' and the group's experiences of on-line collaboration or the different roles learners' adopt. The specific features of the LMS communication tools, if any, are not necessarily important matters of concern.

The way these two types of systems are thought of, their expected role or the expected impact of the software properties are thus very different. However, in both cases, it would be misleading to think that the software used defines the setting and defines what happens. Fundamentally, software is only a mediator (and just one mediator) of learners' activity, and learners' activity is something that will

---

[7]Jones, C., Asensio, M., & Goodyear, P. (2000). Networked learning in higher education: practitioners' perspectives. *ALT-J, The Association for Learning Technology Journal*, 8(2), 18–28.

contextually emerge and dynamically evolve in relation with many dimensions of which software is only one factor.

As an element of the setting, software has some impact, in any case ("neutral software" in an oxymoron). An ITS's and an LMS's expected roles and structuring impact are very different. However, whether the software has features that have been designed to structure the setting and learners' activity in one way or another does not guarantee this will happen. The setting may unfold very differently from what was expected. We will come back to this "impact" notion in Chap. 3.

1.6 Summary

Within an educational software design perspective, TEL may be defined as the scientific field addressing CBPSs and the software used for implementing these settings. This view conveys the following ideas:

1. What is considered is the use of a specific technology (software, i.e., programs to be run) as a means to contribute to the addressing of some pedagogical objectives and, as an overall objective, to enhance learning.
2. The educational considerations are defined with respect to CBPSs or types of CBPSs.
3. Within a CBPS, the software role may correspond to different realities, and may relate to a variety of pedagogical objectives.
4. When addressing the TEL field in general, the considered software may be educational software (i.e. software designed for educational purposes) or basic software (i.e., software not designed for educational purposes but used in educational settings).
5. Software may participate in the definition and structure of the setting to different extents, and in different ways.
6. Software is not to be thought of as prescriptive of how the setting will unfold.

At the very core of the educational software notion is the consideration of how to *design* software that presents functions or properties studied according to educational considerations.

2 Examples

2.1 Examples of Computer-Based Pedagogical Settings (CBPSs)

We introduce hereafter three different examples of CBPSs, based on different types of software and different ways of considering software: the *Java programming*, the *biology inquiry learning* and the *learning theories forum* CBPSs. These examples are only superficially sketched to introduce the concept; they will be reused later on. An effective description would require going into details and addressing many other issues (teaching setting, etc.).

2.1.1 The Java Programming CBPS

The *Java programming* CBPS is typical of a tutoring setting, i.e., a setting within which software analyzes learners' actions and provides tutoring feedback.

The addressed pedagogical objective is that learners should develop some knowledge related to object-oriented design and programming, using as a means the Java programming language.[8]

The setting is individual. Learners are asked to consider a task that consists of a set of exercises, each exercise corresponding to the creation of a Java program according to some given specification.

Within this context, software is thought of as a means to (1) allow learners to build and edit their solution and (2) support them by providing individualized hints.

2.1.2 The Biology Inquiry Learning CBPS

The *biology inquiry learning* CBPS is an inquiry learning setting, i.e., a setting based on "(...) an approach to learning that involves a process of exploring the natural or material world, and that leads to asking questions, making discoveries, and rigorously testing those discoveries in the search for new understanding".[9]

The addressed pedagogical objective is that learners should develop skills related to experimental methods and become able to engage themselves in processes within which they identify interesting questions, define different hypotheses, test these hypotheses and draw rational conclusions. For this purpose, a given application domain in biology is used.

The setting is collective: learners collaborate in front of the software (i.e., two learners use the same computer) and/or via the software (i.e., an individual or a group of two learners sharing a computer may collaborate with another group via communication tools and shared access to some of the software features). Learners are asked to consider a task that consists of building and describing a model (and underlying theoretical elements) to explain the way cells react when immerged in a given salty liquid. It is expected that working collaboratively helps them elaborate and discuss different hypotheses.

---

[8]*Object-oriented* is an approach to design and implementation of software within which focus is on defining *classes* (which allow creating *objects*) and the relationships between these classes (e.g., *inheritance*). *Java* is an object-oriented language.

[9]de Jong, T. (2006). Computer simulations – Technological advances in inquiry learning. *Science*, 312, 532–533.

Within this context, software is thought of as a means to (1) offer a computer-based simulation that simulates the cell behavior and allows testing of hypotheses, and (2) offer collaboration tools.

2.1.3 The Learning Theories Forum CBPS

The *learning theories forum* CBPS is a networked learning setting promoting connections between learners on the basis of an LMS.

The addressed pedagogical objective is that learners should develop some general understanding of a set of learning theories from the behaviorist and cognitivist paradigms, and practice argumentation skills.

The setting is collective. Learners are asked to consider a task that consists of developing a scientific discussion related to the differences and similarities of explanations these theories provide for a topic (e.g., "how learners learn" or "how skills developed in formal teaching may transfer to real-life problem-solving"). The task is broken down into different subtasks (e.g., gathering and structuring some data related to one or the other theory, identifying key concepts, identifying controversial issues or making explicit the underlying hypotheses) and learners are given different roles (e.g., an option is that each learner addresses all the subtasks for a given theory; another option is that each learner addresses the same subtask for all the theories). Learners are supposed to deliver a final common document.

Within this context, software (the LMS) is thought of as a means to (1) deliver the instructions (what learners are supposed to do) and some material (documents related to the theories) and (2) allow learners to upload their final document. Implicitly, it is supposed that the general means provided by the LMS (e.g., the communication tools) may also be of interest.

2.1.4 Discussion

These examples illustrate different issues (some of them already mentioned) that will be addressed in more details in the following chapters:

1. Software may be more or less central in the definition of the setting. For instance, in the case of the *Java programming* and *biology inquiry learning* settings, the software role is different but in both cases of major importance, while this is less the case for the *learning theories forum* setting.
2. Software may be introduced as a central feature of the pedagogical setting or as only a possible means. For instance, in the *learning theories forum* case, it is not imposed that the different tasks should be addressed via the LMS. The way the CBPS is defined implicitly acknowledges the fact that learners may achieve these tasks in a variety of ways and may use whatever means they find to be convenient.

3. Pedagogical objectives (and considerations) are usually multiple and mixed. For instance, in a setting such as the *biology inquiry learning* CBPS it is likely that meta-level dimensions and skills (related to inquiry processes) and domain-related ones (related to biology) coexist.

Finally, these examples illustrate the fact that, in some cases, both basic and educational software may be used. Learners may address the *learning theories forum* CBPS with basic communication software. Similarly, the *biology inquiry learning* CBPS may be implemented with a simulation dedicated to education or not. However, the contextual and individualized hints required for the *Java programming* setting requires specific software.

2.2 Examples of Educational Software

We sketch hereafter four theoretical examples, i.e. imagined systems that do not exist, but are inspired by the field literature: *JavIT* the ITS, *Bio-sim* the simulation-based learning environment, *GeLMS-1* the generic LMS (a counter-example) and *Argue-chat* the graphical argumentation chat tool. More detailed presentations (and other examples) are presented in Chap. 4. These examples will be used throughout this book to illustrate different ideas.[10]

2.2.1 *JavIT*, the ITS

JavIT is an ITS designed to implement the *Java programming* CBPS.

Consistently with the targeted setting, *JavIT*'s principle is to introduce programming exercises and to ask learners to enter a certain number of constructions (the different Java classes, their relationships, the way notions such as inheritance or polymorphism are used, etc.), which constitute different steps towards the solution they propose.

JavIT's specificity lies in (1) the interfaces it provides for editing the solving steps, which are defined to make learners consider some particular concepts in a precise way, make explicit their constructions and justify their propositions and (2) the diagnosis and feedback capabilities, i.e., the system's ability to analyze learners' output and provide individualized epistemic feedback.

JavIT presents both of the characteristics of educational software we have raised in Sect. 1: (1) its design is based on specific educational conceptualizations and models, and (2) it presents educational-related specific functions and properties.

---

[10]The purpose of using theoretical examples is to highlight issues contrasting differences in perspectives while avoiding describing the details of actual systems.

2.2.2 *Bio-sim*, the Simulation-Based Learning Environment

Bio-sim is a simulation-based learning environment designed to implement the *biology inquiry learning* CBPS.

Consistently with the targeted setting, *Bio-sim* offers a computer-based simulation of cell behavior. When using the simulation, learners can make different variables vary and observe what happens.

Bio-sim's main role is to provide a simulation that makes salient features identified as pertinent for the CBPS (e.g., cell nucleus, cell membrane or liquids) and hides or gives less importance to some others. When using the simulation to test hypotheses (e.g., what happens if the salt concentration is changed from value v_1 to value v_2), only some notions may be used as variables. Moreover, the simulation is complemented by additional data visualized via different indicators (e.g., electric charge) which, here again, are meant to make learners consider some particular notions in some particular way, using different representations (e.g., numerical or graphical). These affordances[11] have been defined on the basis of a specific study of learners' cognitive processes and difficulties in such settings. The environment also presents learners with specific editors that help them to model the phenomenon at stake or to relate hypotheses to experimental data. Different communication tools allow distant learners to collaborate. Finally, different methodological hints are provided in order to help them to conduct the inquiry process, e.g., to properly separate variables.

Here again, *Bio-sim* presents both of the characteristics of educational software: its design is based on specific educational conceptualizations and models; it offers functions presenting educational-related specific properties (e.g., the simulation affordances) and specific functions (e.g., the additional cognitive tools, the hypothesis management tools or the model editors).

2.2.3 *GeLMS-1*, the Generic LMS

GeLMS-1 is a generic LMS, i.e., a Web platform managing learners' access to pedagogical resources such as documents or videos and to basic communication tools such as chat rooms, forums, whiteboards or file exchange zones.

GeLMS-1 is, in fact, an information system used (after some cosmetic customization) in the context of education: it manages how users (in this case, learners) access resources (in this case, pedagogical material), and it offers basic communication tools.

GeLMS-1 does not meet any of the characteristics raised in Sect. 1: its design is not based on specific educational conceptualizations or models, and it does not present any educational-related specific functions or properties. The only aspect related to education is the nature of the documents and resources managed by the

---

[11] *Affordances*: here, aspects suggesting how (in this case) artifacts may be used.

system. However, this dimension, or the expected educational use of the communication tools, does not have any influence on the design. *GeLMS-1* is basic software (see discussion).

2.2.4 *Argue-chat*, the Graphical Argumentation Chat Tool

Argue-chat is a graphical argumentation chat tool designed to support learners in conducting argumentative interactions.

Argue-chat is not dedicated to the implementation of a precise CBPS but, rather, to CBPSs within which whether learners develop argumentation is of importance. Its rationale is that, in mediated collaborative learning settings, it is a classical strategy to make learners learn one from another (and/or make them develop interactions on the basis of which teachers will build) by making them argue about the domain or task at hand. The *learning theories forum* is an example of such a setting although, given the way it is defined, the argumentation dimension is not put to the fore.

Argue-chat's role is to address different difficulties that have been identified when learners use basic chat tools to argue, which often lead them not to develop very productive interactions. For instance, learners often build sentences whose intention is unclear, use complex sentences mixing different ideas and arguments, or have difficulties in relating ideas and arguments to one another. For this purpose, *Argue-chat* provides a set of graphical shapes (boxes and connections) denoting specific argumentation notions such as *statement*, *argument*, *counter-argument*, *approval*, *question* or *answer*, and allows their connection.

Argue-chat meets the first characteristic: its design is based on specific educational conceptualizations and models. Whether it meets the second one may be argued (see next section).

2.2.5 Discussion

Bio-sim illustrates that CBPSs may be implemented with both basic and educational software. In this case, the rationale for developing a specific simulation and environment is to support learners by providing cognitively-studied affordances and tools. *Bio-sim* also illustrates the variety of concerns that may be considered: whether the environment may be built (i.e., the conceptual and technical issues addressed); whether it supports learners in an effective way; the impact on learning outcomes; whether it fits teaching settings or not or economical considerations; etc. All these different dimensions may be regarded as such and in relation to one another (the other examples could be used to illustrate this point in the same way).

GeLMS-1 highlights the fact that presenting software as "educational" requires emphasizing what educational dimensions are taken into account, how this is done, and what the results are. In this case, the system is used in education (and might be perfectly satisfactory for some settings), but no educational considerations impacted design.

We have introduced *GeLMS-1* as an information system incidentally used in an education context. Now, if such a system were originally constructed for education purposes, should it be considered as educational software? It may be argued that the first characteristic (design is based on specific educational conceptualizations or models) is met, as designing a platform such as *GeLMS-1* for educational purposes is not free of educational perspective, but, on the contrary, denotes a particular (and very poor) perspective of on-line teaching: e-learning is e-commerce whose product is data (text, video, etc.) considered to be pedagogical. Moreover, it may be argued that the second characteristic (software presents educational-related specific functions or properties) is also met as effective systems of this kind usually present specific functions related to the back-office dimension, e.g., managing learners' registration or marks. Such "educational" considerations are qualitatively different from the ones put to the fore in the *JavIT* or *Bio-sim* cases.

The educational software definition we have introduced is not meant to contrast effective and ineffective systems, or what may be "legitimately" considered as educational software, but design considerations. As a matter of fact, most existing LMSs can hardly be considered as educational software as they provide very few properties dedicated to educational issues (however, this is not intrinsic to the notion of LMS, and counter-examples do exist, see Chap. 4). Anyway, LMSs, because of their generic character and the fact they consider back-office dimensions more than educational considerations, are not very good examples for exploring educational software issues.

Argue-chat highlights the proximity that may exist between educational software and, more generally, software specifically designed to influence users' processes.

Finally, we have introduced *Argue-chat* as educational software because its specificities have been studied and designed according to difficulties that have been identified when learners use basic chat tools to argue. *Argue-chat* is explicitly designed to help learners develop productive interactions. However, addressing the argumentation difficulty may be useful in other contexts (e.g., coordination in collaborative work) and for other non-pedagogical objectives (e.g., collective problem-solving efficiency or collective-design-rationale documentation). If *Argue-chat* had been designed within such a context, this would not change its interest for education.

This example highlights that it would be very unproductive and misleading to separate efforts and work related to educational software from other efforts related to, for instance, Computer-Supported Collaborative Work and interaction (if considering *Argue-chat*-like systems) or, as another example, problem-solving (if considering ITS-like systems). More generally, designing software to influence learners' activity or knowledge is a particular case of designing software to influence users' processes, and shares the more general objective of understanding what *designing software to support human activity* means and how it may be addressed (see Chap. 6, Sect. 3.2). For instance, educational software greatly benefits from work studying how to design software to support interactions (and how such software is used) because such work addresses the relation software/(interaction)-objectives in an explicit way (and, of course, because interaction is closely related to learning).

3 Design of Educational Software: Different Realities

Designing software with respect to educational concerns may correspond to very different realities. We contrast and exemplify here two prototypical cases, which illustrate different prototypical education/CS interplays, and discuss them in Sect. 3.3:

1. Designing and implementing new software, i.e., defining the software specifications from the analysis of the pedagogical setting and implementing them. Technically, this implementation may be addressed in various ways such as programming from scratch or interoperating preexisting software components.
2. Articulating and/or customizing already existing software components to educational needs.

Other options are possible, e.g., instantiating generic software (e.g., an ITS framework) or a basic high-level framework. For instance, a system such as *Argue-chat* may be implemented by instantiating a generic graph-tool.

3.1 Designing and Implementing New Software

Bio-sim is a prototypical case of educational software that is likely to be designed as new software, i.e.: specification of the software is established from the targeted CBPSs (and, possibly, teaching setting) analysis, implemented, tested and iteratively refined. More generally, if one considers complex systems such as ITSs or simulations, building new software is prototypical.

At the basis of design are a given learning theory and an identified set of issues to be addressed. In *Bio-sim*'s case, the rationale[12] is that inquiry learning appears to be a promising approach to make learners learn how to regulate their own learning, gain new knowledge and update their existing knowledge. However, the positive impact of inquiry learning settings may be hindered by the difficulties learners often encounter when facing inquiry processes such as choosing the right variables to work with or implementing the experimental processes. The problem to be studied is less to allow learners to solve the task than to lead them to do so in a knowledge-productive way. The targeted system is meant to play an important and precise role, providing specific affordances and cognitive support. The exact software properties

---

[12]See de Jong, T. (2006). Computer simulations – Technological advances in inquiry learning. *Science*, 312, 532–533.

are important issues, and the requested properties are defined from the pedagogical needs.

It may be noticed that such software is "new" in the sense that, fundamentally, educational specifications are identified, and software is constructed so as to match these specifications. However, from a technical point of view, *Bio-sim* may be implemented from scratch or by reusing and adapting different existing software components (a simulation, a generic editor, etc.). Pushing forward this idea, *Bio-sim* may be just one of a set of inquiry learning environments to be constructed and, from a technical point of view, the strategy may consist of building technical frameworks (pieces of software dedicated to a general set of related features) from which different variations may be constructed according to the precise specifications of one or another system.

3.2 Articulating and/or Customizing Software Components

ICT has considerably changed the TEL field and, if one considers systems used in effective settings, educational software is often a particular selection, adaptation and/or inter-connection of already existing ICT-based software components. Typically, within on-line learning centers, so called "learning technologists" are in charge of understanding, with the involved teachers, what already existing technology may be adapted to their needs, and customize it as necessary.

Let us consider the *learning theories forum* CBPS. A basic LMS offers little support for learners engaged in such a setting. An option may be to build a specific environment from scratch, but this is rather expensive. A more rational process is to study how some of the technical possibilities of the LMS, together with additional software components, may be locally aggregated, customized and interoperated so as to build a kind of task-related activity framework (let us call it *Colab-edit*). Such an environment may for instance be created by adapting and gluing together an editor, a versioning system and a forum as a way to offer learners a collaborative editor that allows them to edit text, track other learners' modifications, submit and comment on work-in-progress reports and launch mediated discussions associated with particular pieces of text. Such an approach may involve both basic tools and specific tools such as *Argue-chat*.

A "mash-up" such as *Colab-edit* is an example of educational software built by selecting and adapting existing components and articulating them in a particular way: it is software that has been designed with respect to educational purposes, and which is meant to influence learners' processes. A different but related example of this type of process is the way a basic information system (named *GeLMS-1* for commercial reasons) may be re-engineered into *GeLMS-2*, technically a new version but, now, a system that takes into account educational considerations and addresses drawbacks highlighted by the practical use of the previous version.

3.3 Education and CS Interplays

Let us consider in more detail the education and CS interplay in the *Bio-sim* and *Colab-edit* cases:

- In the *Bio-sim* case, the educational software is imagined and created from the pedagogic idea. *Bio-sim* is designed as new software. Technically, it may be implemented upon existing software, but the existence of the software used to build *Bio-sim* is not a matter of concern for educationalists.
- In the *Colab-edit* case, the educational software is imagined and created from (1) the pedagogic idea and (2) the existing technology or, more precisely, the way educationalists and computer scientists interpret the existing software affordances with respect to the pedagogical needs. The existence of already existing software is at the basis of the design process (and, also, of the implementation process).

Colab-edit exemplifies the fact that building educational software by articulation and/or adaptation of components can be seen as a movement from two existing constructions (the initial pedagogical idea and the existing software or components) to a third (the designed system). Such a movement is submitted to multiple different influences such as the individual educationalists' and computer scientists' views, their mutual understanding, the common conceptual constructions they may build together (or fail to build), their perception of the existing technologies, the general teaching context, the general technological context (e.g., the technology availability and scalability or economical constraints) or the project's lifespan. The process is usually not linear but iterative, ideas and software being iteratively tested and improved.

However, in fact, such a process occurs in all cases, including when building software from scratch. It is difficult to imagine educationalists (and computer scientists of course) imagining and designing software without any influence from already known systems or, at the least, a certain perception of technology and of what can and cannot be done.

It may also be noticed that a technological framework designed to fit some given pedagogy, once deployed, often leads one to find some of its aspects or assumptions were not noticed, and requires reconsideration of the design.

Therefore, as a general principle, highest importance should be given to the educational dimensions and not to the technical dimensions, and the start point of any project involving the design of educational software should be the pedagogical setting (which is itself to be considered within the more general teaching setting), and not the technical system. Technology should adapt to pedagogical needs and not the contrary. However, what happens is usually a bit more complicated and balanced. In all cases (inventing new software on the basis of a pedagogical idea or a technical opportunity, adapting existing software, gluing together existing components, building CBPSs upon the limited means offered by a platform such as *GeLMS-1*, etc.), there is not a pedagogical idea on the one side and CS work on the other, but co-constructions, adaptations, compromises and/or taken opportunities.

Designing software with respect to educational concerns may thus correspond to very different realities, with significantly different education and CS interplays. This is part of the reason why, if general methodological considerations may be highlighted (CBPSs and teaching levels must be considered; CBPSs are socio-technical contexts; technology is not prescriptive of what will happen; individual characteristics of learners, but also groups' phenomena, institutional or sociological dimensions are of major influence; iterative or participative approaches are useful; effective use of systems is not necessarily related to their properties and impacting effective practices requires considering other factors; etc.), listing precise guidelines or managing projects requires going into specifics of the setting.

4 Addressing Educational Software Design

4.1 Considering Software Properties

It has been raised in Sect. 1 that how learners use software is subject to many influences and that the software does not define what will happen. This may lead one to consider that whatever the software properties are, their effects may be rendered anecdotic by other dimensions, and thus they may be considered contingent.

We argue that addressing the level of software properties is necessary and of interest as these properties have an influence on what is going to happen or not, and how.

First, whatever software is, software properties do impact users' behavior. Software is in no way neutral. Software properties (whatever their design rationale is) define part of the socio-technical system with which users or, in this case, learners, are engaged. They play a role in the development of users' perception and representations of the task and/or of how software may be used as a means, and of course in what actions are possible. Studying how software properties influence or not (and how, when, why, etc.) the unfolding of pedagogical settings is necessary to, at the minimum, avoid raising pedagogically unproductive representations or constraints.

Second, in formal learning settings, the fact that learners are asked to use a given system to achieve a given task in the context of a given institutional setting creates a very specific context. This is the case for still rather open settings such as the *learning theories forum* and, more importantly, for more constrained settings such as the *biology inquiry learning* CBPS implemented with *Bio-sim* or tutoring contexts implemented with *JavIT*. In such cases, as reported in the literature, learners' behavioral and cognitive processes are influenced by software properties.

It makes sense to consider the objective of influencing by the software design what is going to happen.

However, software influence is to be considered in the light of the different points raised in Sect. 1, and with respect to precise contexts. For instance, the objective of influencing by the software design what is going to happen corresponds to very different realities in the *learning theories forum* and the *Java programming* CBPS implemented with *JavIT*. This gives particular importance to the clarification of the setting, the software role, and what the expectations are.

4.2 Making Explicit Matters of Concern and Perspectives

Considering educational software design requires drawing relations between pedagogical considerations, software properties, software usage and the outcomes of this usage. This is the case in both development and research projects studying how to base design on theoretical elements or attempting to capitalize knowledge. With respect to design, a central issue is that of thinking, problematizing and making explicit the relationships between (1) the discourse that is used to denote the considered pedagogical objectives and settings, and the underlying assumptions, and (2) the design and implementation decisions, and the corresponding software properties.

In the preceding sections, we have introduced the *Bio-sim*, *JavIT*, *Argue-chat* and *Colab-edit* examples by making salient (1) the description of the considered CBPSs and (2) the description of the systems' features. Such a presentation allows the general idea to be grasped, but drawing precise relations between pedagogical considerations, software properties and usage requires both broadening the scope and going into other details.

As examples, we highlight hereafter a few dimensions whose clarification is required.[13]

4.2.1 The Way the Pedagogical Setting and Software Role Are Thought of

An important dimension underlying educational software design projects is whether the targeted computer-based setting is expected to present additional value in terms of learning or it is thought of as an alternative to a non-computer-based setting. For instance, a system (and the underlying constructions) such as *Bio-sim* must be considered and evaluated very differently according to whether it is designed to produce better learning outcomes than inquiry learning not based on simulations, as an alternative to in-classroom settings (the notion of "better learning outcomes" is not central anymore), or as an additional means to be used with some others

---

[13]The examples of analysis axes introduced here are part of the list developed in Chap. 7.

(which raises concerns such as the coherence of these different means). Similarly, *Colab-edit* will be considered very differently if it is thought of as a response to a limitation (the fact distant learners cannot attend classrooms) or as a means for a different pedagogy. Such considerations may impact analysis and design decisions and, if not clarified, may be at the origin of misunderstandings and confusions between the project actors.

As a second example, another important dimension is whether software is thought of as something that will impact the way learners conceptualize the domain or it is thought of as merely a resource. For instance, the importance of the fact that learners use *JavIT* editors, and the importance of the way they use them, is very different depending on whether these editors are supposed to impact the way learners will conceptualize object-oriented notions such as inheritance or polymorphism (i.e., act as cognitive tools) or not.

4.2.2 The Considerations That Have Been Taken into Account at Design Time

An important dimension underlying educational software design is whether the project is based on a reference to a non-computer-based setting or not. If the analysis is conducted in reference to such a setting, what is the level of granularity of this reference? Which objects are considered? For instance, an important dimension for analyzing *Bio-sim* is whether it is meant to mimic authentic inquiry (and to what extent, for what notions, etc.) or not.

As a second example, another important dimension is whether the learning domain specificities (notions, objects, assumptions) are taken in account in the analysis and, in this case, how. For instance, some biological knowledge is necessary for designing *Bio-sim* simulation, but the way the system scaffolds learners' processes may have been addressed in reference to generic inquiry principles or in a way that mixes generic principles and domain issues. Addressing *JavIT* feedback on the basis of generic principles or on the basis of a domain-specific analysis of how learners may develop knowledge related to object-oriented design leads to very different issues. Etc.

As a third example, design may or may not be based on, or use, theoretical bases. For instance, *JavIT* feedback properties may have foundations in some given cognitive theory; *Bio-sim* simulation may have foundations in theories relative to knowledge representation, cognitive load or how skills may transfer from one domain to another; *Argue-chat* may have foundations in interaction theories; etc.

As a final example, another important dimension is how the different considered features (theoretical context, domain specificities, etc.) impact the analysis. Do they provide a general way of thinking? Do they provide guidelines? Do they provide concepts? For instance, *JavIT* design may be influenced by theories explaining how learners learn by solving problems in different ways, from very general concerns (e.g., the importance of learning-by-doing) to very precise ones (e.g., the fact *JavIT* should consider learners' zone of proximal development[14]).

4.2.3 The Impact of Pedagogical Considerations on Design

An important dimension is to clarify which of the objects considered at the level of the pedagogical setting are taken into account in the software design. For instance, *Colab-edit* rationale is related to the fact that learners may learn from one another by arguing and co-constructing knowledge. Considering this objective, part of the issues related to making learners *argue* and *co-construct knowledge* may be addressed by the structure of the CBPS (e.g., grouping learners whose background is different as a way to increase the chances they have different views and, thus, have to argue) and another part taken into account in the software design, for instance offering a collaborative editor that allows versioning pieces of text. In other words, design is only impacted by some of the pedagogical considerations, and clarifying these is of crucial importance.

As a second example, another important dimension is whether the considered objects impact design only and/or they also are reified in one way or another in the system. For instance, considering *JavIT*, the fact that learners are expected to make explicit their different problem-solving steps may impact the way the system introduces the exercise (the instructions) and/or the design of the editor which is to be used by learners to edit their solution (the editor may for instance impose the use of constructions such as "I create class C because ..." or "I use inheritance as a way to ..."). Going a step further, the notion of "explicit solution" may also be reified in the system as a specific software component capable of evaluating the extent to which a solution has been made explicit and is properly justified.

As a third example, another important dimension is how features or properties thought of as dedicated to educational dimensions relate to the pedagogical objectives and constraints. For instance, which *Bio-sim* properties are meant to provide specific affordances for learning (and which others are just introduced for the environment to be usable)? How does the use of *Argue-chat* and properties such as offering *sentence openers*, considering *balanced interactions* or imposing *turn-taking rules* relate to the CBPS it is used within? etc.

As a final example, another dimension is the precise processes of the system (data acquisition, data analysis, accessibility management, etc.) and how they relate to the pedagogical objectives. For instance, when *Bio-sim* provides learners with hints, does it analyze learners' hypotheses in terms of biological knowledge or does it only react to general features such as the number of variables involved? If

---

[14]The *zone of proximal development* is "the distance between the actual developmental level as determined by independent problem solving and the level of potential development as determined through problem solving under adult guidance, or in collaboration with more capable peers". Vygotsky, L.S. (1978). Mind and society: The development of higher psychological processes. Cambridge: Harvard University Press.

building a system enhancing *Argue-chat* by a component that analyzes learners' interactions, what type of process is implemented? Are sentences' semantics analyzed using a Natural Language analyzer? Are they categorized according to the sentence openers used by learners (independently from the effective text, which may not correspond)? Does the system just sum up the number of sentences?

These different examples highlight that the description of the considered CBPSs and of the system features is far from capturing all the different dimensions underlying design of educational software. As a consequence, if analysis is limited to these considerations, many misunderstandings and confusions may develop between actors from different disciplines and/or with different matters of concern.

4.3 Importance of Explicitness

Making explicit the details of work related to the design and implementation of educational software is important for different reasons, in particular:

1. It increases the chances of the actors engaged in design and analysis to develop a shared understanding. This is an issue of particular importance and difficulty in TEL due to the intrinsic complexity and multidisciplinarity of the field, and to the variety of possible matters of concern, perspectives or approaches.
2. It increases the chances to benefit from and/or reutilize constructions (e.g., models, processes, software components or lessons learned) from other projects, and the chances to get the constructions elaborated in one's projects to be reusable for other projects, by other persons. In a less positive wording, it helps in avoiding wasting time due to the erroneous idea that some constructions are innovative and avoiding replicating mistakes already made with the previous wave of technology, which is indeed a recurrent pattern of TEL history.
3. It provides a basis for the definition, the evaluation, the criticism and the dissemination of scientific results.

Making explicit design details is a *sine qua non* condition for knowledge capitalization, which may take different forms: understanding of an issue; statement or lesson learned; model (for thinking and analysis, for prediction, for run-time control, etc.); process (general approach, engineering or re-engineering process, benchmark); conceptualization (i.e., a set of concepts proposed as a substratum for some given work); software component; etc. (see Chap. 7).

As an example, one of *Bio-sim*'s specific designed features is to support learners in making connections between the simulation, the data and learners' hypotheses. From such a project may be capitalized lessons learned related to the impact, influence, usage (etc.) of such support, and of how learners may develop and manage hypotheses in such a setting; lessons learned related to the issues raised within such a project; the first steps of an approach or an engineering process related to inquiry learning environment design or to cognitive scaffolding, to be tested in other projects; software components as construction bases for inquiry learning settings; design patterns; etc. Considering *Argue-chat*, which imposes the use of a certain number of graphical constructions related to argumentation, similar knowledge may be capitalized, and *Argue-chat* features (issues, impact, usage) may be compared to those of other approaches to interaction structuring (e.g., using sentence openers), etc.

As will be emphasized in Chap. 6, CBPS and educational software are artificial objects, and knowledge develops via the design and analysis of systems: advances are derived via engineering projects involving, within a larger pedagogical study, the design and implementation of software. As a consequence, both research and development projects may be productive of knowledge. In research-oriented projects, the objective is usually not to build some given software to be used in some effective setting, but to identify and understand issues to be considered, phenomena to be understood, or possible approaches. The constructed software is both the resource and the objective of scientific work. In development projects, whose objective is to build systems to be used in effective settings, knowledge or lessons learned may be elaborated from the analysis of design decisions and their impact. In fact, as discussed in Chap. 6, research and engineering dimensions are to a large extent intertwined.

4.4 Difficulty and Limits of Explicitness

The way the examples of CBPSs and educational software have been introduced in Sect. 2 is typical: researchers or engineers engaged in the design of educational software usually present their projects by focusing on the way they imagine the setting and the innovative features they attempt to introduce, which is related to their perception of the field, the spectrum of the issues they consider, etc.

However, this conceptual context is often largely idiosyncratic, and difficult to share.

> The *raison d'être* of this book is the fact that there is an intrinsic difficulty in making explicit (in detail) work related to the design and implementation of educational software. This book introduces notions, analyzes, examples, characterization items and methodological considerations as means to support such a process.

In this book, we refer to "clarifying" or "making explicit" (design) matters of concern as the efforts made by an actor or a set of actors to render these features intelligible by some other actors (and, by the way, improve their own analysis and understanding).

"Explicitation" is a goal that, however, raises fundamental problems. At a theoretical level, the notion of explicitation leads to considering notions such as accountability (see ethno-methodology studies) or shared understanding.

In particular, considering shared understanding, intelligibility is not only related to language issues (i.e., sharing a common interpretation of language items), but also to many other material, social, historical or cultural dimensions. The documentary artifacts that may be considered by an actor (or a set of actors) as an explicitation of his/her concerns are the result of an encoding by a sender, and will in turn be decoded by a receiver. These encoding and decoding processes are of course context-dependent, and related to many dimensions. In other words, what has been considered as comprehensive and unambiguous by a given actor in a given context may be understood differently by another actor who has a different history, a different culture or a different view of the field and what the important notions or matters of concern of this field are, and is presently facing some given tasks within some given context.

When arguing for the interest of explicitation and attempting to support such processes, these fundamental issues are not to be ignored. They do not mean efforts for explicitation are meaningless, but that they must be considered with these difficulties and intrinsic limitations in mind.

In particular, highlighting and analyzing issues, approaches or characteristics only makes sense, and is only intelligible, if the considered notions are properly defined. In other words, it is not possible to say anything more or less precise, consistent and, above all, shareable, if there has not been proposed some prior clarification of the conceptualization that underlies the proposed constructions.

A conceptualization is a differential system of notions. A given conceptualization emphasizes some aspects of a field (some notions, some dimensions, some properties, etc.) and not others. Because a conceptualization is never neutral, the underlying perspective on the domain must be clarified: the fact that it is useful to denote a given notion or to dissociate two notions that appear similar, or the reasons why a given definition draws attention to particular aspects, only makes sense within a general view of the considered domain.

When addressing complex domains, using differently-oriented conceptualizations allows precision, when attempting to address different issues within a single common view (a kind of "all-in-one conceptualization") often leads one to be rather abstract and general. TEL poses different types of issues and thus requires different views, drawing attention to different dimensions and providing different conceptual means.

In this book, the focus is on the relationships between the discourse that is used to denote pedagogical issues (settings, considerations, objectives, etc.) on the one side and, on the other side, the elaborated software. This is addressed within a software-design-oriented conceptualization that has been sketched in this introductory chapter and is described in detail in Chap. 2. This conceptualization is to be seen as a tool dedicated to conducting multidisciplinary work related to educational software design in TEL.

As a way to emphasize that a given conceptualization draws attention to some dimensions and not to others, let us consider notions such as *learning* or *educational practices*. When focusing on educational software design, these dimensions are not put to the fore. This is not to say learning is not important or that design issues are disentangled from educational practices. Of course, for any TEL project, at a general level, the issue is to address the fact that some targeted CBPSs will allow a better (or a different type of) learning, and will make sense with respect to teachers' practices and institutions. However, if one considers these objectives as such, different analyses on different plans are required. For instance, considering whether a pedagogical setting allows *better learning*, or a *different type of learning*, requires means to describe and analyze TEL settings in terms of learning and properties of learning (e.g., to define what is meant by "a better learning"). In other words, this requires a conceptualization of the field that allows these issues to be addressed. Such a conceptualization may, however, make it hard to grasp some other dimensions, for instance, *the way the pedagogical intention is reified within the system* or *the way the computer-based artifact properties impact learners' activity*, which are not first-class matters of concern and may be completely contingent when addressing the project within a learning-focused view. On the contrary, these dimensions are at the very core of an analysis considering CS-oriented design issues, and the conceptualization underlying such an analysis must allow these dimensions to be grasped. Viewing the domain from the point of view of teachers' practices is again a different view, and leads to the consideration of other notions (and/or addressing notions in a different way).

Coming back to the need for explicitation efforts, from a long perspective, putting into evidence the pragmatic interest of explicitation, and proposing constructions (such as conceptualizations or lists of characteristics) as examples of explicitation tools, may lead communities (researchers or communities of practice) to collaboratively develop and adopt shared conceptual tools.

As a pragmatic feature, efforts at explicitation may finally be related to the following point: designers may associate some logos to the designed software or may not ("technology" in the etymological sense) but, in any case, other actors and, in particular, users, will do. Associating some logos to the designed artifact from the start could be seen as a means to "impose" the designers' view but, anyway, users will take possession of the artifact according to their purposes and needs. Rather, this may help in tracing and understanding the way, in some sense, "design is continued in usage".

5 Content and Structure of the Book

5.1 Objective

TEL projects considering the design and implementation of educational software are intrinsically multidisciplinary and complex. As such, they present the difficulty of conducting detailed analyses allowing the different involved actors to understand respective matters of concern and build common constructions. Another difficulty, related to the previous one, is to benefit from lessons learned in the literature, and to contribute to this capitalization of knowledge.

Within this context, the general objective of this book is to highlight the importance of making explicit the details of work related to the design and implementation of educational software, and to propose a substratum to do so.

More precisely, this book concentrates on the very core difficulty of providing a framework to think about and make explicit the relationships between (1) the discourse that is used to denote the considered pedagogical objectives and settings, and the underlying assumptions, and (2) the elaborated models and software components.

5.2 Content Synthesis

The overall content[15] of this book is:

1. A highlight of the fact that what is referred to by the "design of educational software" may be subject to very different perspectives, and the importance of making explicit matters of concern.
2. A general conceptualization that helps in disentangling issues and clarifying matters of concern with respect to educational software design and implementation.
3. A set of items that may be used to characterize (1) the way the pedagogical setting is considered and (2) the software properties and construction processes.
4. A review of some methodological dimensions.
5. A perspective on the field anchored in an engineering approach, and propositions on how to push the field forward.
6. Different examples used to raise issues and illustrate propositions.

Although this book addresses the field in a transversal way and does not describe a particular methodology, its content (the description of issues, concepts, approaches, examples, methodological considerations) has heuristic value for conducting projects.

5.3 Rationale for the Organization

This book presents two dimensions: analyzing issues and proposing means. These dimensions are intertwined (as opposed to an analysis and then proposals), the general structure being:

- Chapter 1. Introduction
- Chapter 2. A general conceptualization for educational software
- Chapter 3. Understanding differences in perspectives
- Chapter 4. Review of prototypical examples

---

[15]We will come back to this list of contributions and its rationale in Chap. 6, in the context of the analysis of educational software engineering developed in that chapter.

5 Content and Structure of the Book

- Chapter 5. CS perspectives and TEL
- Chapter 6. Educational software engineering
- Chapter 7. Characterizing the design context and the software artifact
- Chapter 8. Methodological considerations
- Chapter 9. Conclusions

5.3.1 Analysis Dimension

Analyzing perspectives within which educational software notions and issues may be considered is specifically addressed by Chap. 3, which provides different examples of how a given project and some important notions may be thought of and managed. In Chap. 4, several examples of systems are studied, highlighting differences with respect to these notions in particular. Chapter 5 also contributes by analyzing the different ways in which CS contributes to the TEL field, and the different ways in which computer scientists may conceptualize their involvement.

This analysis dimension is also more or less indirectly addressed in all the other chapters, as for example in the preceding sections of this introductory chapter and in the concluding chapter, which analyzes some issues for TEL development.

5.3.2 Propositions Dimension

Contributions consist of means for thinking, problematizing and describing educational software design and implementation work and outcomes.

The first proposition is a software-design-oriented conceptualization of the TEL field. This dimension is specifically addressed by Chap. 2, the general perspective (and preliminary definitions) having been introduced in this introductory chapter, and being completed by all the other chapters.

The second proposition is a list of items for characterizing, within a given project, the way the pedagogical setting is considered, and the software properties. This dimension is specifically addressed by Chap. 7. Listing such characteristics is useful because it ensures that specific attention is paid to a certain number of important dimensions. This helps to clarify projects in several ways. First, the listed characteristics that appear pertinent given the considered project can be used as an analysis grid: the list provides a resource for describing projects with respect to an external reference. Second, checking whether the proposed characteristics are pertinent and whether or not they apply leads to identification of variants or other characteristics that best denote some dimensions of the project, which here again helps in clarifying projects. The proposed list is based on the general conceptualization introduced in Chap. 2 and the CS and engineering dimensions analyses developed in Chaps. 5 and 6.

The third proposition is a review of methodological dimensions, consideration of which is of particular importance. This dimension is specifically addressed by Chap. 8, and is present in some way or another in most of the others.

The fourth proposition is an argument for addressing TEL as an engineering field, which defines the rationale for making specific efforts in making explicit matters of concern and elaborating multiple descriptions of projects. This dimension has been sketched in this introductory chapter, and is specifically addressed by Chap. 7. This is completed by a perspective on how to push forward the educational software engineering field (Chap. 9).

5.4 General Comments

5.4.1 Keeping Context in Mind

Writing a text addressing a complex multidisciplinary domain for a multidisciplinary audience opens many opportunities for misunderstandings. This is particularly the case when the entry point is software, the domain is education, and the text is long. Sentences or paragraphs picked up in the text may be misunderstood if considered out of their context. As restating this context in every section would be difficult, it is assumed the reader keeps this context in mind.

As an example, we use the notion of *impact of software properties* to denote the fact that software properties have an influence on what happens or does not. This is to be understood in the context of other considerations introduced before such as the facts that software is not definitional, software is only a mediator of learners' activity, and learners' activity is something that contextually emerges and evolves in relation to many dimensions of which software is just one factor. Not keeping this in mind may result in over-interpreting or misunderstanding the "impact" notion.

As another important dimension to be kept in mind, we have emphasized that a conceptualization is never neutral. In a field such as TEL, a conceptualization emphasizes notions that are of importance given an objective. The proposed conceptualization is related to the adopted orientation, that of the design of CS artifacts (software design; not to be confused with a technical point of view, e.g., addressing languages or platform architectures, or with a techno-centered approach). This is only one of the different possible perspectives that can be developed, and must be developed, when considering the TEL field.

5.4.2 What This Book Is Not

First, this book does not attempt to propose a unified view of notions, theories or any other specific constructions related to TEL. For instance, it does not present a list and a particular definition of notions frequently used in TEL such as *feedback*, *learner model*, *cognitive conflict* or *interaction analysis*. Similarly, it does not propose a unified process for building or evaluating educational software.

The reason for this is that TEL projects may be of very different natures, consider very different types of objectives and/or address them at different levels of granularity, use different theoretical or empirical foundations, etc. It is within a given project that notions such as *feedback*, *learner model*, *cognitive conflict* or *interaction analysis* will find a particular precise definition, will correspond to precise challenges, will be subject to particular attentions and treatments, and will lead to particular processes or methodologies. Attempting to build a kind of unification is useless and meaningless. It may be done, but at a level of granularity and abstraction that will render it of little interest for effective use. Moreover, this could easily fall into an attempt at normalization, which has indeed no sense, for ethical and, if nothing else, practical reasons given the heterogeneity of perspectives, settings and systems.

Second, this book does not attempt to explain how to build some given software or component or how to conduct research, although its content is useful for such tasks.

Here again, given the diversity of TEL projects, addressing such issues "in general" would lead to listing trivial generalities or, here again, to a kind of normalizing view. How to conduct TEL projects and build educational software cannot be reduced to a set of recipes. Every project (which may involve design of one or several systems) requires a detailed analysis in order to understand matters of concern, to adapt to context and to build on lessons learned from the literature.

In this book we address a conceptual level in the sense that emphasis is on proposing means for thinking and problematizing, which may be used for conducting different types of work. This may be inspiring for inducing a methodology or a set of guidelines for a given project, but this dimension is not addressed *per se*. Other books address contextually defined issues such as user-centered software engineering techniques, research methodologies, evaluation procedures or how a given type of problem may be addressed (e.g., building a specific type of system such as ITS).

Chapter 2
A General Conceptualization for Educational Software

Abstract This chapter disentangles different notions related to educational software. The result is a design-oriented conceptualization, i.e., a differential system of notions that puts to the fore dimensions and differences of importance when considering design and analysis of educational software properties.

In this chapter, we introduce and discuss definitions of different notions related to educational software. For this purpose, we first introduce some reference educational notions. For instance, being more precise than in Chap. 1, we define educational software as "software specifically designed to lead a learner to develop an activity that is favorable to the addressing of the considered CBPS pedagogical objectives". This definition is constructed upon previous definitions of the notions of *CBPS* and, beforehand, the notions of *pedagogical setting*, *pedagogical objective* and *activity*.

In Sect. 1, we propose basic definitions for the educational notions whose clarification is required. On this basis, we propose in Sect. 2 basic definitions for different notions related to educational software. In Sect. 3, we focus on some important dimensions and issues put to the fore by these definitions, and we synthesize the distinctions they introduce.

In total, the different notions defined in this chapter are:

- Pedagogical setting
- Teaching setting
- Activity (and task)
- Pedagogical objective
- Pedagogical setting design
- Computer-Based Pedagogical Setting (CBPS)
- Educational software
- Pedagogical-setting support software
- Software pedagogical rationale (SPR)
- Technology Enhanced Learning (TEL) field

For these different notions, we propose definitions or views with the intention of proposing a conceptualization, i.e., a differential system of notions. The rationale is to allow one to identify, characterize and contrast different types of work with respect to design considerations. All these definitions are thus working definitions in the sense introduced in Chap. 1, i.e., definitions convenient for the purpose of making salient dimensions which are of interest and importance within the adopted perspective, that of design and analysis of software properties.

1 Reference Educational Notions

The following working definitions address the considered notions in a broad way, i.e., at a high level of granularity and independently from a particular theoretical or methodological context. They definitely ignore some distinctions that may be of interest *per se* or given other operational views such as instructional design.

1.1 Pedagogical Setting

A program does not have any pedagogical advantages as such. A program allows something to be computed, means to be provide to users, etc. How these features are implemented and their properties (e.g., the software interfaces or the constraints imposed by the program on the users) may have some interest for implementing a pedagogical setting and addressing its pedagogical objectives, e.g., presenting learners with some information, tutoring learners while they solve a problem or supporting them when they interact with peers.

Presenting or analyzing software from an educational point of view thus requires making explicit the considered *pedagogical setting* or type of pedagogical setting. From this perspective, a pedagogical setting may be defined as follows:

> A *pedagogical setting* is a setting designed to lead learners to develop an activity propitious to the fact that some given targeted pedagogical objective(s) will be achieved.

This definition puts to the front the *design* dimension and, more precisely, design *with respect to pedagogical objectives*. This leads one to consider the role played by software with respect to these objectives. As mentioned in Chap. 1, this is a prototypical case. Software may also be used in informal settings, not designed in relation to pedagogical objectives, and analyzed with respect to the characteristics that the settings may present or to users' activity within such contexts.

Pedagogical setting is a broad notion, which has many definitions elaborated on the basis of different perspectives and highlighting different dimensions. Other definitions may, for instance, put to the fore dimensions related to the relationships with institutional structures. From the educational software design point of view, what we need is what is useful when thinking about, elaborating, describing or

1 Reference Educational Notions   33

implementing software: Who are the actors? What are their roles? What is the specific role attributed to the system? How does it relate to the tasks learners are set? And so on.

It may be noted that some types of systems are closely correlated to particular types of settings, which often means the setting is kept more or less implicit. For instance, it may be thought that *JavIT*'s or *Bio-sim*'s pedagogical interest may be understood from the description of the system. However, this is rather dangerous as it may misleadingly lead one to think that the system defines the pedagogical settings. Implementation of pedagogical settings consists of taking different design decisions (the task, the actors, the actors' roles, the timing, etc.) of which the software to be used is just one dimension.

1.2 Teaching Setting

A pedagogical setting is not a standalone construction.

Let us consider the *JavIT* system. At present, it has been introduced in reference to a given pedagogical setting: learners are asked to consider a task that consists of the creation of a Java program according to some given specification. Within this pedagogical setting, the software role has been defined: provide learners with means that allow the solution to be edited within a particular system of support and constraints that have been identified as favorable to the targeted learning.

However, "solving a Java programming exercise" is not an event that happens in the middle of nowhere:

1. It takes place within a physical space (e.g., in a classroom or at home), possibly with some people (teachers, peers) nearby or on-line.
2. It takes place as just one of many pedagogical events related to Java and programming (in-classroom or on-line courses, individual and collective exercises, pre- and post-teaching, exams, etc.), within a history of interactions that learners have developed with Java, with programming, with CS and with science and technology.
3. It takes place within some teaching program and curriculum.
4. It takes place within a history of interactions that learners have developed with the teacher, with this type of setting, with ITSs (etc.).
5. It takes place within the context of an institution.
6. It takes place within a view of how to teach programming (and, more precisely, object-oriented programming; and, more precisely, Java) and how learners learn programming (object-oriented programming; Java) that has been influenced by the evolution of CS, of CS teaching, of the place of CS and programming in the curricula and the institution and, more generally, in society.

A pedagogical setting thus takes place within a context that is composed of, and impacted by, many dimensions of very different natures that, themselves, are related to one another. For instance, the institutional context influences the representations that learners may develop of how they should react to stimulations (the fact there is an exercise to solve, the fact there is a request from the teacher, the fact the system asks a question or suggests recommendations, etc.) and, more generally, what they should do and what they should not do, and how. Previous interactions with ITSs or with programming exercises may have led learners to develop representations that influence their understandings and behaviors, etc.

These different dimensions are studied by specific work. We will refer to them as the *teaching setting*, which may be defined as follows:

> Considering a given pedagogical setting, the *teaching setting* is the context created by the general institutional, human and material features within which this pedagogical setting takes place.

When focusing on educational software, which is principally to be considered with respect to the pedagogical settings within which it is used, the teaching setting may be addressed as the context surrounding the studied setting. In fact, seen from a wider perspective, it is rather the opposite: the teaching setting features lead to the design of particular types of pedagogical settings and systems.

The teaching setting may have more or less impact on CBPSs and educational software design but, in any case, is not to be ignored. Acknowledging this dimension is important in order not to develop a naïve understanding and approach to the pedagogical setting notion. In particular, the teaching setting notion helps one to understand that what happens within a pedagogical setting, which is a local and temporal event, is not only related to this setting's features. This has a direct consequence: designing software or analyzing the way software is used may require consideration of a wider context than that of the considered pedagogical settings. The nature and importance of this dimension varies according to the considered matters of concern, types of settings and/or types of systems.

As an example, let us consider the design of an LMS for an on-line University. Such an LMS may be used to organize the way learners manage administrative issues (registering on courses, etc.), access on-line resources and participate in individual and collective actions. For such a project, the notion of teaching setting and the institutional, human and material features must be considered at the level of how the overall LMS architecture and features are to be thought of. For instance, such a project may consider as an objective to stick to what University students are used to or, on the contrary, attempt to reinvent this. When analyzing how learners use such an LMS, the teaching setting dimensions are indeed central.

As a different example, let us consider the design of an ITS such as *JavIT*. The purpose is to allow learners to practice object-oriented design and programming, in addition to or instead of practicing these topics with other means (a pencil, a piece of paper, a basic editor and a Java compiler). Here, the system is introduced in a context that it does not completely change. It could be considered that there is an existing type of pedagogical setting whose modality is changed by the use of software. However, when designing the system, this does not allow limitation of the analysis to the pedagogical setting. First, the system must be designed in order to be coherent with the teaching setting within which it is used. For instance, the way the system scaffolds learners must be consistent with what happens outside the system, e.g., the teacher's lectures and recommendations. Second, considering the teaching setting may be required in order to design and implement some of the system features. For instance, interpreting learners' behavior may require consideration of the perception of the institutional demand that learners have developed, which may explain part of their actions (see Chap. 3, Sect. 3.3).

Finally, the teaching setting and, more generally, the cultural and institutional features, may have some influence on the way educational software (as a notion) is to be considered. For instance, in some countries or cultures, it is accepted that the institution decides how pedagogical settings should be organized and managed by teachers in their classrooms. Differently, in other countries or cultures, teachers have more flexibility and, for instance, the fact that teachers may be reluctant to use some software that is not perfectly in line with their usual teaching should be taken into account. In such a context, teachers' acceptance becomes a matter of concern. This may lead, for instance, to introduce tailorability as a basic requirement for the software to be designed, i.e., to design software in a way that makes it adaptable in context by the teachers.

1.3 Activity

Ergonomic work has introduced a distinction between the notions of task (the prescribed work) and activity (what people actually do). In the context of a pedagogical setting, it may be considered that:

- The *task* corresponds to what learners are suggested to do, i.e., the instructions explicitly or implicitly set by the teacher and/or the setting (pedagogical setting, associated software and, more generally, teaching setting).
- The *activity* is what learners do.

In the context of a pedagogical setting, the activity developed by learners is related to the task they have been asked to consider (solve a programming exercise, build a synthesis, interact with peers, etc.), but not only this. The perception of the task that learners develop (and its evolution) may be significantly different from what is expected, in relation to different factors such as the learner's personal characteristics, the learner's motivations and how these motivations evolve, the interactions with the other actors and/or the setting features (e.g., the software properties), the teaching setting or previous experiences. These factors may impact both learners' perception and enaction of the setting.

For instance, at some given time, a learner using *Bio-sim*'s simulation may effectively be considering different (non-exclusive) tasks: discovering the system, testing hypotheses, playing with the simulation, exploring the simulation's limits, respecting the teachers' perceived expectations, showing or explaining something to a peer, teasing a peer, wasting time, etc.

The fact that a learner's activity may differ from the expectations given the prescribed task is not a dysfunction of the learner, it is intrinsic to the notion of task and human activity. Much research originating from ergonomics or activity theories address this issue.[1] They insist on the fact that when considering how to support humans' actions the focus must not be limited to what is prescribed (in this case, the teacher's or system's instructions): it is also necessary to take into consideration many other dimensions such as the context and, in particular, what is effectively considered by (in this case) learners.

Learners do not learn because a task is suggested to them, but because they do something in relation to this task. As a consequence, if one considers designing software meant to support learners when (for instance) solving a problem, rather than software whose role is limited to introducing the textual description of the problem on the screen, software must be designed with respect to what learners do in relation to the problem (the activity) and not only to the problem as such, or as thought of by teachers.

This task/activity duality and how it may be acknowledged will be examined in more details in Chap. 3, Sect. 4.

Activity (here, what learners do) may be addressed in many different ways according to matters of concern and/or adopted theoretical backgrounds.

In educational sciences, activity is often addressed on the basis of a differentiation of the *behavioral activity*, which is directly observable (e.g., learners are producing some Java code, drawing boxes and relations with *Argue-chat* or using the *Bio-sim* simulation) and the *cognitive activity* (for instance: learners are generating, inferring, evaluating, analyzing, planning, selecting, organizing, integrating, etc.). Both may be described at different levels of granularity. For instance, "considering hypotheses" may be a pertinent level of granularity for some context or purposes, but disentangling "generating hypotheses" from "adapting existing hypotheses" may be required in other cases.

Inferring *cognitive activity* from *behavioral activity* may be conducted in the light of very different theoretical approaches, from views based on a brain-computer analogy (learners as "rational data processors") to views taking into account social, cultural, historical, technical, affective, motivational (...) dimensions. The type of analysis that may be conducted is also related to the nature of the considered setting. Interpretation rules (i.e., rules allowing a certain interpretation of behavioral activity in the light of a given theoretical background or empirical knowledge) may be relatively easy to produce for a well-defined task, in a well-defined context, for a well-defined set of actors. Things may be more

---

[1]See for example Leplat, J. (1990). Relations between task and activity: elements for elaborating a framework for error analysis, *Ergonomics*, 33 (10 & 11), 1389–1402 or Engeström, Y., Miettinen, R. & Punamäki, R.-L. (1999). Perspectives on Activity Theory. Cambridge: Cambridge University Press.

1 Reference Educational Notions

difficult in open and complex contexts, which are also more prone to task/activity differences.

As an example, let us consider an inquiry learning CBPS within which a given set of learners are told to use *Bio-sim* under teachers' supervision. Learners' activity may be analyzed on the basis of a model of inquiry processes, for instance dissociating different processes ("orientation", "hypotheses", "experiment" and "conclusion") and/or sub-processes (e.g., refining "defining hypotheses" into "generating new hypotheses" and "adapting existing hypotheses").[2] The fact that the setting is more or less controlled allows application of experimental psychology methods. Pertinent data (e.g., learners' skills as demonstrated by a test) can be acquired before, during and after the setting. This is very different from, for instance, analyzing on-line learners' activity that may use *Colab-edit* (or some other means) during the 6 weeks they will, among many other things, collaborate in the context of the *learning theories forum* CBPS.

1.4 Pedagogical Objective

The notion of pedagogical objective is a very broad one. It may correspond to significantly different realities within conceptualizations originating from (and/or mixing) cognitive theories, learning or teaching theories, generic or domain-related views, institutional or professional views, etc.

Developing a typology of possible pedagogical objectives is not in the scope of this book as this would require listing, defining and exploring different approaches and theories related to education and learning.

As a way to introduce this complexity, it may be noticed that matters of concern may be defined with respect to learners (and in different ways) and/or with respect to other considerations.

Examples of concerns defined with respect to learners are:

- Learners are set a task.
- Learners engage in some activity.
- Learners practice some skills.
- Learners develop some knowledge or some skills.

Examples of concerns defined with respect to other considerations are:

- Some teachers' task is facilitated.
- Some social relations are modified.
- Some institutional dimension is modified.

---

[2]van Joolingen, W.R. & Zacharia, Z.C. (2009). Developments in Inquiry Learning. In: Balacheff, N., Ludvigsen, S., de Jong, T., Lazonder, A. & Barnes, S. (Eds.) Technology-Enhanced Learning – Principles and Products, Berlin: Springer, 21–37.

Different concerns lead to different emphasis and the consideration of different notions. For instance:

- Considering as an objective the fact that learners are offered something (e.g., a task to achieve or some given simulation) places emphasis on the need to provide resources (to be contrasted with: focusing on what learners do with these resources).
- Considering as an objective the fact that learners engage in some activity (e.g. reading, communicating, arguing, solving problems or building models) places emphasis on what learners do. This may however be analyzed in different ways (see for example the behavioral/cognitive dimensions) and in the light of different theoretical perspectives.
- Considering as an objective the fact that learners practice some skills places emphasis on the notion of skill (i.e., the ability to perform something successfully) and, more particularly, on the fact that learners' activity relates to some given specific skills. With respect to activity this is not another level, but a different perspective. Moreover, emphasis is on the fact that learners practice something, and not on the fact that they have acquired or developed something.
- Considering as an objective the fact that learners develop some knowledge (or acquire or improve some skills) places emphasis on learning outcomes. This is again a different perspective.

As a first example, let us consider a CBPS making use of *JavIT*. Considered objectives may be related to both behavioral and cognitive dimensions, and in different ways. For instance, it may be observed whether learners define classes and draw inheritance relations, practice inheritance-based modeling (i.e., there is an effective epistemic dimension to their manipulations), develop their understanding of the inheritance notion or develop their capacity to use inheritance properly. These different objectives are not exclusive and are not independent from one another. However, if one considers evaluation, what is to be observed and the evaluation processes are different.

As a second example, let us consider the *learning theories forum* CBPS and the *GeLMS-1* platform. The setting's pedagogical objectives are that learners should "develop some general understanding of a given set of learning theories" and "practice argumentation skills". The platform allows a certain form of implementation of the setting. However, the platform features are not addressed at the conceptual level at which the pedagogical objectives are defined. Rather, they correspond to a level which is that of "equipping learners with something", in this case pedagogical resources (from which come the description of what is to be done or texts related to the learning theories to be studied) and tools that allow on-line communication (forum and chat).

These examples illustrate important issues further addressed in Sect. 3:

1. Pedagogical objectives may be multiple and/or interrelated, and clarifying the software role or features may require them to be disentangled.

2. There may be important differences between the pedagogical objectives considered at the level of CBPSs and at the level of the software design. In order to clarify this dimension we introduce the *software pedagogical rationale* in Sect. 2.4.

1.5 Pedagogical Setting Design

How to design pedagogical settings is at the core of many studies, and different methodologies are reported in, for instance, the instructional design literature.

Within the previously defined general framework, designing a pedagogical setting may be viewed as generally consisting of the definition of[3]:

1. One or more pedagogical objectives.
2. A task, i.e., something that learners must do.
3. The actors, i.e., a learner and, potentially, several learners and one or more teachers (in the broad sense: teacher, tutor, facilitator, etc.).
4. A context that defines the timing, the place, the concerned artifacts (etc.).
5. A teaching task that ensures consistency of these elements, i.e., addresses the objective that the activity developed by the considered learners(s), in relation to the considered task, within the considered context, allows the pedagogical objectives to be addressed.

In other words, it consists of the creation (and the management, when this dimension is addressed) of a *pedagogical setting* within which learners are going to engage in interactions related to the task defined by the teacher, interactions that will lead them to develop an *activity* considered to be favorable to the achievement of the targeted *pedagogical objectives*.

A pedagogical setting is often associated with a *pedagogical scenario* (also referred to as a *learning* or *teaching scenario* in the literature), which may be defined as follows:

> A *pedagogical scenario* is a more or less formalized description of a teaching sequence defining the targeted pedagogical objectives and the means to be implemented to address these objectives. A scenario generally describes the actors (learners, tutors), the resources (documents, software, etc.), the tasks and subtasks learners should address, the roles of the various parties concerned and the constraints to be respected.

The notion of "design of a pedagogical setting" refers to the teacher (in the broad sense) and to the definition of the task, resources and associated constraints that learners are provided with. The way this designed setting unfolds may differ from what is anticipated (see the duality task/activity).

---

[3]Tchounikine, P. & Tricot, A. (under press). Environnements informatiques et apprentissages humains. In: Garbay, C., Kayser, D. (Eds.), Informatique et Sciences Cognitives : influences ou confluences? Ophrys/MSH, 167–200.

2 Educational Software Notions

2.1 Computer-Based Pedagogical Setting (CBPS)

A basic definition of computer-based pedagogical setting has already been introduced in Chap. 1:

> A *computer-based pedagogical setting* (CBPS) is a pedagogical setting involving some software that is meant to play a role in relation with the considered pedagogical objectives.

As mentioned in Chap. 1, a CBPS may be implemented with basic software (in the sense defined in Chap. 1) or with educational software. Examples have been introduced in Chap. 1: the *Java programming* tutoring setting (which may be implemented with *JavIT*), the *biology inquiry learning* setting (which may be implemented with *Bio-sim*), the *learning theories forum* networked learning setting (which may be implemented with basic network and communication means such as proposed by *GeLMS-1* or more specific software such as *Colab-edit*).

As pedagogical settings, CBPSs may be addressed by considering different objects from different levels: cognition and individual or collective psychological issues; knowledge and knowledge construction mechanisms; teaching settings issues; appropriation and usage phenomena; learning phenomena; integration in basic practices phenomena; social evolution phenomena; educational politics; etc. The software role may thus be addressed with very different matters of concern, and at very different levels of granularity, depending on whether the software is considered as allowing CBPSs to exist (e.g., Web-platforms allow on-line learning settings) or is viewed as supporting precise cognitive processes.

The rationale for the adopted CBPS definition is to put to the fore the relationships that may be made (by designers, analysts, institution representatives, etc.) between the software properties (and thus, for educational software, the design decisions), the software roles, and how these dimensions relate, directly or indirectly, to the considered pedagogical objectives.

Within CBPSs, software may play a more or less central role. As an example, the role played by *JavIT* in the *Java programming* tutoring setting is definitely more central and important than the role be played by *GeLMS-1* in the *learning theories forum*. A more qualitative definition may thus be envisaged, e.g., defining a list of possible roles and deciding which ones would be eligible (would be sufficiently important) to decide which settings may be called CBPSs and which ones should be discarded (e.g., the case of a slide presentation program when lecturing in classrooms, which is indeed not a type of setting we will consider in this book). However, this may be hazardous (one of the reasons being the fact the intended role and the effective role may be different) and, anyway, is not necessarily very useful: the purpose of the adopted definition is to draw attention to important dimensions and to not build a taxonomy of systems.

2.2 Educational Software

Building on the premise that what is important is what learners do, we define educational software as follows:

> *Educational software* is software specifically designed to lead a learner to develop an activity that is favorable to the addressing of the considered CBPS pedagogical objectives.

2.2.1 Examples

Different examples have been introduced in Chap. 1 (*JavIT*, *Bio-sim*, *Argue-chat*, *Colab-edit*). Regarding types of systems, educational software may correspond to a variety of cases such as:

- Intelligent Tutoring Systems, i.e., software that leads learners to address a task and can manage different issues arising from human teaching in a way adapted to learners' individual characteristics, for instance: capacity to solve the task at hand, explain and justify the solving process; capacity to manage different teaching issues such as selection or elaboration of a pedagogical strategy, analysis and interpretation of learners' actions to elaborate understanding and representation of their behavior, knowledge and/or profile; selection or elaboration of the feedback to be provided (correction, help, explanations, adaptation of the task to be addressed, etc.); etc. Such software may powerfully build on a specific analysis of the domain and/or of learners' difficulties or misconceptions. *JavIT* is an example.
- Microworlds, simulations or virtual reality pedagogical environments, i.e., software that allows learners to immerse themselves in a virtual world designed so as to present properties that will favor the addressing of the targeted pedagogical objectives: modeling of a domain specifically adapted to some targeted learning; taking advantage of features such as reversibility of actions, replay of sequences or *a posteriori* analyses; etc. *Bio-sim* is an example, based on a simulation.
- Hypermedia learning environments, i.e., environments based on the integration of different types of resources (text, images, videos, audio), their organization using different types of semantic relations (e.g., *hierarchy*, *consequence*, *part-of*, *pre-requisite* or *example*), and the pedagogical use of these relations' semantics. Such hypermedia may be static or adaptive (dynamic adaption on the fly, on the basis of learners' individual characteristics such as their profile and/or their trail within the hypermedia).
- Recommendation software, i.e., systems that can prompt learners. Such prompts may be based on comparing learners' actions with a specific reference (in such case, recommendation systems may be seen as close to an ITS's matters of concern) or with other learners' behaviors (e.g., diagnosing what learners are attempting to do and prompting them with what other learners are doing or have done under similar circumstances). Recommendations may also include other

dimensions such as calendar and deadline reminders or changes of topics as the course progresses.
- Collaborative learning environments, i.e., environments designed to favor the emergence of some kind of interaction among peers (e.g., building on each others' ideas) and providing support and constraints designed to favor the addressing of the targeted objectives. Such environments often build on collaborative-learning scenarios. *Colab-edit* is an example (in this case, with a very basic scenario).
- Specific communication tools, i.e., tools providing support and constraints designed to favor interaction properties identified as favorable to the addressing of some targeted pedagogical objectives. Such support and constraints may, for instance, be introduced by graphical constructions, turn-taking rules, sentence openers such as "I propose an argument" or interaction patterns such as "proposition – arguments – counter-arguments". *Argue-chat* is an example.
- On-line learning platforms, i.e., platforms providing access to resources (e.g., courses, exercises or links to external resources) and associated features (e.g., communication tools or supervision tools for teachers) and organizing these features in a way that matches learners' needs (supporting autonomy, etc.). *GeLMS-1* is a counter-example highlighting the absence of effective educational concerns.
- Mobile learning devices, i.e., software making use of mobile devices (e.g., laptop, PDA, mobile phone or tablet computer) to implement CBPSs for which context is an important dimension. For instance, learners may be provided with tasks or resources specifically related to the fact that they are visiting a museum, so that they benefit from both the context (the museum) and on-line facilities (links to additional resources, communication with peers, etc.).

It may be noticed that there is no bijection between types of systems and settings: a given piece of software may be powerfully used within different types of settings (for similar or different issues), and a setting may be implemented with different types of systems (see how the *learning theories forum* CBPS may be implemented with *GeLMS-1* or *Colab-edit*).

The above examples highlight the diversity of systems that may be considered. It is far from being exhaustive. Efforts to build a comprehensive list may help to clarify the domain. However, it is not necessarily the best way to explore design issues. First, if nothing else, building such a list is difficult, in particular because many systems correspond in fact to blended approaches and/or mix constructions in different ways. For instance, learning scenario players (not listed above) may be standalone systems and/or embedded as a component in an on-line learning platform, and themselves may embed specific communication tools or mobile devices as means offered for a particular scenario. Moreover, differentiation criteria may be arguable. For instance, collaborative learning environments such as *Colab-edit* may be viewed as particular cases of communication tools within an extended definition of communication. Second, systems may belong to the same category but their design relate to very different matters of concern and, conversely, systems that may be seen as very different in nature may share similar issues (see *infra*). This is the rationale for the approach adopted in this book, i.e., providing means for making explicit particular projects rather than classifying systems and addressing these classes.

For instance, is the type of system known as an LMS to be considered as educational software? If considering the broad use of the term educational software as "software smartly used in education", the answer is: yes. If considering educational software according to the definition we have introduced, the answer is: it depends. *GeLMS-1* is an educational software counter-example. In Chap. 4 we introduce *GeLMS-4*, an evolution of *GeLMS-1* designed not only to act as a resource provider, but also to address issues on-line learners often face such as understanding curricula structure and teachers' expectations, developing a group spirit or managing time. Here, educational concerns have governed design or, more precisely, re-engineering. Similar examples may be given for mobile learning systems or drill and practice systems (i.e., software that leads learners to address a very limited task in a repeated way), which may be designed in the light of very different considerations, stemming from the use of a basic algorithm "repeat the question until the right answer is given and then skip to the next question" to the management of individualization issues. Similarly, designing editors offering carefully studied conceptual notions reified in the software interface (such as in *JavIT*) raises issues which, for some of them, are similar to some of the ones to be considered when designing microworlds or simulations such as *Bio-sim*, although the overall systems are of different natures.

2.2.2 Rationale for the Adopted Definition

The rationale for the adopted educational software definition is to put to the fore:

1. The fact that educational software is to be considered in reference to a pedagogical setting (or a type of setting).
2. The fact that educational software embeds and carries out a pedagogical intention: it is designed with respect to pedagogical objectives.
3. The specific importance of considering effective activity.

The point is to draw attention to the relationships between designed software properties, pedagogical objectives and the way the setting unfolds.

2.2.3 Technical Dimensions

Nowadays software has often a complex architecture based on the articulation of different pieces of code and/or on-line services (see approaches such as component-based design or "software as a service"). The articulation may be implemented by a variety of technical approaches such as physical articulation (components are glued in some way or another) or logical articulation (components are connected to one another using middleware).

A first implication is that educational software implementation may be addressed on the basis of strategies consisting of developing and/or reusing software components. As a consequence, when designing or selecting such components, generality and genericity dimensions become important issues (see Chap. 9), as well as how components may be locally articulated or customized to fit contextual needs. For instance, a system such as *Bio-Sim* may be addressed within a strategy targeting the development of a series of inquiry learning systems. When such a strategy is limited to the implementation dimension, users (learners, teachers) are not affected. However, as raised in Chap. 1, Sect. 3.3, this type of approach may influence the design process and the education/CS interplay.

A second implication, more fundamental, is to reconsider the very notion of software as a well-studied artifact offered to users. As an example, supporting learners' mobility may be addressed by the design of an architecture gluing together a set of interoperable pieces of code allowing learners to access means (resources, communication tools, etc.) in a way that is adapted to their context (classroom, home, museum) and available technological means (e.g., desktop, laptop or smart phone). However, another approach is to consider that learners will use whatever tool they will contextually find available and convenient: the applications running on their smart phones, software they have installed on their laptop, available Web-services (etc.), which may vary from learner to learner and from session to session. Within such an approach, in some sense, software used by learners is a contextual construction, and what is to be considered is the on-the-fly interconnection of the different tools contextually used by learners, both in terms of pedagogy (relationships to the pedagogical objectives) and in terms of technology (interoperability, coherence, etc.). Such an approach is consistent with the fact that some learners are no longer technologically dependent on the teaching institution: they have their personal computer and other electronic devices, are familiar with handling these technologies and, for instance, installing and customizing software. Another case where such a view makes sense is informal learning. Within such contexts, what is to be considered is no longer the software offered to learners, but the software learners decide to use.

Generally speaking, consideration of the evolution from standalone programs to components-based architectures or to "software as a service" requires special care when defining the relationships between software and pedagogical issues as the very notion of software is changed. On-the-fly organized architectures, when they make sense, require reconsideration of the way the relationships between the pedagogical intention and the technical features are thought of.

It may be noticed that the articulation/disarticulation dimension is not only a technical concern. For instance, it is a central design dimension for systems such as LMSs. LMSs design faces two different and sometimes conflicting concerns. One is to allow a variety of organizational forms and pedagogic intentions, and thus offer various available tools whilst keeping the organization stand outside of the software design. Another is to take care of (for instance) learners' difficulties or specific needs, which may lead to provision of specific tools, but may also require organizational dimensions of how these tools are provided to be addressed.

Social networks or Communities of Practice (CoPs) are other examples of the fact that the very notion of "software" may require reconsideration. For instance, with respect to pedagogical concerns, a CoP may be seen as implementing a kind of "recommendation system".

2.3 Pedagogical-Setting Support Software

In the preceding sections (and in the rest of the book) the focus is on software dedicated to learners. However, software may also be dedicated to teachers (in the broad sense). In order to avoid confusions, such software may be referred to as pedagogical-setting support software:

> *Pedagogical-setting support software* is software designed so as to be useful to actors concerned in the design, management or analysis of CBPSs.

Different types of software fall into this category: authoring tools for designing CBPS components such as hypermedia resources or learning scenarios; software for analyzing learners' activity or supervising learners' actions; etc.

2.4 Software Pedagogical Rationale (SPR)

With respect to a given CBPS, software is given a role and is designed so as to present the properties that will allow this role to be played. This role is in relation to some of the features of the CBPS. However, CBPSs usually come with several interrelated pedagogical objectives, and educational software may only address part of these. Moreover, what is considered at the level of software design may only be part of the CBPS and teaching setting considerations.

In order to clarify what software design relates to, we introduce the software pedagogical-rationale notion and define it as follows:

> The *software pedagogical-rationale* (SPR) is the part of the CBPS and teaching setting objectives and related features that is taken into account when designing educational software and has a tangible impact on this design.

2.4.1 Examples

Let us consider the *biology inquiry learning* CBPS introduced in Chap. 1.

The general strategy is to lead learners to *engage themselves*, *explore the natural or material world*, *ask questions* and *make discoveries*. More precisely, the considered objectives are that learners *identify interesting questions*, *define hypotheses*, *test hypotheses* and *draw rational conclusions*. Going into details, these objectives are instantiated in biology (cell nucleus, cell membrane, electric charge, liquid exchanges, etc.).

If one considers *Bio-sim* as we have introduced it, its design has been impacted by a certain number of considerations related to the fact that learners define biological hypotheses, test them and draw rational conclusions. These considerations form what we define as its SPR: the software nature (a dedicated simulation enhanced by cognitive tools) is thought of as a means for defining and testing hypotheses; the system suggests making explicit hypotheses, provides means to edit them and to relate them to data; it provides support such as hints related to how to properly separate variables; etc.

However, the considerations taken into account when designing *Bio-sim* only correspond to part of the CBPS pedagogical considerations or, put another way, some other considerations are not taken into account. For instance, the inquiry orientation phase (which involves gathering data and activating prior knowledge[4]) is not considered. This is not to say it is not acknowledged that such a phase exists and is important, but the way it is acknowledged has no impact on the software design. As an example of a different nature, *Bio-sim* allows learners to edit hypotheses and conclusions. With respect to hypothesis management, it provides specific support (dedicated editor, links with the simulation data, hints, etc.). With respect to conclusions, the system offers editing facilities. However, analyzing whether the conclusion is correct or whether the data provided by learners provides evidence for the proposed conclusion is not a matter of concern for the software design. In other words, if one disentangles objectives, *define hypotheses* or *test hypotheses* are considered both in terms of general behavior and of qualitative analysis of learners' processes, while *draw rational conclusions* is only addressed in terms of general superficial behavior (whether a text has been written). This example is different from the previous one because it does not relate to phases that may or may not be taken into account, but to the matters of concern when addressing the phase (e.g., relating hypotheses to data or analyzing conclusions).

As another example highlighting that what is important is not only whether some features are taken into account or not, but also the level at which they are taken into account, and how, let us consider the *learning theories forum* CBPS. This setting may be addressed according to a basic functional perspective. The corresponding SPR may be something such as "learners must have access to a file exchange zone and a forum", and the corresponding software may be a website offering such tools (in such cases, the usual approach is rather to make learners use a platform such as *GeLMS-1*). Adoption of such a perspective does not necessarily mean designers are not aware of the difficulties learners may encounter in working together, but that these difficulties are not taken into account in the design or the selection of an appropriate system. Alternatively, the SPR may be something such as "learners must be supported with respect to their identified difficulties when managing

---

[4]van Joolingen, W.R. & Zacharia, Z.C. (2009). Developments in Inquiry Learning. In: Balacheff, N., Ludvigsen, S., de Jong, T., Lazonder, A. & Barnes, S. (Eds.), Technology-Enhanced Learning – Principles and Products, Berlin: Springer, 21–37.

work-in-progress documents, discussing particular pieces of text or dealing with multiple versions", which may lead one to consider systems such as *Colab-edit*.

It may be noticed that pedagogical intentions usually underlie both the CBPS design and the software design and that, in most cases, they are reified in multiple ways (e.g., in the teachers' instructions, the scenario and the system properties), whose different dimensions are related to one another.[5]

2.4.2 Rationale for Introducing This Notion

CBPSs and teaching settings are complex constructions, mixing many dimensions. In order to clarify design processes, it is important to make explicit, within the general CBPS and teaching setting features, those that correspond to objectives or considerations taken into account for software design. This helps to make more explicit and more precise the way software is thought of, and should be addressed. Not defining what the SPR is may create misunderstandings related to the fact that the part of the overall considerations that may impact software design (and how) is different in the educationalists' and computer scientists' mind.

Returning to the definition of educational software, it may be said that educational software is software that has a non-empty SPR, i.e., some features or properties exist for some precise pedagogical reasons, and both these reasons and their impact on the software can be exhibited.

2.5 The Technology Enhanced Learning Field (TEL)

On the basis of the different working definitions introduced in this chapter, a more precise characterization of the TEL field as considered in this book is:

> *Technology Enhanced Learning* (TEL) is the scientific field the objective of which is to study scientific issues related to CBPSs.

Work related to TEL may address different (interrelated) issues such as design of CBPSs, design of educational software, analysis and evaluation of CBPSs, analysis of educational software usage or impact, effective practices, policy issues, sociological issues, etc.

---

[5]On this point, see for example the concept of embodied conjecture in Sandoval, W.A. (2004). Developing Learning Theory by Refining Conjectures Embodied in Educational Designs. *Educational Psychologist*, 39(4), 213–223.

3 Important Dimensions and Issues Put to the Fore

In Sects. 1 and 2, we have selected and defined in a particular way a certain number of notions. In this section, we analyze important dimensions and issues that this view leads one to consider.

3.1 Disentangling Pedagogical Objectives

As mentioned in Sect. 1.4, it is very common that pedagogical settings refer to different interrelated objectives. Within a perspective of design (of CBPSs, of educational software), making explicit, disentangling and thoroughly explaining the considered pedagogical objectives is of crucial importance. In particular, this is necessary to make clear which of the considered objectives (or considerations related to objectives) are taken into consideration and influence design, i.e., the SPR. It is also of importance for evaluating systems and design principles: design impact may only be evaluated if what has been considered is made explicit.

3.1.1 Pedagogical Objectives and Learning Objectives

The *raison d'être* of pedagogical settings is usually that learners are led to learn something. Settings are usually associated with a learning objective defined as a piece of domain knowledge or a skill (e.g., a mathematics notion or the capacity to achieve a task) or as some transversal competency (e.g., argumentation or synthesis skills, or learning-to-learn capabilities).

However, as already emphasized by the examples listed in Sect. 1.4, settings may be associated with an overall learning objective but, when going into details, design may only effectively consider pedagogical objectives which are not learning objectives. For instance, objectives such as the fact that learners *get familiar with a topic* or *discover their conceptions are not relevant for a given problem or context* are pedagogical objectives which have a learning rationale, but are not learning objectives as such.

The fact that "learners learn something" is just one of the different types of objective that may be considered when designing pedagogical settings or educational software. In fact, more precisely, learning is always in the picture, but not necessarily addressed as such, which often creates confusion.

3.1.2 Intermediate Objectives and Indirections

The fact that pedagogical settings may be associated with different objectives is closely related to the facts that objectives are often intertwined, some objectives may serve as intermediate objectives and/or teaching strategies may use some indirections.

For instance, let us consider Computer-Supported Collaborative Learning (CSCL) scenarios, also referred to as CSCL scripts.[6] Such scenarios are designed to increase the chances that learners engage in interactions related to the knowledge at stake. For example, a classical structure is to group learners known to have different knowledge or views relative to the studied topic and to make them solve together a task requiring that they share their knowledge and actions.

The rationale for considering the objective *make learners engage in interactions related to the knowledge at stake* is anchored in both theoretical and empirical studies showing that whether learners engage in some particular types of interactions (knowledge-generative interactions such as explanation, argumentation, negotiation, mutual regulation or conflict resolution) is positively correlated to learning. Seen from a general perspective, considering this objective is thus part of the strategy for making learners develop some learning. However, with respect to design, what is considered is limited to the intermediate objective of making learners collaborate and interact.

As other examples of intermediate objectives and indirections:

- An objective such as *confront learners with a new type of problem* may be both a pedagogical objective *per se* and a way to address the more general objective of *make learners challenge their current knowledge*. Similarly, *make learners challenge their current knowledge* may itself be a way to address the more general objective of *create conditions for making learners discover* (by themselves, via hints, etc.) *some target knowledge*.
- Objectives such as *generate learners' interest* or *develop some social relationships between learners* may serve other objectives such as *enhance motivation* or *develop positive bases for future fruitful collaboration*.
- Objectives such as *provide automatic answers to learners' basic questions* may be addressed as a means to allow human tutors not to be overwhelmed and to concentrate on key issues.

As another type of example, the design of educational software may also consider objectives such as facilitating the introduction of CBPSs in institutions, for instance considering how to allow teachers to customize some software features as a strategy to ensure their involvement in the use of computers in their classrooms.

3.1.3 Pedagogical Objectives, Learning Objectives, and Design Evaluation

Disentangling objectives and clarifying the ones that are considered when designing software is of major importance for avoiding misunderstandings, for evaluating

---

[6]See for example Fischer, F., Kollar, I., Mandl, H. & Haake, J.M. (Eds.) (2007). Scripting Computer-Supported Collaborative Learning – Cognitive, Computational, and Educational Perspectives. Computer-Supported Collaborative Learning Series v. 6, New York: Springer.

design and for knowledge capitalization. The distinction between learning objectives and pedagogical (but not learning) objectives allows this point to be illustrated.

Let us consider CSCL settings designed in relation to what has been identified as a means for learning: the emergence of knowledge-generative interactions. If one considers such a CBPS, two different dimensions may be analyzed and evaluated: (1) whether learners develop the targeted types of interactions and (2) the learning outcomes. However, if one considers the software dimension (and, possibly, what lessons learned may be capitalized), analysis and evaluation are to be limited to the fact that learners develop the targeted types of interactions, which is what the system has been designed for (i.e., what is its SPR). Analyzing the software role and impact with respect to the overall learning objective is not meaningless, but is subject to many biases as, given the introduced indirection, the learning outcomes may be impacted by many factors: the fundamental hypothesis that the targeted interactions increase the chances that learners learn may not hold for this type of setting or domain, or some other CBPS or teaching setting features may create noise. Analyzing the software role and impact with respect to the learning outcomes is a shortcut that may lead to confusing conclusions with respect to, for instance, the impact of software properties on learners' activity.

With respect to learning objectives as such, software may thus be designed in relation to different goals:

- Software may address a precise learning objective, and be designed in a way that takes into consideration learning mechanisms. What is expected from the software usage is defined in terms of learning outcomes, and the software role is directly related to this learning: the relationships between the computer-based system properties (and usage) and precise learning objectives and mechanisms are explicit. For instance, *JavIT* is designed to make learners develop knowledge and skills related to *inheritance in object-oriented design and programming*, and evaluating learning outcomes is the system's natural evaluation.
- Software may be designed to address what is considered an intermediate objective related to learning. Here, very different cases exist. Intermediate objectives may be very precise and closely related to learning mechanisms such as in the case of CSCL scenarios and building a scenario player with respect to an interaction-related objective. Software may also be designed to play a role that corresponds to some CBPS requirements whose object and/or how it is tackled is much more distant from learning considerations. For instance, offering learners pertinent documents or videos (an "access-to-resource" objective) is a *sine qua non* condition for on-line pedagogical settings to exist. However, here, what is considered at the software level has little to do with learning mechanisms (effective learning issues may be studied in some other dimension of the work, when defining the content of the documents). This may have important consequences with respect to design issues. For instance, in such a case, the possible influence of software properties on the task/activity duality may not be an important matter of concern, while it is of major importance for CSCL scenario players or ITSs.

As a way to emphasize differences, let us consider what type of criteria could be used to stop the system. For the CSCL system, criteria to stop could be something such as *learners came to the end of the scenario, learners do not interact anymore* or *learners had sufficient interactions*, i.e., something related to the software rationale. This is to be compared with an ITS designed to teach and (for instance) engage in epistemic interactions with the learner, for which a criteria to stop could be *the learner's knowledge is now correct* or *the learner's misconceptions cannot be destabilized*, which is coherent with the system rationale. In the CSCL system (as we have introduced it), knowledge-related criteria make no sense as this dimension is not part of the SPR, is not represented in the system and cannot be grasped by it. Knowledge-related criteria can be considered by a human teacher as the actor of the CBPS in charge of managing the learning objectives, but not by the system, which has not been designed for this purpose.[7] Similarly, if software is only designed according to the objective of offering access to resources it may only consider whether learners access them or not.

3.1.4 Issues and Limits

The fact that disentanglement of objectives is an important dimension does not mean it is easy, or that it can necessarily be done in a totally satisfactory way. It may also not be pertinent in some cases.

As a way to illustrate the difficultly (and possible non-pertinence) of disentangling objectives, let us consider the rise of Web-based on-line education in the 1990s. One of the issues that appeared in many effective projects was the difficulty teachers encountered when they were asked to "make explicit" their objectives, strategies (etc.) as a requirement to build these on-line learning systems. "Making explicit" objectives and means was presented as a positive side-effect of these projects, and its underlying difficulty or even feasibility was neglected. However, as mentioned previously, from a theoretical point of view, there is an issue related to explicitation (see Chap. 1, Sect. 4.4). Moreover, pedagogical settings may be addressed by teachers in many ways, some not necessarily very detailed or planned (e.g., creating a situation known to be a rich context opening opportunities for different considerations). In such cases, attempting to disentangle and define precisely all possible objectives is not only difficult: it may appear irrelevant and pedagogically counter-productive.

---

[7]This is not, however, intrinsic to this approach. CSCL scenarios may be explicitly associated with domain-related knowledge or transversal skills, and the designed systems address these dimensions, see for example Tchounikine, P., Rummel, N. & McLaren, B.M. (2010) Computer Supported Collaborative Learning and Intelligent Tutoring Systems. In: Nkambou, R., Mizoguchi, R. & Bourdeau, J. (Eds.), Advances in Intelligent Tutoring Systems, SCI 308, Berlin: Springer-Verlag, 447–463.

As a way to illustrate that disentangling objectives cannot necessarily be done in a totally satisfactory way, let us consider the previous CSCL example: although the reference for the design decisions will be whether learners collaborate and interact, the system design is likely to be also influenced by the overall learning objective (e.g., the way teachers may build on learners' interactions in a debriefing phase). Moreover, when engaging in the system design, other objectives and constraints may apply (e.g., objectives such as *allowing an operational representation of the scenario*, *allowing teachers to customize the scenario on-the-fly* or *allowing teachers to supervise learners' actions*).

When designing software, disentanglement of pedagogical objectives is thus to be seen as a direction to follow as far as it is requested and useful to the design and evaluation needs. The process is to be conducted within this perspective, while being careful not to fall into epistemological traps or a naïve kind of "positivism".

It should be noticed that we have here contrasted the notions of *pedagogical objective* and *learning objective* as a way to highlight and illustrate this complexity, and not as a fundamental issue. In this book we use *pedagogical objective* as a way to denote the broad notion that corresponds to *an objective in relation to some teaching or learning objectives*. This is convenient for discourses of a general scope for which, given what is to be said, there is no particular interest in detailing the nature of the objective, when the setting is associated with different objectives of different natures, or when characterizing precisely the learning issues is not pertinent, or not possible, at the current level of analysis.

3.2 Analyzing the SPR/CBPS Relationships

The process of going from educational descriptions of a pedagogical setting to a program is not that of a simple translation from an abstract level n to a less abstract level $n - 1$. It must be decided what will be considered and the level at which it will be addressed. Different types of processes interplay, such as restrictions of the matters of concern, transformations of these matters of concern or projections on some conceptual or technical plans.

Matters of concerns may be transformed from one level to another in different ways. For instance, the issue of *providing technical support for on-line collaboration* may be addressed at the level of very general considerations (e.g., the existence of synchronous and asynchronous communication means) or at the level of more precise features (e.g., the fact that learners *practice argumentation skills* or *co-elaborate some concepts*): the implications for design are very different.

Moreover, as mentioned in Chap. 1, Sect. 3, the process may appear to consisting of going from educational considerations to CS considerations but, when one goes into details, what is constructed may in fact be the result of both the "top-down" process of implementing educational considerations and the "bottom-up" process of conceptualizing what technology offers and/or what can technically be done, and how. For instance, the definition of the properties that *Bio-sim* should present is the result of a process that takes into account pedagogical requirements and how CS constructions (interfaces and their affordances, constraints and the influence they may have on learners' behavioral or cognitive activities, etc.) may best respond to these requirements, this being addressed through iterative cycles.

The notion of SPR leads to clarification of the issues considered at design time and the nature of these issues: the objectives and considerations that may influence design processes, the design dimensions that may be influenced and how, the considered notions and the way they are addressed and, consequently, the related problems and possible solutions. This clarification allows characterization of the way the pedagogical setting is considered and the targeted software properties (see Chap. 7). Conversely, not clarifying the SPR is a source of many misunderstandings during design and afterwards (e.g., when studying software usage or impact).

Another reason to pay specific attention to the SPR explicitation is knowledge capitalization. Analyzing software independently from the considerations underlying its design and drawing general conclusions from this is misleading. For instance, considering on-line communication, it does not make much sense (and it is very unproductive) to consider and analyze in the same way tools such as *GeLMS-1*, *Argue-chat* and *Colab-edit*. Making explicit what pedagogical considerations have impacted software design (and how they have impacted it) is necessary to keep a correspondence between (1) the theoretical elements used as foundations, if any, (2) the models and (3) the constructed pieces of code (see Chap. 8). This is an important feature for software maintenance and evolution, for testing ideas and alternatives, and for capitalizing knowledge.

A major difficulty is that the SPR is not a direct implication of the description of the CBPS or of the decision of what type of system (ITS, microworld, etc.) will be used: it is a specific construction. This is why it is to be made explicit and not to remain implicit (and, likely, pretty different) in the heads of the educationalists on one side, and the computer scientists on another.

As a way to highlight issues, we exemplify hereafter how an SPR may be impacted by both general and specific considerations. A more detailed example will be developed in Chap. 3, Sect. 2.

Let us consider the *Java programming* CBPS. When considering the general orchestration of the setting, different options are possible, which lead to very different systems:

1. Software is designed to manage the different CBPS major roles. This is the way we have introduced *JavIT*: the system is supposed to introduce the exercise, provide means for learners to build and make explicit their solution, and implement support and feedback. The SPR (i.e., what is to be considered when designing this ITS) is not very different from the overall setting specification. In other words, the software role is so central to the CBPS that almost all of the setting considerations impact software design.
2. Software is given the much more limited role of allowing learners to edit the diagram representing the classes they propose to create and the relations between

these classes (the class diagram). In other words, the system is thought of as a means to build and test constructions that may be useful to complete the considered exercise. The setting is orchestrated by the human teacher, who decides which exercise is selected, how learners should explain their process, when to provide feedback and what this feedback should be.

Let us now consider, in the case of a setting orchestrated by the teacher, the more precise issue of providing learners with means for editing the class diagram. Here again, different options are possible:

1. Consider a generic graphical tool that may be used to draw circles and boxes, draw lines between these constructions, and tag these constructions with some open text as a way to denote what they are meant for.
2. Consider a domain-specific editor that provides predefined structures for the useful object-oriented notions (e.g., *class*, *inheritance relation* or *aggregation relation*).
3. Consider an education-specific editor that provides predefined structures whose definitions and associated constraints have been studied according to pedagogical decisions. For instance, the environment (the notions it makes salient, the constraints and properties) may be defined according to the way teachers phrase problems or provide feedback, and manage in a specific way the fact learners draw meaningless relations or change one relation for another.

These different approaches illustrate different ways of addressing what may be considered as a single role. However, matters of concern vary greatly. In the first approach, the model editing issue is addressed at a level that is independent of the knowledge at stake and the pedagogical use: the considered specification corresponds to that of a basic model editor. The SPR is empty. In the second approach, the model editing issue is addressed at a domain-related level but, here again, the SPR is empty. In the third approach, the model editing issue is addressed in relation to the knowledge at stake and educational considerations, in this case coherence with teachers' practices. The SPR includes the different pedagogical considerations related to the notions and relations to be proposed, and the underlying semantics ruling their use. Its design requires addressing considerations such as: what notions and relations should be presented? What may be the influence of one representation or another on a learner's conceptions or misconceptions? How should the editor react when learners attempt to draw relations that are not semantically coherent? Should learners be allowed to draw any incorrect constructions, or be limited to incorrect constructions corresponding to classical misconceptions the teacher may productively build on? etc. The design process is a problem-solving task whose problem is: how can one impact learners' activity in a way which is consistent with the pedagogical objectives? By comparison, in the first two cases, design does not require consideration of any teaching or learning phenomenon, and the considered problem is just how to allow drawing boxes and relations or respecting Java and object-oriented rules.

3   Important Dimensions and Issues Put to the Fore   55

At a high level, what is captured by the SPR notion thus corresponds more or less to classical possible roles of educational software: orchestrating the setting; providing meaningful means for a task; suggesting some notions or ways of proceeding; constraining, scaffolding or engaging in teaching interactions such as epistemic dialogue; etc. Defining the general software role is, however, not sufficient: defining the SPR requires going into more details and, in particular, making explicit what precise features are taken into account and do impact. At this level, as mentioned in Sect. 2.2, systems of similar types may be related to very different matters of concern.

3.3 Synthesis of the Introduced Dissociations

In this chapter, we have highlighted a set of notions of importance when considering educational software design and we have adopted working definitions that allow matters of concern to be contrasted. Figure 2.1 synthesizes the conceptualization (i.e., the system of notions) introduced by these definitions.

This schema dissociates, within the "pedagogical" zones (e.g., the pedagogical setting zone), the more precise "learning" zones (e.g., the learning setting zone, to be understood as pedagogical settings explicitly targeting precise learning objectives). As stated previously, this is not to oppose these notions, but to highlight and draw attention to the fact that software may relate to some learning settings but its design only relates to "pedagogical-but-not-learning objectives", e.g., raising interest or enhancing interactions. The reason for this emphasis is that this pedagogic/learning objective confusion is a frequent cause of misunderstandings.

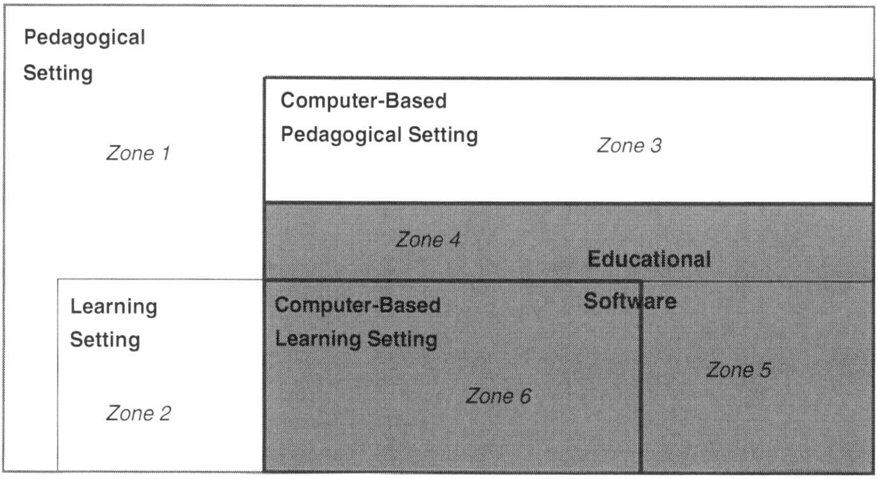

Fig. 2.1 Synthesis of the introduced differentiations

Zone 1: Some pedagogical objectives are defined, but not in terms of precise learning outcomes; the setting does not involve any software.
Zone 2: Some learning objectives are defined (and, possibly, some other more general pedagogical objectives); the setting does not involve any software.
Zone 3: Some pedagogical objectives are defined, but not in terms of precise learning outcomes; the setting involves basic software, i.e., software whose design does not take account of the considered pedagogical objectives (its SPR is empty). *GeLMS-1* is an example.
Zone 4: Some pedagogical objectives are defined, but not in terms of precise learning outcomes; the setting involves software, and this software has been specifically designed to take account of the considered pedagogical objectives (the SPR is not empty). *Argue-graph* is an example.
Zone 5: Some learning objectives are defined (and, possibly, some other more general pedagogical objectives); the setting involves software, this software has been specifically designed to take account of the considered pedagogical objectives, but it has no specific role with respect to the more particular learning objectives (the SPR is not directly related to the learning objectives, but to other -possibly intermediate- objectives). *Colab-edit* is an example.
Zone 6: Some learning objectives are defined (and, possibly, some other more general pedagogical objectives); the setting involves software, this software has been specifically designed to take account of the considered learning objectives (and, possibly, of the more general pedagogical objectives). *JavIT* is an example.

The grey zone denotes the educational software notion: pedagogical (or learning) objectives are defined and software has been specifically designed to take account of them.

To allow one to denote all literature and projects referring to TEL, one might consider adding a *Zone 0* corresponding to the unfortunate situation in which a pedagogical discourse is associated with some given computer-based system, but the hypothesized pedagogical advantage of this system is not explicitly associated with any well-founded and analyzed pedagogical objective or setting.

Chapter 3
Understanding Differences in Perspectives

Abstract This chapter highlights and analyzes a certain number of dimensions that are particularly prone to lead to misunderstandings when considering educational software design issues.

Design of educational software may correspond to very different realities. As a consequence, many notions or issues may be addressed in different ways according to perspectives or matters of concern. Confusion or misunderstanding may have their origins in actors' disciplinary backgrounds but this is far from being the only cause.

In this chapter we explore different dimensions that may lead to differences in perspectives, both as a means to illustrate the necessity of clarifying matters of concern and to study a set of issues of particular importance: the used conceptualization (Sect. 1), the nature of the setting analysis (Sect. 2) and the way complexity of influences (Sect. 3), uncertainties related to learners' effective activity (Sect. 4) or disciplinary dimensions (Sect. 5) may be addressed.

1 Notions and Definitions

There are many teaching or learning approaches.[1] Many misunderstandings may occur in relation to the fact that different approaches associate different meanings to otherwise general terms. Moreover, different cultural dimensions also create confusion. We explore hereafter a few examples.

---

[1] See for example the summary of 50 major theories of learning and instruction (and their relevant concepts) compiled in: Kearsley, G. (2010). The Theory into Practice Database (http://tip.psychology.org; retrieved November 11, 2010).

1.1 Examples

1.1.1 Activity

Activity is a term that may be contrasted with that of task. This is how we have defined it in Chap. 2. Used in this way, it allows one to denote the difference between what learners are asked to do and what they do.

However, this term is also often used in many other constructions such as "pedagogical activity". This usage makes the distinction between what learners are presented with *vs.* what they actually do unclear.

Along with this distinction, *activity* also has some specific definitions. For instance, in Activity Theory,[2] a precise definition and a precise model for this notion are given, together with notions such as *actions* or *operations*.

1.1.2 Didactics

Didactics is often used as a broad term denoting the scientific study of how to teach.

Alternatively, in some European countries in particular, didactics refers to the process of teaching and learning within a particular knowledge area. This dramatically changes the perspective.

Considering disciplinary dimensions gives particular importance to a comprehensive analysis of the knowledge at stake and the specifics of this knowledge construction. This may lead one to give particular importance to the diagnosis of learners' domain conceptions and misconceptions (or "alternative" conceptions; as examples: "electrons are circling like planets around a star"; "3.62 + 4.56 = 7.118"), the reasons why such misconceptions may occur (curricula dimensions, epistemological dimensions, etc.) or the elaboration of epistemic feedback that may destabilize them. It may also lead one to take into account the social, historical and institutional dimensions of how the domain's concepts have been elaborated and are taught. As an example, mathematics education studies have led to the elaboration of different specific teaching theories, models, methods and notions.

1.1.3 Setting, Environment and Milieu

In TEL, the term *setting* may be used to denote the broad notion of *the general context within which activity takes place*. This is the way we use it, as when introducing CBPSs in reference to notions such as pedagogical objectives, tasks, actors, timing, place or teaching setting.

---

[2]Engeström, Y., Miettinen, R. & Punamäki, R.-L. (Eds.) (1999). Perspectives on Activity Theory. Cambridge: Cambridge University Press.

1 Notions and Definitions   59

Another perspective is to have in mind what is referred to in some work as the *epistemic milieu*, i.e., to consider the significations carried out by the resources or organizational features with which learners are presented, in particular with respect to a domain-specific analysis. In such a context, the constructivist perspective "learners learn by adapting to the setting" takes on a particular meaning and leads one to consider the epistemic dimensions of software interfaces (e.g., the way they may lead the learner to conceptualize the domain or the studied problem), control of learners' actions or offered hints.

In CS, the terms *software*, *computer-based system*, *program* or *computer-based environment* are often used as synonyms. Environment, however, often suggests more or less implicitly the fact that the user is offered a consistent and comprehensive set of tools and facilities for performing a task or a type of task. In relation to the setting notion, this set of tools may be thought of as a platform offering different means or as forming a kind of epistemic *milieu*. However, the underlying matters of concern are very different. Taking as an entry point this notion of "environment" and epistemic or feedback dimensions, it would be very confusing to consider in the same way *GeLMS-1* and *Bio-sim*.

Clarification of these dimensions is of particular importance as, in many projects, there is a more or less implicit hypothesis that the software environment is part of (or forms) the "context of activity" and, as such, plays a role in (or, determines) the way its users will conceptualize the domain and/or the problem, and will act. However, such a perspective corresponds to very different realities (hypotheses, levels of analysis, expectations, etc.) in projects such as *GeLMS-1* and in projects such as *JavIT* or *Bio-sim* (see example developed in Sect. 2), and perspectives are again significantly different in *JavIT* (in which emphasis is on tutoring) and in *Bio-sim*.

1.1.4 Interaction

As a final example, *interaction* may refer to a variety of realities such as *learner-teacher* or *learner-learner interaction*, *learner-software interaction*, or *learner-epistemic milieu interaction*. The considered level may also vary. For instance, regarding *learner-learner interaction*, what "interaction" refers to is very different if one considers the fact that learners *exchange some data* (e.g., send each other e-mails) or if one considers the content and nature of the data and underlying process (e.g., the fact that learners *discuss some issues* related to the knowledge at stake or the fact that they *build on each others' propositions*).

1.2 Discussion

Generally speaking, a central issue of the TEL field is that work is often conducted or described on the basis of rather implicit or idiosyncratic conceptualizations.

Misunderstandings may develop because of different disciplinary backgrounds, but also because of non-acknowledged differences in the adopted matters of concern, general view, theoretical foundations, focus, considered objectives and/or conceptual notions. This phenomenon is amplified by the fact that concepts may falsely appear similar and/or intuitively understandable, and the fact that similar wordings may refer to very different notions and ideas.

In Chap. 2 we have introduced general notions that provide a substratum that can be used to describe work at a high level of granularity, that of the educational software concept. However, this is not sufficient when addressing precise work. Such a conceptualization effort may be pushed forward, addressing more precise notions and going into more details. However, as raised in Chap. 1 and further exemplified in this chapter, educational software projects may be of very different natures. As a consequence, attempting to build a fine-grained conceptualization that would fit all projects is meaningless. Such a process only makes sense when conducted in the context of a precise project (which may encompass design of a series of systems) or when building on a precise theory or engineering methodology (see Chap. 6).

Within this perspective, Chap. 7 lists different characteristics that may help to clarify the adopted perspective and conceptualization. As an example, when considering the software pedagogical rationale, matters of concern may be very different: the technical provision; the usage of software that learners may develop; whether this usage will lead to better or different learning than with some other software, or without software; whether pedagogical settings using this software are consistent with the considered overall teaching setting, fit into the teachers' practices and/or modify them, fit curricula or material conditions such as learners' access to computers; etc. Considering possible alternatives (for this dimension and other characteristics) helps to clarify concepts and approaches.

2 Nature of the Setting Analysis: An Example

The examples introduced in Sect. 1 suggest TEL settings may be analyzed within radically different perspectives. In this section, we exemplify this diversity by contrasting two different analyses of a given setting.

The example we consider is about building educational software to support learning of addition of fractions. The general specification is to build a system that will support on-line learners in the collaborative solving of addition of (complex) fractions exercises.

The way the setting is presented is, of course, very general and vague, thus allowing a large variety of implementations. We explore hereafter two possible analyses of this setting, the general *Pedagogical Analysis A* and the domain-specific *Pedagogical Analysis B*, and associated technical analyses.

2.1 A General and a Domain-Specific Analysis

2.1.1 Analysis A

[Pedagogical Analysis A]

- Randomly create groups
- Present exercise to the groups
- Provide the groups with access to some textual resources related to addition of fractions (course, solved exercises, etc.)
- Provide the groups with collaborative means
- Provide the groups with means to send their solutions to the teacher

This may lead to an analysis of required software features and properties such as:

[Technical Analysis A]

- Accessibility features:
  - Shared resources management system allowing access to resources (exercises, courses, etc.)
  - Workflow/dataflow (control of access to resources)
- Communication features:
  - Synchronous and/or asynchronous communication tools (e.g., chat or forum)
  - Collaborative tool (e.g., whiteboard)
  - File transfer system

2.1.2 Analysis B

[Pedagogical Analysis B]

- Conduct a domain-specific (mathematical) analysis of the fraction notion, of how this notion and related features are taught in the curriculum and why (arithmetic, ratio, etc.), and of the epistemic obstacles that may be encountered by learners when learning to add fractions.
- Elaborate domain-specific models of learners' conceptions, misconceptions and knowledge-construction processes, as a way to support the understanding of learners' activity and productions and to identify how to support learning by destabilizing misconceptions.
- Identify what exercises may be used to make learners challenge their knowledge, strengthen correct conceptions, destabilize misconceptions or face cognitive conflicts.
- Group together learners whose conceptions, misconceptions and/or knowledge-construction processes models are different, on the basis of learners' knowledge and skills as demonstrated in preliminary individual exercises.

- Present the groups with exercises that maximize the chances for learners to engage in epistemic interactions.
- Scaffold the groups' fractions and calculus work, and the epistemic interactions.

This may lead to an analysis of required software features and properties such as:

[Technical Analysis B]

- Diagnosis and elaboration features:
  - Diagnosis algorithm allowing the construction of learners' models from the analysis of their solutions to the preliminary exercises.
  - Pairing algorithm allowing learners to be grouped according to their models and to the analysis of the domain knowledge-construction processes.
  - Elaboration of pertinent exercises according to learners' models and groups' composition.
- Editing features:
  - Specific editor of fractions based on the notions and constraints identified by the domain-specific epistemological analysis.
- Communication features:
  - Argumentation tool, e.g., chat tool imposing a set of sentence-openers based on the domain-specific epistemological analysis.

2.2 Differences and Implications

2.2.1 Description of the Setting and Considered Objectives

Analysis A considers a pedagogical objective ("support a group of on-line learners in the collaborative solving of exercises"), which is not further defined in terms of learning. Taken this way, the evaluation of a system constructed according to this analysis would be: are learners supported? This remains a broad notion, but analysis A is indeed of a superficial nature.

Analysis B gives a specific meaning to the broad notion of "support": support should be related to the epistemic obstacles encountered by learners when learning to add fractions and to the epistemic interactions that may develop when collaborating. This leads one to consider the creation of conditions that are likely to favor the fact that learners cross these obstacles by challenging the coherence or pertinence of their present conceptions while interacting with peers, and refine their present knowledge.

It may be noticed, however, that Analysis B does not explicitly state any learning objective. If we analyze the setting, there are two different objectives. One is to make learners challenge their knowledge (which may be further disentangled with respect to solving and epistemic interactions dimensions). The other is to make

2 Nature of the Setting Analysis: An Example

learners develop the targeted knowledge. The latter is the rationale for the former. However, only the former (and, in particular, the interaction dimension) is taken into account in software design. The system is designed to detect learners' profiles and pair them. It does not, for instance, provide hints highlighting why learners' present conceptions are inadequate.

This example illustrates the importance of clarifying what pedagogical objectives are addressed and how, and different issues raised in Chap. 2: different pedagogical objectives may be considered, objectives are often meshed, and software may relate to only part of these objectives (SPR notion).

2.2.2 Nature of the Pedagogical Analyses

A is based on a general pedagogical analysis: it addresses teaching and learning issues at a level of general principles, independent from the taught domain. If the studied domain is *ecology* and not *addition of fractions*, nothing changes except the type of resources that will be used.

B is based on a fine-grained disciplinary (in this case, mathematics) analysis, which addresses teaching at a level that takes into account the disciplinary specifics of the construction of knowledge. It builds on specific notions such as *conception* and *misconception*, *epistemic obstacle*, *cognitive conflict* or *argumentation* and their domain-dependent instantiations *(the way learners conceptualize what a fraction is, the epistemic obstacles learners face when learning to add fractions,* etc.), considering how to present to a learner an epistemic *milieu* (the system, the peer) confrontation with which will lead to the expected outcomes.

Pedagogical Analyses A and B are just possible analyses of the setting (in fact, the premises of an analysis). Both make sense and can be argued. Analyses such as A are very common in on-line learning projects. The implicit underlying way of considering education is: how to give learners access to pertinent resources and provide collaboration means? It matches technical infrastructures such as LMSs and, in fact, this type of analysis is often implicitly influenced by the fact that it is known in advance that an LMS will be used. Analyses such as B are preferably conducted when building ITSs or microworlds for instance.

2.2.3 Technical Analyses

Technical Analyses A and B are again just possible implications of the pedagogical analyses. Both make sense and can be argued. They correspond respectively to Pedagogical Analysis A and B in the sense that they are consistent with these pedagogical analyses: issues are addressed at the same levels of granularity.

Analyses A and B lead to considering very different SPRs. In the A case, issues are considered in terms of access to data and to communication means: what springs immediately to mind are the features related to workflow and dataflow as this is the level of granularity of the pedagogical analysis. In the B case, some workflow and dataflow features will also be addressed. However, they are not the entry points. The central issue is less to give access to a communication tool than the characteristics of the communication tool as a way to stimulate epistemic interactions. Similarly, the focus is not on sharing or making documents to circulate, but on providing learners with conceptual scaffolding that will lead them to face some cognitive conflicts and to conceptualize the domain in a certain way. The issue of making documents circulate will also be tackled, but this has little impact on the way the setting is addressed and the notions that are considered. As other examples of design issues impacted in different ways:

- The software genericity and reusability dimensions. Typically, Analysis A may be implemented using generic structures (e.g., an LMS). By contrast, Analysis B requires specific features whose spectrum is partially related to the domain and partially related to the way issues such as learners' modeling is implemented.
- The importance given to how the system is used. In the A case, whether learners use one communication tool or another is not of great importance as there are no particular assumptions underlying the use of these tools. In the B case, the tools provided are thought of as carrying particular significations: whether or not learners use these tools, and how they use them, is of particular importance.
- The evaluation. The way evaluation (of the built system, of the obtained CBPS, of learners' usage of the proposed tools or of the impact of design decisions) is to be processed is very different in the A and the B cases.

Considering the way Pedagogical Analysis B impacts design issues, it may be noticed that some dimensions help one to conceptualize the overall approach and inform the elaboration of some software components (e.g., modeling the domain conceptions or the knowledge-construction processes helps one to conceptualize how learners may be led to face cognitive conflicts or how to group them) and, in addition, some dimensions are reified in software (e.g., the sentence-openers).

As a final remark, it may be noticed that although it is unlikely that high-level generic analyses such as Pedagogical Analysis A lead to low-level analyses such as Technical Analysis B, it is quite often the case that a detailed analysis such as Pedagogical Analysis B is implemented within a high-level generic approach similar to Technical Analysis A. In other words, the Pedagogical Analysis B may be implemented by considering a SPR similar to that of Analysis A, i.e., only addressing the dataflow and workflow issues of the analysis, management of the other pedagogical issues being left to learners and/or teachers.

2.3 Conclusions

In this section, we have taken a very general description of a TEL project and showed that it may lead to very different types of analyses, involving different matters of concern and notions.

In fact, joint presentation of Analyses A and B immediately reveals their lack of completeness and the fact that they both rely on many implicit issues. If designers wrote Analysis A and then considered an analysis such as B, they would immediately refine their analysis to make it more precise, explain that it does not consider some issues, that of course the overall objective is as follows, etc. In other words, contrasting analyses is a means of making explicit and unambiguous (for oneself and for others) one's matters of concern, objectives, decisions, etc. As already mentioned, this is the rationale for listing possibly pertinent characteristics in Chap. 7.

3 Acknowledgement of Influential Factors: Examples

Building artifacts or analyzing settings requires one to define what factors are considered as having an influence, and how this influence is considered. In the context of TEL, given the variety of levels, matters of concern and/or theoretical approaches that may be considered, very different perspectives may develop. As a way to exemplify this, we explore three topics, very different in nature: first, the notion of *impact* of software; second, the role of the socio-technical dimension of TEL on the effective usage of educational software and the field's development; third, elements that might be considered when analyzing learners' activity.

3.1 Impact of Software

For a computer scientist (and, possibly, other actors), the major dimension of the concretization of a TEL project is classically the construction of software presenting the required specific properties. These properties may be related to algorithms, interfaces, functions, etc. When conducted in a research project, the objective is not simply to build systems, but to elaborate knowledge – models, techniques, processes, etc. – that may be used as foundations, guidelines or tools for the design and implementation of the considered type of system or properties.

Introducing software into a pedagogical setting changes the setting, in any case. The *raison d'être* of giving a system some particular functions and/or some particular properties (and of capitalizing knowledge or components facilitating design and implementation of such systems) is that this makes (or contributes to) a difference. The underlying notion is that of *the impact of a specific system*: system s_1, because of its properties, has a different impact than another system s_2.

As an example, the rationale for the design of synchronous communication tools such as *Argue-chat vs.* basic tools allowing the message to be typed directly (or other tools proposing sentence-openers forcing learners to first select an item such as *I think that* or *I provide a counterargument* before typing the message, or other structuring means) is that these differences are of importance, and will have different impacts on learners' interactions.

Anticipating that a system will be used as expected and will have the expected impact on learners' activity is a rather naïve and techno-centered approach. What is to be considered is not learners' expected usage, but learners' effective usage, which often differs from what has been anticipated. This is why the definition of educational software proposed in Chap. 2 builds on the notion of learners' activity. The properties of a given system are only one of the different dimensions that may influence the activity learners will develop when considering the learning setting and using this system (see Sect. 4).

Nevertheless, the *raison d'être* of designing educational systems is related to a perception of technology as having an impact on the setting and on learners' activity and learning: the impact is not necessarily the one that was anticipated, it is not necessarily a major impact, it is not necessarily the same impact on all learners at any time, it is not necessarily an impact that has an overall positive effect given the considered objectives but, in any case, there is an impact. This dimension is central in the context of analyses such as Analysis B developed in Sect. 2, which puts to the fore detailed relationships between the pedagogical setting and the system properties. See also *JavIT* or *Bio-sim*.

The notion of "impact of software properties" may, however, be considered very differently. For instance, let us consider other entry points such as the general teaching setting within which CBPSs takes place. Within such a view, the specific properties of s_1 or s_2 may be relegated to the status of contingent elements, and disregarded as key components of the setting. The "impact of a specific system" dimension may be completely ignored and not considered, in a way similar to how techno-centered approaches do not consider the individual characteristics of users or the effective usage dimensions.

The concept of "impact of a specific system" may even be challenged as a relevant concept itself. It may for instance be argued that as it is impossible to anticipate the effective usage of software, which is related to too many different factors (see Sect. 4), and as learners' activity is a complex construction for which software is only one element whose influence is impossible to disentangle from other dimensions, taking as something useful for design the notion of "impact of a specific system" is irrelevant. This is an argument that often underlines more or less implicitly the use of basic software rather than specific software, or building disarticulated environments such as LMSs (see Chap. 2, Sect. 2.2).

This notion of "impact" illustrates that if, when considering a given CBPS or the very concept of CBPS, the role attributed to software may be thought of and considered very differently, this is also true of what is expected from this role and the influence of software. As a consequence, the importance given to design issues and to usage issues may vary greatly. Typically, computer scientists may consider with great care some interface details that are in no way a matter of concern for educationalists and, *vice versa*, may consider as technically equivalent what is considered by educationalists as presenting very different affordances.

Reasons for considering or not considering detailed software properties may vary. For instance, in Chap. 1 we have introduced the *learning theories forum* networked learning setting and highlighted that it may be implemented by presenting learners with a basic LMS (e.g., *GeLMS-1*). Such an implementation approach may be based on the fact that the CBPS is not analyzed in detail (with respect to the example introduced in Sect. 1, it is of the "Analysis-A" type), the fact that software issues are considered as contingent, and/or other considerations such as economic considerations. Presenting learners with *Colab-edit*, which is related to a more precise analysis of learners' needs, only makes sense if this particular software is thought of as something that is likely to have some impact on learners' activity (which impact may be related to whether some difficulties disappear, some processes are eased, etc.).

As a matter of fact, it may be recalled that software is never "neutral". For instance, when designing a chat tool, an interface must be designed, and this interface will have properties. A chat interface may be more or less structured (graphical shapes, sentence openers, etc.), but deciding that the interface is unstructured or that sentences appear chronologically is a design decision, is a particular property of some chat tools, and has some impact.

3.2 Software Usage and Socio-technical Dimensions of the Field

TEL is intrinsically a socio-technical field. Influences are complex and multiform at the different levels of organization of teaching settings, evolution of practices, dynamics of some given types of systems and software usage.

With respect to the dynamics of some given types of systems, let us consider the way the CSCL paradigm has gained importance when, at the same time, the ITS paradigm has become less dominant. From a teaching and learning point of view, this change in paradigm may be analyzed in the light of the rise of socio-cultural approaches to learning. From a technical point of view, this change in paradigm may be analyzed in the light of the emergence of ICT. In fact, taking a more general perspective, a variety of interrelated reasons may be highlighted[3]:

1. Work conducted in the 1970s and 1980s on modeling of the learner and of the addressed domain to allow the computer to play the roles of a human tutor (and, in particular, provide individualized feedback on the learners' actions at each stage of problem-solving) turned out to be much more difficult than expected. Except in delimited domains, this approach appeared very difficult to implement, and few systems have been successfully implemented.

---

[3]This analysis is inspired by: Tchounikine, P., Mørch, A.I. & Bannon, L.J. (2009). A Computer Science perspective on TEL research. In: Balacheff, N., Ludvigsen, S., de Jong, T., Lazonder, A. & Barnes, S. (Eds.) Technology-Enhanced Learning – Principles and Products, Berlin: Springer, 271–284.

2. Advancements in network communication and interfaces brought to the fore the fact that the computer could be seen as a mediating mechanism between learners and teachers or other learners. Such systems are inspired by a socio-cultural view of learning, as well as by progress in computer-supported cooperative work and groupware. This view does not require any attempt to model substantive aspects of the learners or of the domain. Rather, learners are provided with resources for action through the computer medium, allowing flexibility and control to be in the hands of the users, not the system.
3. The complexity of the technologies underlying ITSs and CSCL systems is very different. ITSs raise issues such as the understanding by the system of learners' activity and output, problem solving and interaction control. All these issues are difficult and not yet solved Artificial Intelligence problems. On the other hand, most CSCL work does not address these issues. CSCL also raises tricky CS issues (e.g., Human Computer Interaction issues), but these are less binary and less non-contingent problems than in ITS (i.e., the problem is solved or not, the software can be programmed or not). Most CSCL projects are based on simple and stable technologies.
4. Dissemination and usability of technologies underlying ITSs and CSCL systems are very different. Teachers are unlikely to customize AI-based systems, but often have no difficulty in using the ICT features underlying CSCL applications. Moreover, ICT is well disseminated and almost freely available.
5. The demand for skills in collaboration and knowledge integration (e.g., to critically evaluate information resources found on the Web) has been brought to the foreground, making the teaching of these skills more important than ever. While the ITS paradigm is associated with teaching and learning domain-specific skills (physics, mathematics, etc.), CSCL is often about general skills (e.g., working in teams, collaborating or synthesizing).

This example illustrates that why one type of system appears to be used rather than another is subject to many different influences. The virtues attributed by some actors to CSCL approaches (*vs.* ITS approaches) may be related to very different considerations: a given view of learning and teaching, the fact that CSCL software is more easily implementable, the fact that CSCL settings make more sense for teachers or for institutions, economical reasons, etc.

Moreover, if one considers similar systems, success may be related to many other features than these systems' differences in properties. In particular, the fact that software s_1 is used in effective settings (rather than software s_2) does not say anything about the respective qualities of s_1 and s_2. It may be the case that experiments have shown that for some given setting and some given objectives s_1 has a more positive impact than s_2, but other reasons (related to economical or institutional reasons, to teachers' practices, etc.; see Chap. 9, Sect. 2) lead to a predominant use of s_2.

Acknowledging the fact that many features may influence CBPSs or the use of software is not in contradiction with considering the fact that specific software may have specific impact and, *vice versa*, considering specific software has specific impact is not in contradiction with acknowledging that software is usually not definitional of the setting, that this impact may be influenced by many different features and, possibly, may be rendered contingent by other factors. These are different dimensions, to be disentangled.

Among many other issues, not disentangling these dimensions prevents knowledge capitalization and scientific perseverance. For instance, laudation of the CSCL approach and criticisms of ITSs often mix two dimensions, the fact that the underlying views of teaching/learning are different and implementation dimensions. The fact that it is considered, on the basis of some theoretical view or some empirical studies, that the CSCL approach (or the ITS approach) has some virtues should be disentangled from the fact that CSCL systems are usually easy to implement while ITSs raise serious difficulties. As a matter of fact, from a CS perspective, technical difficulty is part of the explanation for the movement from the ITS to the CSCL paradigm.

3.3 Diagnosing Learners' Activity

As a final example of the importance of defining what factors are considered as having an influence, and how this influence is to be thought of, let us consider the issue of perception and understanding of learners' activity, taking *JavIT* (the ITS dedicated to object-oriented design and programming) as an example.

A central feature of ITSs is feedback (or retroaction): learners act, the system retroacts, and the system's feedback must be consistent with the pedagogical objectives. Addressing feedback issues requires three main issues to be tackled: (1) perception and understanding of learners' activity; (2) elaboration of the feedback to be processed; (3) implementation of the feedback. We will focus here on the first of these.

As in the example analyzed in Sect. 2, perception and understanding of learners' activity may be considered in very different ways. For instance, one may consider behavioral dimensions (use of the *JavIT* editor's features), generic cognitive dimensions (e.g., *generating* or *analyzing*) or domain-specific processes and skills (e.g., *elaboration of inheritance relationships* processes).

In order to process diagnosis, interpretation rules may be used, using patterns corresponding to correct and incorrect constructions. Such patterns may be elicited from an accurate analysis of the domain or by an automated data-mining analysis of a significant mass of learners' productions.

When defining these rules, according to the adopted approach, different dimensions may be considered as having a potential influence on learners' productions. We contrast hereafter two possible options.

A first approach is to consider learners as rational actors using in a rational way (although possibly incorrectly) their knowledge (which may be correct, correct for some spectrum or incorrect) to solve the problem. Learners' output is considered as direct symptoms of their conceptions, misconceptions and application processes.

Within this view, an erroneous inheritance construction may be diagnosed as the fact that the learner has a misconception of the inheritance notion or an erroneous application mechanism. For instance, the inheritance notion ("class-B inherits from class-A") may be used in different ways[4] corresponding to different perspectives: *conceptual* (*a* and *b* being objects created by instantiating class-A and class-B respectively, "a *b* is an *a* which is more specific"), *set-oriented* ("set B is included in set A"), *logical* ("if *o* is a B, *o* is an A"), *behavioral* ("a *b* can do anything an *a* can do") or *structural* ("*a*'s features are part of a *b*'s features"). Diagnosis may suggest that a learner applies a perspective on inheritance, which, in this case, may explain the error. Following this line of thinking, feedback may address issues such as destabilizing learners' misconceptions by suggesting consideration of another perspective or introducing an example that, given the learners' adopted perspective, may emphasize the error.

Another approach is to consider learners (and settings) as natively and fundamentally influenced by the conditions and constraints that determine the controlled diffusion of knowledge and skills in society, in an anthropological perspective.[5] The way learners' activity is addressed is now different, considering it may be less powerfully explained in terms of conceptions and rational use of knowledge than in terms of compliance with the social, institutional and historical context: the way the institution expects learners to solve the problem as carried out by the curriculum, the text books, the way CS design and programming has developed and is addressed (e.g., the place of the *object-oriented* perspective with respect to other paradigms such as the *functional* or the *logic* perspectives), etc. As a consequence, the bases for elaborating the interpretation rules are very different than in the conception-oriented perspective.

These two approaches, contrasted here, are not necessarily in direct opposition. The point here is to highlight that what may be considered as the influential factors to be considered, and their importance, may vary to a great extent. Here, in contrast to the example introduced in Sect. 2, analyses are quite similar in terms of objectives or levels of granularity (interpretation rules). However, the adopted approaches lead one to consider very different dimensions.

4 Acknowledgement of Activity-Related Uncertainties

In this section, we come back to the *activity* notion, highlighting that learners may consider a task other than the one set by teachers, that effective use of the provided technology is subject to uncertainties, and that these dimensions may be acknowledged and considered very differently.

---

[4]Meyer, B. (1996). The Many Faces of Inheritance: A Taxonomy of Taxonomy. *Computer*, 29(5), 105–108.

[5]See for example: Chevallard, Y. (2007). Readjusting Didactics to a Changing Epistemology. *European Educational Research Journal*, 6(2), 131–134.

4.1 Uncertainties Related to the Effectively Considered Task

As introduced in Chaps. 1 and 2, in the context of educational settings, teachers set *tasks* (the prescribed work), and learners' *activity* (what they actually do) is a more or less rational response to their interpretation of this task.[6] In other words, learners may consider *another task* than the one set by the teacher or the system.

As an example, let us consider the *biology inquiry learning* CBPS and *Bio-sim*. The task defined by the teacher is: "build and describe a model (and underlying theoretical elements) that may explain the way cells react when immerged in a given salty liquid". Different features complement this instruction in different (more or less implicit) ways: the setting is collective, which suggests learners should collaborate; learners are provided with *Bio-sim*, which suggests they should use it; it takes place within a teaching setting, which may influence learners' perception and representation in many ways; etc. However, learners may develop different representations of what (for instance) "build and describe a model" should correspond to, for instance:

- The task consists of elaborating a model of the phenomenon and representing it using *Bio-sim* editors.
- The task consists of modeling the phenomenon with *Bio-sim* editors.
- The task consists of collaborating with peers to elaborate and discuss a model.
- The task consists of using *Bio-sim* communication as means to discuss with peers the biological notions that may be involved in the model.
- Etc.

Differences may be subtle, but change important dimensions with respect to software. For instance, if considering elaborating a model of the phenomenon and then representing it using *Bio-sim* editors, the editors may only be considered after the model is elaborated: if they are meant to influence the elaboration (see the notion of epistemic *milieu*), this goal is missed. This may even lead the provided software to appear as an obstacle to learners' collaboration as they enact it.

With respect to software itself, different representations may also be developed, for instance:

- *Bio-sim* simulation is a means to understand the domain.
- *Bio-sim* simulation is a means to test hypotheses.
- *Bio-sim* simulation is fun (but its relation to the task is unclear).
- Etc.

---

[6]Goodyear, P. (2001). Effective networked learning in higher education: notes and guidelines. Volume 3 of the Final Report to JCALT: Networked Learning in Higher Education Project (http://csalt.lancs.ac.uk/jisc/; retrieved November 11, 2010). See also Jones, C., Dirckinck-Holmfeld L. & Lindström, B. (2006) A relational, indirect, meso-level approach to CSCL design in the next decade. *International Journal of Computer Supported Collaborative Learning* 1(1), 35–56.

The effective tasks considered by learners may be related to the above-mentioned features, but also to dimensions related to other different objectives and motivations of different kinds, for instance:

- Receiving a good mark.
- Being proud of one's work.
- Collaborating with a peer.
- Imposing oneself as a leader.
- Demonstrating one's superiority over a peer.
- Preventing the group from failing in the task.
- Avoiding tensions within the group.
- Acting just enough so as to be decently allowed to say to the teacher one did make some efforts.
- Etc.

What learners think they are doing or have done may differ from what actually happened (or was perceived by other actors), and may correspond to different realities. For instance, learners may think they use *Bio-sim* as expected by the teacher when elaborating a model on a sheet of paper and then editing the result with the *Bio-sim* editor, when the fact that learners would elaborate the model with the editor (and be influenced by the notions provided by this editor) was considered to be a key dimension of the setting. As another example, learners may think they save the group from failure by solving the problem on their own when in fact they prevent peers from contributing.

In summary, the effective task(s) considered by learners may differ from the ones defined by the teacher. The relationships between prescribed and effective tasks may be complex and not straightforward, and evolve in time.

4.2 Uncertainties Related to the Effective Use of Technology

From a technical point of view, a computer-based system allows capabilities: a chat tool allows synchronous exchange of text-based sentences between different computers; a shared modeler offers a set of representations that can be manipulated, means to organize them graphically on the interface and means for different connected users to access the model; etc. These capabilities may be defined by general textual presentations (as described above) or using formal and unambiguous representations (e.g., formalisms based on logics).

This functional dimension, however, only defines a technological capability. The fact that learners appropriately understand the underlying assumptions (e.g., that learners will use the provided shared modeler, will associate with the modeler notions with a semantics that is similar to that of the designers or will interact while editing the model) is not a given.

Without going into detailed theoretical considerations, two points may be highlighted.

First, an object of complex design such as software is not something that is understood in the same manner by different persons. A piece of software presents affordances, i.e., aspects that suggest how it should be used.[7] These affordances will be perceived differently by different users (and also by the same user in different contexts or at different times), which will influence the usage.

Secondly, theoretical frameworks such as Activity Theory[8] help one to understand that designers do not provide users with instruments. Designers create *artifacts* on the basis of how they imagine their future usage. However, an artifact only becomes an instrument for users in the context of their activity, when and through the fact that it allows these users to achieve the tasks they consider in the way they consider them: it is the user that gives the status of instrument to the artifact.

As an example of how this may be conceptualized, according to the instrumental-genesis theory,[9] the instrument is an abstract notion that can be seen as constructed from the artifact (the technical object) and the functions users assign to it in the context of their activity, in a double process of *instrumentation* (adaptation of the user to the artifact constraints) and *instrumentalization* (attribution by the user of functions to the artifact, functions that may correspond to or differ from those anticipated by the designers). An instrument may thus be considered as composed of a technical dimension (the artifact), originating from the design process, and a psychological dimension (the usage *schemes*, specific to the user and/or socially defined) developed by the user, in use. Ergonomic work related to this artifact/instrument dichotomy suggests that the artifact impacts but does not define the instrument.

In other words, software features and properties must not be considered as passively received by actors in a form that corresponds to those that underline their design, but as co-constructed by these actors, in the context of their activity, according to their expectations and needs, and thus with psychological, historical and cultural influences.

As a way to illustrate this issue, different classical examples of unexpected usages of educational software may be highlighted:

- Usage of chat as a means of perception for mutual presence or actions.
- Usage of a function meant to edit a result as a "support for thinking" or, *vice versa*, editing of a result (elaborated via other means) with tools meant to elaborate the result, thought of and considered as a "support for thinking" and a vector for the targeted learning.

---

[7]For a comprehensive comparative analysis of different definitions of the affordance notion, see: McGrenere, J., Ho, W. (2000). Affordances: Clarifying and Evolving a Concept. In: Fels, S. & Poulin, P. (Eds.) Proceedings of Graphics Interface 2000, Montreal: Canadian Human-Computer Communications Society, 179–186.

[8]Engeström, Y., Miettinen, R. & Punamäki, R.-J. (Eds.) (1999). Perspectives on Activity Theory. Cambridge: Cambridge University Press.

[9]Rabardel, P. (2003). From artefact to instrument. *Interacting with Computers*, 15(5), 641–645.

- Change in the way the environment is used due to the evolution of motivations (and, thus, effective activity), for example from "playing the game of the pedagogic contract and using the platform to meet the teacher's demand" to "deal with urgency and produce the expected result (whatever the means are)".
- Etc.

4.3 Acknowledgement and Possible Implications for Design

4.3.1 Issue

The activity that will emerge from the confrontation of learners with the task and the technological setting may be influenced by different dimensions, and is subject to different contingences. Learners' perception and enactment of settings are intrinsically situated, and therefore difficult to predict. Learners' activity is related to the (different) task(s) learners consider, their different motivations, and how these interrelated dimensions interact. The characteristics of the technological setting will be interpreted in different ways by learners, who will appropriate them, in context, according to their purposes and in terms of their own current interests or needs. Basically, learners do not use the provided software to solve the set task, they consider some task (that may only correspond more or less to that set by the teacher) and take advantage of the means that seem best adapted to them (which may correspond to some usage of the provided software) in the context of their activity. How technical properties will be perceived and used is subject to different contingences and impossible to predict in detail.

To what extent learners' enactment of the technological setting may diverge from expectations is related to different dimensions. CBPS's openness is an important one: a task limited to one or two unambiguous limited actions is less prone to variations than, for instance, a collaborative project involving several learners for several weeks. However, this issue is not limited to open and complex settings, see the way learners use multi-choice questions to see the feedback on alternatives. As other examples of important dimensions: the way the technological tools relate to the task (for instance, tools that are the only way to achieve the task *vs.* tools that are just possible means), software feedback (see differences between *JavIT* and *Bio-sim* based settings) or learners' autonomy.

The task/activity duality is not specific to educational settings. This issue, however, is of particular importance in an educational context as learning is related to what learners do, and not to what they are presented with (which is the reason why, in Chap. 2, the notion of pedagogical setting was defined in relation to the notion of activity and not to that of task). If one acknowledges that the task considered by learners may substantially differ from that expected by teachers as defined in the CBPS, designing computer-based systems according only to the teacher's definition of the task is questionable.

4.3.2 Implications for Design

The task/activity may be acknowledged or not and, if acknowledged, may be addressed or not. As examples of options:

- The task/activity notion is not acknowledged. Matters of concern are limited to the existence of software that presents the features required to solve the task as thought of, and defined, by the teacher.
- The task/activity notion is acknowledged, but is considered to depend on too many contingent issues to be addressed. Therefore, design focuses on providing means that allow the task to be solved, and learners will do whatever they want with it.
- The task/activity notion is acknowledged, and the conclusion that is drawn is that offering complex and articulated tools may render activity difficult rather than support it. Therefore, design should address the objective of providing a set of separate (non-articulated) means, and learners will use them according to what is the most convenient for them, in context. This might be a possible theoretical rationale for developing generic structures such as LMSs.
- The task/activity notion is acknowledged, and addressed using classical CS approaches to the software requirements issue. For instance, software engineering approaches such as UML have popularized the notion of Use Case. In short, when designing a system to be integrated in a given service, priority is to be given not to the theoretical functioning of the service as demanded by the boss, but rather to the effective issues faced by the effective users of the system to be designed, studying the different effective use cases. The task/activity may be addressed within this view, implementing user-centered iterative or participative processes with the objective to fix issues after a certain number of iterations.
- The task/activity notion is acknowledged and addressed as such. It is considered that if software designed within a techno-centered approach is more prone to unattended usages than software carefully designed using user-centered iterative approaches, nonetheless, effective enactment remains subject to intrinsically emergent issues. These emergent and sometimes unexpected usages cannot simply be addressed by an iterative design process that would, after a certain number of iterations, allow the "standard" usage of the technological setting to be fixed: the same technological setting, offered to similar learners and/or at different period of time, may be used very differently. This may lead one to consider designing tailorable software and the technical and usage-related issues.[10]

---

[10]If such an approach appears interesting, it also raises other issues such as whether, for instance, tailoring software is *another* activity, which may break the flow of learners' processes.

4.4 Conclusions

The task/activity duality is a central issue, which may, however, be difficult to understand or accept for technologists.

Moreover, the way this issue is acknowledged and/or addressed may depend on many dimensions: the adopted theoretical background if any; the way the software role is thought of and, in particular, whether a particular usage is considered to be a core dimension of the CBPS by the fact that it leads learners to develop some targeted activity (e.g., testing hypotheses) or to use and conceptualize some particular notions in some particular way; technical difficulties; empirical studies showing that effective usage is not an issue; economic reasons; etc.

How this issue is thought of, and addressed, may thus generate many misunderstandings. Stating the different actors' views is of particular importance.

5 Disciplinary Dimensions

Specific work related to epistemology addresses the formation and evolution of disciplines, the different ways concepts or processes stemming from one discipline can be used in another, and how new concepts may be elaborated on top of existing disciplines. According to the adopted definitions, different interplays of disciplines may be contrasted, for instance:

- *Multidisciplinarity* generally refers to the enrichment of a disciplinary perspective by contributions from other disciplines.
- *Interdisciplinarity* generally refers to the transfer and adaptation of methods from one discipline to another, which contributions and crossings may lead these disciplines to evolve.
- *Transdisciplinarity* generally refers to the integration of different scientific approaches in a proper framework, crossing disciplines' boundaries, which may lead to the development of new concepts or methods.

Clarifying ones use of one term rather than another may be an important issue. In this book, as in most of the literature, *multidisciplinarity* is used as a general term denoting the basic idea that educational software is concerned with different disciplines.

Without going into theoretical issues, we highlight in this section different perspectives related to disciplinary contributions that may develop.

5.1 Mono-disciplinary Work

Implementation (programming) of a given system from a set of unambiguous specifications is a pure CS issue. Similarly, another typical example of disciplinary work in TEL is measurement of the learning outcomes related to the usage of a given system in a given setting, which may be addressed as a purely educational psychology issue. For instance, it may be tackled within an empirical approach:

1. Different groups that will and will not use the system are created.
2. The groups are checked to be sure there are no initial differences in terms of what is to be measured, e.g. the understanding of a given notion or some skills.
3. A pre-test is organized to measure learners' initial level.
4. A set of groups use the system (or the system tuned in some way) while the others use other means (e.g., no system, another system or the system tuned in another way).
5. A post-test is administered to measure learners' final level.
6. The data is analyzed to detect whether learners having used the system have higher final scores than the others (or if some other variable has been impacted).
7. Statistical tests are used to check whether the difference (if any) is significant, i.e., is unlikely to have occurred just by chance.

TEL is a field that leads one to use existing disciplinary knowledge and to develop disciplinary knowledge related to the specific issues it raises. As examples: how to measure learning outcomes in a way that may be connected to the detailed properties of the used computer-based system; how to manage temporal issues such as the fact that meeting new software creates disorientation and requires some familiarization time, and that impact of a system may only be measured over long periods of time; how to conduct experiments in ecological contexts; how to develop software engineering methodologies that facilitate building flexible or tailorable software; etc.

As a matter of fact, if incomprehension may develop between disciplines, it also develops within disciplines. For instance, in the CS discipline, important incomprehension may develop between, on the one hand, computer scientists considering how to develop tailorable tools as an answer to a given theoretical perspective on the activity notion, or how to design interfaces forming an epistemic *milieu* favorable to the development by learners of some target knowledge and, on the other hand, computer scientists who consider that software is meant to be used as specified, or that the characteristics of the elements handled through an interface (for example, in a simulation) or a particular workflow (for example, in a CSCL framework) do not have any particular effect on the way learners may conceptualize a setting.

5.2 Clarifying the X-Disciplinary Dimensions of Projects

5.2.1 Clarifying the Disciplinary Interplay

Let us consider the following overall process:

1. Design and model of a CBPS, the different actors, their roles, etc.
2. Specification of the required software features and properties according to the CBPS.
3. Implementation of software.
4. Usage and impact analyses.
5. Re-engineering as needed.

Such a process may be seen as multidisciplinary if considered at a high level of granularity. However, considered at a lower level, it may be implemented as a sequence of separate disciplinary actions, with no disciplinary interplay.

What is to be considered is thus not the fact that several disciplines are concerned in the project, but how they relate to each other on precise considerations.

For instance, knowledge related to a given learner (the *learner's model*) may be addressed in different ways such as (1) the compilation of all data related to learners that may be accumulated (according to the type of system: number of connections to a website and accessed resources; actions at the simulation interface; etc.) or (2) the behavioral and epistemic models that would suit teachers' (or CS-based tutors') requirements. The first solution is rather techno-centered. The second may appear more appealing. However, defined independently of the effective data that technically exists in the system (logs, etc.) and how it may be diagnosed by an automated system, it may not correspond to any addressable reality. What may be considered is thus rather another interpretation of the learner's model notion, built on the basis of *what would be useful* given the pedagogical objectives and *how this may be grasped* by an automated-diagnostic process *from the data that actually exists* in the considered technical system. This is definitely another notion.

Learners' models and learners' model management (building, evolution) is a prototypical example of the fact that some issues cannot be addressed from an educational point of view *and then* as a CS issue (or *vice versa*), but must be addressed from the start as transdisciplinary constructions, in a way transcending the boundaries of conventional academic disciplines.

5.2.2 Clarifying What the Difficulty Is

In the context of the TEL literature (and in other places), highlighting the multidisciplinarity of the field is often used to suggest complexity and difficulties. Highlighting what the difficulty is, the efforts (methodology, theoretical dimensions, organizations, etc.) mobilized to address it, the skills engaged in work, the established results or the evaluation processes is an important dimension of work clarification.

In TEL, difficulties may be related to different interrelated dimensions: the fact that actors with different backgrounds (disciplines, experiences, views, competences) must understand each others' perspectives; the fact that different techniques or methods must be interoperated; the fact that transdisciplinary concepts must be elaborated; the fact that the field poses difficult disciplinary problems (see *supra*); etc.

As an example, let us consider *Colab-edit* and *JavIT*. In both cases, these systems require different actors to work together. *Colab-edit* (as we have introduced it) does not require any conceptual difficulty to be addressed, but may pose serious technical difficulties (e.g., for interoperating the existing pieces of code). Such issues may also arise in the *JavIT* case. However, *JavIT*'s design also poses the specific transdisciplinary difficulty of defining the notion of "cognitive profile that may be built from the learners' outputs and the computational events generated by learners' actions when using the software", and how to build and manage such profiles.

5.3 Conclusions

Stating that a project raises X-disciplinary issues (X taking its value in *multi*, *inter* or *trans*) may denote very different realities, and be addressed from very different perspectives. Clarifying this dimension is a means to understand actors' underlying perspectives, and enhance the chances of mutual understanding (see Chap. 5). At the level of theoretical or methodological considerations, it may also help thinking about the field's evolution (see Chap. 6).

It may be noticed that X-disciplinarity is a matter of work and not of persons. The fact that a team involved in a given project embeds actors from different disciplines does not define the X-disciplinary character of effective work. Inversely, X-disciplinary work may be conducted by actors originating from a single discipline but acting according to X-disciplinary principles, i.e., pertinently taking into account and/or building on other disciplines' notions, knowledge or methodologies.[11]

6 Conclusions

When considering design of educational software, a variety of differences in perspectives, interpretations or concerns may be developed, which create a lot of room for misunderstandings.

---

[11]Unfortunately, a known unproductive pattern is that of work presented as X-disciplinary when it corresponds in fact to work related to a discipline D_1 that is conducted by actors of the discipline D_2, on the basis of a surface understanding of D_1 issues and methodologies.

Differences and misunderstandings may take their origins in different sources: implicit beliefs, postulates or disciplinary views; considered levels or types of analyses (see the A and B analyses in Sect. 1); considered notions or definitions (see the task/activity duality); ways these notions are acknowledged and their implications perceived and addressed; etc. As examples of implicit beliefs or postulates: users (here, learners) will consider the task they are set and will use the tools in a coherent way (which is the way for which they have been designed); what learners will do is unpredictable and thus going into design details is useless; teaching is fundamentally related to the properties of the taught knowledge and its specific epistemological difficulties, and thus addressing teaching independently of the addressed knowledge is meaningless; analysis should only address the behavioral (or the cognitive) level; etc.

A classic misunderstanding that may occur is that of computer scientists engaging in a detailed design of very specific features that, independently of their potential positive, negative or neutral impact, are just not matters of concern for educationalists. For instance, computer scientists may focus on *Colab-edit* issues such as the features that the system presents learners with (the versioning system, the tagging system, etc.), the detailed specifics of the interfaces (e.g., the details of how learners may refer to a piece of text in the communication tool, or how features are integrated within a common interface dedicated to the task at hand), data flow and workflow issues, etc. By contrast, educationalists may not take into consideration these dimensions, considering issues at a much higher level of granularity. Technological concerns may be limited to the fact that learners access a set of useful tools, i.e., not making much distinction between *Colab-edit* and *GeLMS-1*. Rather, whether learners feel at ease with the notion of collective document or work-in-progress reports may be considered to be more important than the details of a given tool. However, such differences are not a matter of disciplines, but of concerns. For instance, detailed properties are matters of concern for both computer scientists and educationalists in projects such as *JavIT* or *Bio-sim*.

Variety is thus not to be addressed in terms of "good" or "bad" analysis. Projects are contextual, and must be addressed as such. Considering the example presented in Sect. 2, if domain-specific issues are a matter of concern, Analysis A is meaningless. However, if we consider on-line learning settings, Analysis-B is likely not to be tractable. Analysis B is not better than Analysis A. Both analyses make sense. The TEL literature is full of A-like analyses and corresponding systems and (fewer, however) B-like analyses and corresponding systems. Comparing A-based and B-based CBPSs makes little sense. Similarly, apart from general considerations if any, lessons learned from one or the other type of settings and systems are not to be confused. Mixing projects of different natures is meaningless and not productive for design. In fact, it is a methodological error.

Rather, the conclusion to be drawn is that a TEL project and, in particular, an educational software design project, is not understandable, analyzable or comparable with another project if the underlying considerations at stake (general views; matters of concern; targeted CBPSs; considered pedagogical objectives, SPR or notions, and the way they are addressed; etc.) are not properly clarified.

6 Conclusions

As mentioned in Chap. 1, making everything explicit is not possible for both theoretical and pragmatic reasons. However, clarifying a few important dimensions may already make a difference. We have raised some important dimensions that may be considered in this chapter. The definitions introduced in Chap. 2 also draw attention to important dimensions and to their clarification. Chap. 7 lists various more precise items.

Chapter 4
Review of Prototypical Examples

Abstract This chapter reviews different educational software examples, and illustrates a variety of approaches with respect to the notions and issues introduced in Chaps. 2 and 3.

In this chapter, we contrast different examples (some of them already introduced) with respect to notions and perspectives addressed in the preceding chapters. These imagined systems illustrate a variety of approaches, matters of concern, types of educational software and design rationales. Here, they are introduced in a way that is consistent with their rationale. This leads one to put emphasis on different dimensions. In Chap. 7, we will come back to two of these systems to illustrate how the proposed list of characterizing items helps in conducting a more analytical presentation. The featured systems are:

1. *GeLMS*, the Generic Learning Management System
2. *Phys-edit*, the physics modeling editor
3. *Argue-chat*, the argumentation chat tool
4. *Colab-edit*, the collaborative editor environment
5. *Bio-sim*, the inquiry setting environment
6. *JavIT*, the Java Programming Intelligent Tutor
7. *Scen-play*, the scenario player
8. *Colab-solver*, the collaborative problem-solving environment
9. *Geo-world*, the mathematics graphical microworld

1 *GeLMS*, the Generic Learning Management System

GeLMS-1 is a Web-based information system used as a means to address the objective of providing local or distant learners with pedagogical resources and means. It is not designed according to pedagogical considerations: it's a basic platform whose features are interpreted according to pedagogical concerns, and used accordingly. It is considered an adequate response to the considered objective thanks to the fact that it allows implementing a website from which different types of resources (documents, videos, etc.) and generic tools (chats and forums, whiteboards, file exchange zones, agendas, awareness tools such as information related to who is connected or an internal messaging system, etc.) may be made accessible. The resources made available introduce the overall presentation of the educational program, the courses comprising the program, what is to be done (read documents, watch videos, fill in a questionnaire, produce a text, etc.) and the corresponding content resources (documents, etc.).

In the preceding chapters, we have used *GeLMS-1* as a counter-example. In order not to assimilate all LMSs to such a limited platform, we may consider *GeLMS-1* upgrades.

GeLMS-1 offers learners an interface structured in terms of functional spaces: a content resource space and a communication space. *GeLMS-2*'s interface was redesigned to offer learners an interface structured in terms of programs and courses. When connecting, learners have access to general features (general agenda, institutional messages, etc.) and to the specific sections corresponding to their courses and these courses' resources, which appears to have improved usability. Building on this line of more accurately considering learners' needs, *GeLMS-3* introduced the notion of *advancement indicator*. Learners are supposed to indicate via a form to what extent they have currently addressed the different courses' tasks. When learners' actions may be diagnosed by the system (e.g., when the fact that learners have completed an on-line questionnaire denotes some task or subtask is completed) the advancement indicator is filled in automatically. These indicators allow learners to be aware of each other's advancement, and also facilitate the way tutors can supervise learners and provide more accurate support. Finally, *GeLMS-4* introduced workflow features, allowing the definition of scenarios scheduling access to resources.

With respect to matters of concern, *GeLMS-1, 2, 3 & 4* are identically thought of as information systems. Emphasis is on providing access to resources that are thought of as files (text, videos) or tools (chat, etc.). However, the software pedagogical rationale of these systems is different. *GeLMS-1*'s SPR is empty. *GeLMS-2&3*'s SPR relates to the learners' needs for resources organized according to the teaching structures (courses, etc.), awareness and supervision support. *GeLMS-4*'s SPR relates to orchestration dimensions. These are examples of phenomena and issues that are classically considered when the entry point is the broad idea that learners are on-line, and emphasis is placed on identifying structures that best allow learners to be provided with adequate resources in adequate time. Such a system may be associated with pedagogical-setting support software allowing teachers to describe the required structures (program and course descriptions, links to resources, scenarios, etc.) and supervise learners' usage of the platform.

If one considers the impact notion, *GeLMS-1*'s impact is about changing the very notion of distant learner, how one may access educational resources, and how to introduce on-line communication with teachers and peers. Its evolution is in line with educational analyses studying how such platforms impact distant and blended education (e.g., difficulties encountered by distant-learners, such as isolation or autonomy). As such analyses are of a rather high level, they provide bases for general upgrades such as extending means of communication or introducing awareness tools as a way of addressing isolation. The addressed level of granularity is not that of (for instance) the particular impact of *GeLMS* chat tool and what would be changed if one of its specific properties were to be modified.

If one considers learning, *GeLMS*'s underlying rationale is that learners will learn by accessing pertinent resources (documents, videos, etc.) and achieving the proposed tasks (exercises, etc.) with the help of the proposed tools. The analysis does not go into more detail, for instance taking into account specific domain-related difficulties or particular learning theories. This does not mean that designers are not aware of these dimensions, but that they are not matters of concern and do not affect the SPR.

GeLMS is a typical generic system. It may indifferently be used for a course in mathematics or in history, introducing inquiry-learning based tasks or collaborative problem-solving tasks as long as these courses and tasks are modeled following the structuring notions required by *GeLMS*, i.e., program, course, text file, video file, chat, forum, scenario, etc. *GeLMS*'s SPR does not consider any dimension related to the epistemological specifics of a given domain or a given type of CBPS and its impact on teaching or learning. Similarly, *GeLMS* is not considered to be a particular epistemic *milieu* within which learners are supposed to develop a particular cognitive activity. What is considered is whether learners have completed a course or a module. Dimensions such as *advancement indicators* or *scenario* relate to the instructions (prescriptive tasks) and not to learners' effective activity[1]: the task/activity duality is not a concern.

GeLMS illustrates the fact that a given type of system (LMS) may be addressed with different pedagogical considerations, including none. However, LMS is a very broad notion. LMSs may correspond to very different realities, including that of a generic structure providing, as such, few affordances for learning, rather focusing on institutional issues (formatted courses, back office services, etc.), but offering links to more specific software. The following sections address more interesting examples.

---

[1] As we address here a theoretical system, we may risk an alternative explanation of the fact that *GeLMS* does not consider the task/activity issue: at first, the issue was not understood; designers became aware of this dimension when reading an educationalist's research paper; hopefully, they discovered another paper highlighting that the activity learners develop depends on too many contingent issues to be anticipated; *GeLMS*'s structure and provision of separate "neutral" tools was reinterpreted as a rational response to this issue; the implementation difficulties of this "theoretically-based" response *vs.* other possible ones did not discourage the designers.

2 *Phys-edit*, the Physics Modeling Editor

Phys-edit is a model editor dedicated to physics phenomena. It provides a set of graphical shapes (boxes, connections, etc.) denoting specific physics notions. These shapes are stored in a library, and the ones used for a given setting can be selected by the teacher (or the learners). For instance, for an exercise related to movements of solids, *Phys-edit* may be used with graphical shapes denoting notions such as velocity, acceleration, friction, force or energy. *Phys-edit* may be tuned so as to be used in free mode, which allows learners to draw any constructions, or in constrained mode, which prevents learners from drawing inconsistent relationships.

Phys-edit's rationale is a learning theory suggesting that the fact that learners build models (here, models of physics phenomena) helps them to develop pertinent conceptions (here, in physics), and empirical data suggesting learners do have difficulties in building such models and must be supported.

With respect to CBPSs, *Phys-edit* is considered to be a tool to be used in settings within which learners benefit from such a support. The considered prototypical setting is to provide learners with some resources introducing a phenomenon (texts, videos or a simulation – in a similar way to *Bio-sim*), and to ask them to build a model of this phenomenon. There are various possibilities: the exercise is introduced in classrooms, as a means for learners to become familiar with the problem, and as a way for the teacher to build on each learner's output within a second phase; the exercise is entirely on-line and associated with an explicit scenario; the exercise is collaborative (here again, different cases are possible: two peers solve the exercise together; each peer solves the exercise individually and then the group has to discuss and merge the different models, etc.). However, the SPR is related to a given task (modeling) known to be useful in different CBPSs rather than to a precise CBPS.

If one considers the domain dimension, *Phys-edit* is not a generic system: it considers a particular domain and addresses particular notions related to this domain. More precisely, SPR is concerned with the epistemological analysis of the constructions (shapes and relations) to be provided in relation to the domain notions, learners' possible conceptions and misconceptions, the domain semantic constraints, pedagogical constraints or how these constraints may be relaxed. In other words, *Phys-edit* differs from a non-pedagogical editor by the fact that the notions it highlights and the way they may be used are not the physics notions, but the notions that have been defined as useful in learning physics in the context of a given type of task (modeling).

Technically, *Phys-edit* is a tool that may be implemented at a generic level, i.e., as a generic modeler that allows manipulation of shapes and relationships, the semantics associated with these shapes and relationships (and the constraints governing their usage) being represented as separate data. This makes it possible, for instance, to easily develop an instantiation of *Phys-edit* dedicated to solid movements (shapes and relationships denoting notions such as velocity, acceleration, friction, force or energy, etc.) and another instantiation dedicated to electricity (shapes and relationships denoting notions such as generator or resistance). This exemplifies the fact that the notion of SPR may be defined at an instantiated level (that of a precise domain) or at a more abstract level, coupling it with additional data. It may be noticed that here there is room for divergent views: *Phys-edit* is both domain-specific software (when considered according to what it provides its users with) and generic software (when considered from a technical point of view).

If one considers the impact dimension, *Phys-edit* may be viewed in different ways. Let us consider the use of *Phys-edit* in an inquiry-learning setting, e.g., learners manage a physics experiment, elaborate hypotheses and model them using *Phys-edit* in the free mode; later, these models serve as a resource for classroom work. Seen from this broad perspective, the considered impact is not due to *Phys-edit*'s particularities but, rather, due to the fact that learners have means to build models. Within this view, *Phys-edit* could be changed for another graphical modeler. By contrast, the same setting may be addressed at a more fine-grained level of granularity, similar to that of *Bio-sim*, by tuning *Phys-edit* (denoted notions, associated relations, constraints) in a way that is meant to impact the fact that learners develop a certain number of conceptions or behaviors. In such a case, one may consider the specific impact due to *Phys-edit*'s particularities.

Phys-edit illustrates systems thought of with respect to a task that is known to occur in CBPSs and designed as a means to influence the user's conceptualization of a domain (and thus, their activity), although the user's effective activity and the task/activity duality is not really considered. The fact that users may consider a task other than that of building a model of the phenomena when using *Phys-edit* is not a matter of concern for the tool designers.

3 *Argue-chat*, the Argumentation Chat Tool

Argue-chat is a graphical argumentation chat tool that provides a set of graphical shapes (boxes, connections, etc.) denoting specific argumentation notions such as *statement*, *argument*, *counter-argument*, *approval*, *question* or *answer*.

Argue-chat rationale is that empirical studies have shown that graphical representations of arguments help learners in exchanging arguments, understanding each other's positions and, more generally, developing knowledge-generative interactions. The rationale is that such interactions have been positively correlated to collaborative learning. Moreover, the structured reification of the interactions may be a basis for different pedagogical exploitations (e.g., make learners aware they mix different considerations or organize a debriefing).

Argue-chat is introduced here just after *Phys-edit* to raise similarities and differences.

If one considers relation to CBPSs, matters of concern, or how the notions of impact or activity are addressed, *Argue-chat* is similar to *Phys-edit* (although *Argue-chat* is not related to a domain such as physics, but to a transversal skill).

If one considers a technical point of view, *Phys-edit* and *Argue-chat* share the same technical basis. They may be defined as different instantiations of the same generic modeler. Another instantiation of this modeler, dedicated to biology, may be built for *Bio-sim*.

When building these systems, the design issue is thus limited to that of "thinking" the constructions to be offered: many generic modelers exist and may be used, and implementation is trivial. However, "thinking" the constructions (testing usage, evaluating, etc.) to be offered by the modeler is very different in *Phys-edit* (taking into consideration domain-specific epistemological issues) and in *Argue-chat* (taking into consideration argumentative interaction issues and their relation to learning), and is again different if used in the context of *Bio-sim* (taking into consideration the overall process of supporting inquiry dimensions and consistency with the simulation or the other cognitive tools). This illustrates the fact that systems may appear very similar (and, technically, be very similar) but, in fact, relate to different matters of concern and require very different work.

On another dimension, as raised in Chap. 1, while *GeLMS* highlights that the limits between educational software and basic software may be unclear, and a matter of perspective, *Argue-chat* highlights the proximity that may exist between educational software and software specifically designed to support or influence users' processes (in this case, argumentation processes).

4 *Colab-edit*, the Collaborative Editor Environment

Colab-edit is an environment designed to address the pedagogical objective of supporting a group of on-line learners working collectively to elaborate a common document. With respect to this objective, it provides learners with an articulated set of tools: a file transfer system that allows uploading and downloading documents from a shared repository; an editor that allows synchronous work on a shared document; a versioning system that allows different versions of a document text to be managed and other learners' modifications to be tracked; a tagging function that allows sharing of comments; communication tools from which a forum that allows a mediated discussion to be connected to a particular piece of text.

Colab-edit exemplifies a perspective on the notion of activity environment as a consistent set of tools within which learners' activity will take place and will be supported.

If one considers the CBPS notion and matters of concern, *Colab-edit* is designed to address a more precise type of setting than *Phys-edit*. It differs from a non-pedagogical editor not only because of its specific features and properties (e.g., connecting a mediated discussion to a particular piece of text), but also because different tools have been selected and interoperate in a way which is meant to respond to the different interrelated issues faced by on-line learners when engaged in this type of on-line setting. For instance, particular attention has been paid to allow learners to submit and comment on work-in-progress reports. This has resulted in a specific articulation of features related to editing, tagging, communication and management of different versions of text (to be contrasted with the way platforms such as *GeLMS* may offer a comprehensive but disarticulated set of tools).

In Chap. 3 we have referred to the notion of *epistemic milieu* as the objects, resources or organizational features the learner is presented with and an accurate analysis of the significations they are associated with. Using this *milieu* notion in the case of *Colab-edit* as we have introduced it is something that may be debatable as learners' issues are addressed in terms of functional needs and behavioral activity rather than at a cognitive level. However, systems such as *Colab-edit* may also be studied at a more cognitive level.

In terms of reference to the domain or to skills, *Colab-edit* is similar to *GeLMS*: it may indifferently be used for any domain as long as the setting is addressed according to the constructions provided. Whether the nature of the common document to be elaborated raises particular difficulties for learners (e.g., synthesis issues or having to deal with conflicting views) is not a matter of concern.

If one considers the impact notion, *Colab-edit* may be seen in different ways. As we have introduced it, it is meant to facilitate a given task by articulating different means, on the basis of an analysis of difficulties encountered by learners when considering this task and the limitation of other means (e.g., *GeLMS-1*). The targeted impact is to facilitate learners' addressing of the task. Seen from another perspective, in a similar way to *Phys-edit*, it may be thought of as providing affordances as means to influence learners' activity. However, what underlies the analysis (and the targeted objective) is different in *Phys-edit* (domain-specific analysis and learners' conceptions or misconceptions) and in *Colab-edit* (previous systems' usage-analysis and learners' behavior). Assumptions related to the system usage are also different. If one takes as an example the *learning theories forum*, it is expected that *Colab-edit*'s features will allow learners to tag documents or discuss pieces of text, but the setting is introduced in a way that leaves open for learners the use of the technology they want, and there is no particular assumption related to the learners' use of *Colab-edit* except that it may facilitate their engagement and suggest collaborative actions. This is to be contrasted with the assumption that using *Phys-edit* will influence learners' conceptions of some physics notions, and the importance of the fact that they do use the system.

Let us finally recall that in Chap. 1 we have introduced *Colab-edit* to exemplify that educational software design may correspond to adaptation and articulation of existing software components to particular needs. Technically, *Colab-edit* is a mash-up: it is created by adapting, gluing together and interoperating basic tools (a shared editor, a versioning system, etc.).

5 *Bio-sim*, the Inquiry Setting Environment

Bio-sim is a simulation-based learning environment designed to address the pedagogical objective of supporting a group of learners engaged in an enquiry learning process in a sub-domain of biology.

With respect to this objective, *Bio-sim*'s central tool is a simulation that models different notions (e.g., cell nucleus, cell membrane or liquids) and phenomena (e.g., liquid exchanges) related to the considered sub-domain. When using the simulation, learners can make different variables vary (e.g., salt concentration) and observe what happens. In a similar way to *Phys-edit*, the notions and phenomena made salient have been chosen according to the pedagogical objectives, i.e., in this case, supporting learners engaged in an inquiry process as they elaborate, test and validate hypotheses. These notions are thus based on an epistemological analysis of the domain and of learners' conceptions, misconceptions and skills related to the domain and to inquiry processes (e.g., defining and separating hypotheses). Different other tools enhance the simulation, for instance providing different indicators (e.g., electric charge or concentration of the salt) which, here again, are meant as means to make learners consider some particular notions in some particular way. Other tools are provided to support the methodological dimensions of the inquiry process: editors that help in modeling domain phenomena, defining hypotheses or relating hypotheses to experimental data; a recommender system that roughly analyzes the learners' process (e.g., whether they have defined an hypothesis or the number of variables they test) and provides methodological hints (e.g., "not too many variables should be tested at the same time" or "variables should be properly separated"). Finally, various communication tools and sharing mechanisms allow distant learners to collaborate.

Bio-sim illustrates how educational software may be thought of as introducing dedicated epistemic means and cognitive tools for a precise CBPS, in this case the *biology inquiry learning* setting introduced in Chap. 1. This software-based activity is preceded and followed by in-classroom interactions with other peers and with the teacher.

If one considers the impact notion, the objective is not only to provide affordances suggesting some behavior as in the *Colab-edit* case, but also to have a specific influence on learners' conceptions (as in the *Phys-edit* case) and processes. Within this perspective, the duality task/activity is an issue. We have highlighted in Chap. 3, Sect. 4.1, the fact that learners may be using *Bio-sim* in a way very different from the usage targeted by teachers: in such cases, the fact that software is meant to influence learners' cognitive activity is rather challenged.

Bio-sim also illustrates how educational software may consist of different components designed with different SPRs relating to different concerns. Technically, some software components are specific to the setting, domain and teaching intentions (e.g., the simulation); to the domain and teaching intentions (the modeling editor); to the process and teaching intentions (e.g., editor of hypotheses or means to relate hypotheses to data). Others are generic (e.g., communication tools). As in the

Colab-edit case, but with more specific pieces of software, such architecture may be created by articulating different components: a model editor obtained by instantiation of a generic modeler; a recommender system implementing methodological support that may be reused from another inquiry learning setting; etc.

6 *JavIT*, the Java Programming Intelligent Tutoring System

JavIT is an ITS designed to address a precise CBPS, the *Java programming* CBPS introduced in Chap. 1. The approach is anchored in constructivist and cognitive theories: one learns design and programming by building programs and getting some feedback on the built program and the way it is built. Learners are provided with a set of exercises, each introduced by a text that explains what the program they are asked to construct should be able to do; they are supposed to achieve the task by using the system. The considered pedagogical objective is to provide support and individualized intelligent feedback, and teach.

With respect to this objective, *JavIT* provides learners with specific interfaces related to the notions at stake when editing, compiling and running their program, in a similar way to *Phys-edit* or *Bio-sim* for example. For instance, the way learners are led to build their Java programs may be supported to a greater or lesser extent by providing a basic editor, a syntactical editor (i.e., a grammar-guided editor that will avoid syntactical errors) or another kind of more conceptual editor (e.g., featuring the concerned notions). However, *JavIT* also embeds components that allow the system to (1) perceive and diagnose learners' actions and learners' output, (2) define/calculate the feedback to be processed, and (3) implement the feedback.

JavIT illustrates matters of concern and SPR very different from the other examples. Similarly to them, it is a means for a particular type of task learners must address (build programs). However, its fundamental objective is to teach, and this dimension is embedded in the system. For instance, the system implements strategies such as making learners develop a view of inheritance that corresponds to simple-inheritance and, when this view seems correctly understood, introducing a multi-inheritance example: the knowledge learners had developed, which was operational for a given scope, now becomes non-operational. Learners have to reconsider their very conception of inheritance, and their implementation strategies.

Several versions of *JavIT* have been designed, illustrating different types of relationships to the domain and to the teaching issue, and leading to very different SPRs.

JavIT-L (for Language) focuses on the fact that Java is a language governed by precise grammar. The system detects learners' constructions that are not allowed by the language and explains why the construction is erroneous. Technically, learners' constructions are analyzed with respect to constraints denoting Java syntactical and semantic rules. Systems such as *Phys-edit* also embed constraints on the relationships that may be drawn between shapes, implementing passive feedback. On the contrary, in *JavIT-L* feedback is the main concern. The system may decide to render some constructions impossible or on the contrary allow any construction, analyze them and provide feedback as necessary.

JavIT-E (for Error) focuses on the fact that learners' erroneous constructions may denote misunderstandings, e.g., erroneous understanding of the inheritance notion. The system analyzes learners' constructions within this perspective and provides feedback addressing the cause (the misunderstanding) and not only the symptom (the erroneous construction). Different versions of *JavIT-E* have been designed, exploring different approaches. One of these is to conduct a constraints-based analysis of learners' constructions, i.e., analyzing whether learners' constructions are consistent with the specification they must implement. Another is to use a repertory of recurrent errors and patterns. In order to build such a reference, different approaches are possible such as using knowledge capitalized from Java teachers, analyzing learners' constructions with data mining techniques or building on a domain teaching theory. Here again, as illustrated in Chap. 3, different options are open, for instance focusing on conceptions/misconceptions (e.g., misconceptions that may be created by the proximity of the *abstract class* and *interface* notions, or different views on the *inheritance* notion) and/or considering the influence of institutional dimensions.

If one considers the impact notion, *JavIT* may be seen in different ways. *JavIT* may be used as a basis for building general strategies such as providing learners Java and object-oriented concepts courses, studying different examples of Java programs making use of these concepts with the teacher, making learners use *JavIT* to individually confront themselves with programming exercises, and recap in the classroom. Seen from this broad perspective, *JavIT* could be replaced by another system sharing its basic role of "making learners practice Java exercises". However, the rationale for *JavIT* and its different versions is that its specific feedback makes a difference: the specific diagnosis and feedback implemented in *JavIT-L* and *JavIT-E* is meant to make a specific difference with respect to learners' learning (what is put to the fore by the system, e.g., syntax *vs.* conceptual misunderstanding; how these conceptual dimensions are addressed; etc.).

If one considers the task/activity duality, this issue is not brought to the fore by the *JavIT* project. Consistently with the basic principles adopted, emphasis is on reacting to learners' actions. The key issue is to define and implement the most pertinent feedback. Learners' actions are rather constrained: the task to be tackled is precise and has a fine level of granularity, learners are supposed to use specific tools they cannot change, and the system reacts to each of their actions. Within such a view, the fact that learners may develop an activity that differs from expectations is not considered as such. However, the domain-specific analysis conducted for *JavIT-E* may require consideration of issues such as the fact that learners' actions may be motivated by different domain-specific goals (e.g., preserve a kind of equilibrium in the inheritance tree, group attributes as much as possible, use or on the contrary avoid abstract classes; on some other dimensions: ensure consistency with their view of data structures developed from imperative languages or limit the number of classes to avoid documentation burden). In other words, considering learners' output in the light of task/activity duality may be useful.

From a technical point of view, *JavIT* is based on a knowledge-based infrastructure that is used to implement the domain knowledge model (the Java language rules, etc.), the learners' actions and output diagnoses and the pedagogical decisions (e.g., define the feedback to be processed). As in the *Bio-sim* example, such an implementation may mix generic constructions (e.g., the diagnosis or feedback processes) and domain-specific constructions.

7 *Scen-play*, the Generic Scenario Player

Scen-play is a learning scenario player designed to address the pedagogical objectives of (1) allowing teachers to describe learning scenarios (i.e., organized sequences of tasks learners must address), (2) delivering the learning scenarios (i.e., providing learners with instructions and resources according to the scenario), and (3) allowing tutors to supervise and manage learners' enactment of the scenario.

Scen-play exemplifies systems that are from some perspective educational software (software providing learners with an activity framework) and, from another perspective, pedagogical-setting support software, i.e., software designed so as to be useful to people concerned in the design, management or analysis of CBPSs.

In terms of CBPSs, *Scen-play* is designed with respect to on-line settings within which learners are supposed to address a complex task that can be described as a precise sequence of actions. When using *Scen-play*, learners are presented with tasks and resources in a way similar to *Colab-edit*, providing learners with an environment adapted to the set task and the way its enactment is anticipated. As an example, the player may be used to implement the *learning theories forum* in a way that emphasizes roles, division of labor and scheduling of subtasks.

Seen from the teachers' point of view, *Scen-play* offers a graphical editor based on different notions that allow descriptions of what learners are supposed to do (e.g., task instructions or properties such as whether a task is individual or collective), the resources associated with the tasks (documents, tools, etc.) and the associated constraints (e.g., task ordering or under what conditions learners may skip from one task to another). It also offers means to supervise learners' scenario enactment such as a synthetic view of learners' advancement in the scenario or the output produced by learners for a given task.

Technically, *Scen-play* is a workflow, i.e., an engine that allows the different steps of a process to be scheduled and controlled. Its educational specifics lie in the notions that form the workflow language and may be used to represent the steps and the control structure.

With respect to matters of concern and SPR, *Scen-play* is similar to *GeLMS* by the fact that emphasis is on providing access to resources. Domain issues are not taken into account. However, an important difference is that while *GeLMS* acts as an information system, *Scen-play* highlights the pedagogical notion of scenario, proposes a conceptual language to help teachers to model scenarios, and implements this language by providing an editor, a player that controls learners' access to resources and functions, and supervision tools. A platform such as *GeLMS* may be used to provide learners with a textual description of a scenario and the associated resources. However, for instance, scheduling constraints cannot easily be implemented with *GeLMS-1, 2 & 3* versions, while this is a basic dimension of *Scen-play*'s SPR.

If one considers the impact notion, *Scen-play*'s impact may be regarded in different ways. From a general perspective, it allows teachers to build explicit scenarios and provide learners with active settings rather than spoon-feeding settings. From a more precise teachers' perspective, the notions it introduces and tools it offers may impact teachers' conceptualization of the notion of scenario and/or of their elaboration processes. From a more precise learners' perspective, the notions and the player's properties (e.g., the way it schedules tasks) may impact learners' activity.

8 *Colab-solver*, the Collaborative Problem-Solving Environment

Colab-solver is an environment for collaborative learning designed to address the pedagogical objectives of making learners develop knowledge-generative interactions such as explanation, argumentation, negotiation, mutual regulation or conflict resolution. However, in contrast to *Argue-chat*, it addresses a specific type of CBPSs within which learners are supposed to collaborate on-line to solve a problem.

Colab-solver is an example (more complex than the *Argue-chat* and less specific than the *Bio-sim* cases) of a system designed to influence learners' processes according to objectives that are related to educational issues, and whose difference with equivalent basic software is to impose constraints rather than to ease the process. Here, main matters of concern are that the targeted interactions occur, and not that learners solve the problem, which is only a means. Consequently, *Colab-solver* is not designed to ease the process, but to increase the chances that the process presents the expected characteristics. As an example, the system introduces constraints related to how learners may broke down the overall task into different subtasks, divide work, make explicit their collective and individual processes or acknowledge decisions.

Colab-solver also exemplifies the specific importance that the task/activity dimension may play. Many difficulties in preserving productive interactions have been reported in the literature such as learners adopting unbalanced division of labor or conflicting. These difficulties partially stem from the fact that learners often consider different tasks: attempting to build a solution; attempting to build a solution whose characteristic is to be the best solution; attempting to build a solution whose characteristic is to be a collectively agreed solution; avoiding being pin-pointed as not participating; addressing teachers' (supposed) expectations; having social relationships; imposing oneself as a leader; etc. Given the objectives and the level of analysis (the issue is not that learners solve the problem, it is not only that they interact, it is that they develop a certain kind of interactions), taking into account the fact that learners may consider another task than the one defined by teachers and, more generally, the characteristics of their activity, is an issue. For this purpose, *Colab-solver*'s SPR considers limiting the chances that learners adopt inadequate behaviors by introducing constraints such as imposing collective acknowledgements of the group's decisions or providing them with a synthetic analysis of their interactions as a means to make them aware of unbalanced participation or division of labor.

9   *Geo-world*, the Mathematics Graphical Microworld

Geo-world is an environment for direct manipulations of geometrical structures designed to address the pedagogical objectives of making learners develop pertinent conceptions in geometry.

Geo-world illustrates another approach to domain-specific educational software that may be useful for a large set of different CBPSs: what is considered is not a task (e.g., modeling), but a domain as such or, more precisely, an educational perspective on the domain.

Geo-world is designed for settings within which teaching is organized by a human teacher, who sets learners some exercises. It is meant to be used by learners as a means to understand geometrical constructions and their properties, and to test ideas. Learners are provided with a graphical interface within which they can define geometrical structures (parallelograms, lines, circles, etc.) from their mathematical expressions (as a formula) or by drawing them directly on the screen. The two representation modes are kept consistent, i.e., if a learner modifies a structure using the direct manipulation mode (e.g., enlarging a circle with the mouse) the mathematical expression is changed accordingly, and *vice versa*. The system also maintains the mathematical consistency of the objects concerned. For instance, if a line l is defined as a *tangent* to the circle c and c is modified, l is modified accordingly.

Geo-world shares some similarities with *Bio-sim*'s simulation. However, *Bio-sim* is designed to support inquiry learning and, although the simulation may be used for other purposes, some design decisions are related to this type of setting. By contrast, *Geo-world*'s major axis is a model of geometry: its design is related to mathematics education as a specific area, having in mind the variety of geometry exercises developed by teachers and the corresponding needs.

With respect to matters of concern, *Geo-world* is thought of as a tool that provides evidence for the notions and the properties that human teachers want to refer to: point, line, circle, translation, symmetry, infinity, etc. The SPR is about the notions that learners will be presented with and the educational (and mathematical) consistency of these notions when manipulated. For instance, a specific issue is the way infinity should be represented and managed for learners to develop a correct conception of the concept.

10 Discussion

In this chapter, we have introduced different examples highlighting the variety of types of systems, objectives or matters of concern that may be encountered when designing educational software. These examples illustrate how concerns or notions may be interpreted in different ways, have more or less importance, and give rise to very different work.

This variety is again made more complex by the fact that effective systems are often less prototypical than our theoretical examples, pursuing multiple objectives and blending approaches. As an example, generic platforms such as *GeLMS* may be enhanced by specific tools such as *Argue-chat*, *Colab-edit* or *Scen-play* as components or plug-ins. As another example, systems thought of as means for learners to build something (e.g., *Phys-edit*, *Colab-solver* or *Geo-world*) may be associated with scaffolding means inspired from *JavIT*-like systems. For instance, in graphical editors, how shapes may be related to one another may be ruled by constraints that are made more or less salient and/or associated with additional feedback (e.g., hint, counter-example or link to some resource), making learners aware of and/or teaching the semantics associated with the notions at stake; learners' output may be analyzed and individual or collective hints provided, e.g., highlighting domain-related contradictions; etc.

Moreover, the directive ideas underlying systems may be implemented in a variety of ways according to the targeted setting. For instance, a system such as *Colab-solver* may be considered within the context of mobile technologies and the fact that learners may use desktops, laptops, PDAs, smart phones or tablet computers. Similarly, systems such as *JavIT* or *Geo-world* may be considered within the context of virtual reality and tangible interfaces. Although manipulation of tangible objects does not appear straightforwardly pertinent for learning the Java language, it would dramatically change many issues if the taught topic was (for instance) some surgical manoeuvre, and learners' actions are no longer mouse manipulations but tangible surgical material with haptic features.

The conclusion to be drawn is that many different types of educational systems may be considered, associated with very different pedagogical objectives, and these systems may be addressed with different matters of concern and technologies. Given this diversity, and the fact that effective projects often blend different issues, attempting to build a precise map of how types of systems, pedagogical objectives, matters of concern (etc.) and technologies relate to each other is rather challenging.

Unfortunately for simplicity, but hopefully for designers and teachers, projects are to be considered contextually and in their complexity. However, this does not mean that all projects should build from scratch: both knowledge and pieces of code may be capitalized and reused. This however requires careful attention when disentangling and making explicit issues, considered matters of concern and adopted perspective.

Chapter 5
CS Perspectives and TEL

Abstract This chapter analyzes the relationships between CS and TEL: the different roles that CS may play within the TEL field, and the different ways in which computer scientists may conceptualize their involvement.

An[1] intrinsic difficulty in clarifying the relationships between TEL and CS is that the CS field encompasses a number of distinct intellectual traditions, leading to debates about the nature of this field. It can be conceptualized and broken down into different sub-domains in different ways, and is subject to different definitions, interpretations, and misunderstandings.

While we shall not attempt here a tentative definition of CS or a description of its history and different features, it is worth highlighting that what the term CS emphasizes may correspond to different notions, in particular:

- Emphasis on the studies of computation, complexity and formalisms – what is often termed "theoretical CS", and takes its origins from the mathematics tradition.
- Emphasis on hardware and software development, software applications for specific domains, software engineering, etc.

As a matter of fact, very little TEL research or practice may be considered as related to the theoretical foundations of CS. TEL is rather concerned with software development, and may be powerfully addressed as an engineering field (see Chap. 6). In TEL, the human and social aspects of computer system design, usage and evaluation are central issues.

Considering the relationships between CS and TEL is useful for both computer scientists and educationalists as it helps to clarify and understand the nature of the

---

[1] Part of this chapter is inspired by: Tchounikine, P., Mørch, A.I. & Bannon L.J. (2009). A computer science perspective on Technology Enhanced Learning research. In: Balacheff, N., Ludvigsen, S., de Jong, T., Lazonder, A. & Barnes, S. (Eds.) Technology-Enhanced Learning – Principles and Products, Berlin: Springer, 275–288.

work and the dimensions underlying actors' engagement. In order to investigate these relationships, we explore two different perspectives. First, in Sect. 1, we take a TEL perspective and disentangle different roles for CS in TEL: (1) building new technologies or further developing existing technologies to create novel possibilities for supporting human activities; (2) elaborating powerful abstractions; (3) enabling specified models and processes to be run on computers. Second, in Sect. 2, we disentangle three prototypical ways in which computer scientists may conceptualize their involvement in TEL: (1) TEL as a place for clever CS applications, (2) TEL as a field where some CS problems arise and are to be solved and (3) TEL as a proper field. While the first perspective emphasizes a characterization of different types of work, the second emphasizes the different views on TEL that may underlie the work. This analytical analysis is completed, in Chap. 6, by an analysis of why and how developing an engineering perspective to TEL is a productive approach.

1 Roles of Computer Science in TEL

To clarify the different ways in which CS impacts the field, three prototypical (non-orthogonal) roles for CS may be disentangled:

1. Building new technologies or further developing existing technologies to create novel possibilities for supporting human activities.
2. Elaborating powerful abstractions.
3. Enabling specified models and processes to be run on computers (algorithm development and implementation).

These roles are not orthogonal to each other and, in the context of a given project, computer scientists may act at different levels and on different planes. Their separation, however, provides a basis for clarification of the nature of computer scientists' actions (see Sect. 3).

1.1 Creating Novel Possibilities for Supporting Human Activities

As highlighted in the introduction, CS is a broad field that includes work on the creation of new computer-based technologies (i.e., hardware, software or user interfaces). Computer scientists are naturally at the forefront of this activity, which has a spin-off effect in that it opens up new possibilities, that is, creating software or hardware allowing innovative interactions to take place.

The evolution of the TEL field and of the considered types of systems can easily be linked to technological advances in CS:

- Behavioral-inspired systems such as basic drill and practice systems, involving the direct application of algorithmic techniques.

- Intelligent Tutoring Systems based on representation of knowledge and expertise, decision making, Artificial Intelligence and knowledge engineering techniques to model domain expertise or pedagogical expertise.
- Microworlds or simulations based on modeling and visualization (2D, 3D) techniques.
- Hypertext and multimedia based on structuring documents and creating conditional or dynamic access techniques.
- Communication-based systems and CSCL, based on the technological developments in networked computing (basic exchange of data between two computers, speed rate improvements, graphic interfaces, permission or deadlock management allowing the creation of advanced systems such as wikis or workflows) and Human-Computer Interface (HCI) techniques.
- To give other examples: Web-based learning approaches; mobile learning; so-called e-learning 2.0 or Grid-learning; etc.

This list is witness to the impact of the evolution of technology: new types of educational systems not only become possible, but are imagined because some technology, that did not exist previously, creates new possibilities.

It may also be noticed that advancement of technology impacts not only the very nature of systems, but also how some dimensions of already existing types of software are thought of. For instance, the advancement of data mining and text mining in CS has raised interest for interaction analysis. Recent work in CSCL attempts to provide learners with adaptive frameworks and individual or collective support using ITS techniques[2]: the dimensions of collaborating for learning and the intrinsic nature of the system are not impacted, but are enhanced by a new dimension.

Of course, the evolution of technologies is only part of the story of the evolution of the field, see the discussion related to how the CSCL paradigm gained importance and the ITS paradigm became less dominant in Chap. 3.

1.2 Elaborating Powerful Abstractions

1.2.1 Computer Science and Modeling

Modeling is a core issue in CS. Advanced software engineering practices such as the Model Driven Engineering[3] approach push forward the use of models to direct the course of understanding, design, construction, deployment, operation,

---

[2]Tchounikine, P., Rummel, N. & McLaren, B.M. (2010). Computer Supported Collaborative Learning and Intelligent Tutoring Systems. Nkambou, R., Bourdeau, J. & Mizoguchi, R. (Eds.): Advances in Intelligent Tutoring Systems, SCI 308, Berlin: Springer, pp. 447–463.

[3]See for example Model Driven Architecture (http://www.omg.org/mda/; retrieved November 11, 2010).

maintenance and modification of systems implementation. Working at the level of models rather than at a symbolic level facilitates software construction and, in particular, appears to be the only way to address the complexity of today's software and architectures.

Technically, it is now possible to generate a large part of the code required to build applications from abstract descriptions represented in conceptual modeling languages, which allows one to focus on abstract notions and processes rather than on programming language issues (e.g., variables or control structures). This is a step in the direction of software built by automated transformations of models. Software components or frameworks (i.e., high-level building blocks that hide their internal structures or code and expose their external interface and connection points) also facilitate and enhance software construction by addressing issues at a higher level of abstraction than general programming languages allow.

Models and components support the tendency of application developers to act at a level that is closer to that of the domain expert users. For instance, considering the design of software for a bank, some issues will be addressed at a purely technical level (e.g., networking issues), but some computer scientists will also be concerned, along with domain (bank) experts, to help model the notions to be considered (e.g., monetary transactions), and the processes to be operationalized.

1.2.2 TEL and Modeling

TEL is an area where building models that involve software issues is a key dimension, and elaborating (with learning scientists) powerful abstractions is arguably computer scientists' core contribution to TEL.

Modeling may take place at different levels such as CBPSs (which requires consideration of the role and the properties of the computer-based system in the setting) or modeling the notions required to design and implement software. For instance, software thought of as a *milieu* reacting to learners' actions requires consideration of a variety of models related to the taught domain knowledge, teaching scenario, learners' possible actions, learners' actions interpretation process, feedback model, etc. (see Chap. 8, Sect. 2).

Computer scientists are key actors in this type of modeling. They provide conceptual languages and notations (XML-based formalisms, UML-based formalisms, Petri nets, etc.), tools (design tools such as graphical modelers, visualization or simulation tools), and their modeling skills.

It should be noticed that such modeling activities have a value in and by themselves, and not only when used as a base for implementing procedures or processes. Very often, the objective of the work is to elaborate a model that allows one to understand or design the setting, even if no computer implementation is planned or the model is not implemented as such in the computer. For instance, it is very common to address learning scenarios via some given Educational Modeling Language and the associated conceptual notions or manipulation tools.

This modeling is often not made further use of, for example, to generate some code or tune a technical architecture, but it is still a valuable pedagogical tool.

A model is an oriented representation of something, which captures the features that have been decided to be pertinent given one's objectives. Modeling requires the addressed object to be understood, and what is pertinent to be decided. In the context of TEL, this is often not addressable by segmenting it into disciplinary phases, considering educational dimensions and then CS. As examples: the models underlying *Bio-sim*'s cognitive tools; the way problem solving and collaboration may be conceptualized and supported in *Colab-solver*; the way *JavIT* implements diagnosis or feedback; etc. Such situations require the problem to be conceptualized and addressed as a transdisciplinary TEL problem, in a way transcending the boundaries of conventional disciplines.

1.3 Implementing Specified Models and Processes on Computers

Finally, the most obvious way for computer scientists to be involved in TEL is to be in charge of writing the code and implementing a working model on a computer system.

When considering this type of work, if the operationalization process raises some effective difficulties it requires the computer scientist to act as a CS researcher; if not, it requires the computer scientist to act as an engineer.

Implementation of educational software does raise effective CS research issues in some cases. As examples: creating knowledge-based systems that can implement pedagogical decisions; analyzing learners' interactions or outputs; interoperating software components on the fly; implementing tailorability; etc.

2 Engagement of Computer Scientists

In Sect. 1, we have disentangled different roles played by CS and computer scientists in TEL. In this section, we now consider the way in which computer scientists may conceptualize their involvement in TEL. We disentangle three prototypical cases:

1. Considering TEL as a place for clever CS applications.
2. Considering TEL as a field where some CS problems arise and are to be solved.
3. Considering TEL as a proper field.

The rationale for considering this dimension is that in order to understand what actors do, how they do it or the underlying rationale, it is also important to consider what their perspective is. Similarly to the CS roles introduced in Sect. 1, these perspectives are not orthogonal to each other. The purpose of disentangling and contrasting them is to highlight their features.

2.1 TEL as a Place for Clever CS Applications

Educational software may be approached as a place for clever applications of CS work. Within such an approach, emphasis is on innovation and creating novel possibilities. Typically, corresponding work builds on technical advances: a newly developed technology is interpreted as a means for creating pertinent novel possibilities for supporting human activities, and is turned into a new generation of educational systems or features.

This view of TEL is developed and enacted by a much wider audience than computer scientists. It corresponds to the technologically-pushed dimension of the field.

2.1.1 Negative Dimensions of Building on Technological Advances

Considering TEL as a place for clever applications of technological advances leads to technology-driven educational applications. The risk is of course techno-centrism and putting emphasis on the technology *per se* rather than on the pedagogical outcomes for learners. This may lead to the development of smart software that, unfortunately, does not correspond to any educational need or interesting usage.

Considering technology-driven educational applications, a recurrent pattern can be identified:

1. New technology stirs up a wave of excitement among technologically-oriented TEL researchers and early adopters in educational fields.
2. Disappointment appears as the expected pedagogical benefits do not immediately materialize.
3. The simple but core principle that technology is not the answer to a question that must be found, but rather a potential means to address well-defined educational problems, again resurfaces.
4. The importance of pedagogy over technology is once more stressed, and the technology-driven development stalls.
5. A novel technology occurs, followed by a new wave of educationally potentially useful computing innovation. Technologically-inspired visions come to the fore and take center stage for a period.

The fact that every new wave of techniques generates a new type of system, and often tends to replace the preceding one, is an issue that should be analyzed. Rather than deciding whether the new technologies allow one better to solve the educational problems that were already the subject of work with the previous technologies, or provide a better understanding of the educational objectives that should be addressed, the target (considered educational issues) seems to move with the means (the technology). When considering techno-pushed applications, the question to ask is: what is the specific educational advancement that is related to the fact that this particular technology is being used?

2.1.2 Positive Dimensions of Building on Technological Advances

Indeed, it is not because some new technology becomes available that it allows pertinent educational uses. However, it is not because a proposal is based on a technical innovation, and not on an educational requirement, that it is meaningless.

First, some technology-driven applications have encountered success with very few educationally-oriented adaptations. See for example effective uses of communication systems.

Second, technology-driven applications may contribute to the understanding of issues. ITSs are an example of systems based on an emergent technology (knowledge based systems) which created a wave of excitement and a lot of disappointments. The first generation of ITSs was addressed by considering as the central issue the fact that the system should be able to solve the problem submitted to learners and provide a trace of the solution process. Advances related to this problem helped it to be understood that this was not the central issue from an educational point of view. Important distinctions such as the difference between *trace* (report of the problem-solving steps) and *explanation* or the difference between *an expert solution* and *a solution that might make sense for learners* were put to the fore. The importance and difficulties of issues such as *diagnosing learners' actions* or *managing learners' models* were best understood, etc. It may be noticed that this work allowed advances not only in the TEL field, but also in AI and Knowledge Engineering.[4]

Innovation does contribute to the advancement of the field when avoiding the process of producing a technological innovation and an *ad hoc* associated discourse of how interesting this innovation is from an educational point of view, this interest not having been proved and lasting no longer than the time taken for the next innovation to emerge. When the implementation of the approach rather than the approach itself is questioned, conducting long-lasting studies is crucial. This is partly what happened in the case of ITSs, some of these systems, after many years of CS and education co-developments, reaching the stage that allows them to be used in classrooms.

2.1.3 Taking into Account Conceptual and Technological Complexity

If technology-driven applications and techno-centrism are indeed important issues, this may correspond to different realities according to (1) the system and setting complexity and (2) the software structuring role. As an example, we contrast hereafter important differences in the issues, dynamics and success criteria for ITSs and ICT-based systems.

Considering ITSs, how "success" is to be investigated is rather precise: the system is a success if it tutors learners in a pertinent way and, consequently,

---

[4]See for example: Clancey, W.J. (1986). From Guidon to Neomycin and Heracles in twenty short lessons: ORN final report 1979–1985. *The AI magazine*, 7(3), 40–60.

learning outcomes are improved. This requires many different issues to be dealt with: if a solver that can tackle the problems the learners will be presented with cannot be constructed, if the system cannot understand learners' activity and provide scaffolding or if this scaffolding is non-pertinent, the system is unusable. ITSs' teaching features require definitive success on many difficult problems. Such systems cannot be built without considering educational dimensions from the start, and there is little chance that a technology-driven process matches the conditions for success.

Let us now consider systems developed as clever applications of ICT features (synchronous and asynchronous electronic communication; sharing resources; searching for resources; etc.). Such a use of these technologies by actors (computer scientists, educationalists, teachers) having innovative ideas is made easy by the fact that it generally is not necessary to address basic technological dimensions (e.g., network technical issues) but rather how to use services and integrate them in a user-friendly interface. Teachers or learners can make these technologies theirs (e.g., tuning software to their needs), which is unlikely for complex software such as ITSs. Success or failure is therefore much less binary than in the ITS case: the fact that how the different services are integrated in interfaces is not optimal is less an issue than when an ITS unproductively constrains learners or provides non-pertinent scaffolding. Moreover, most of these systems are not meant to teach, but to provide learners with means. As a consequence, "success" may correspond to different dimensions such as the fact that the system generates some interest (from researchers, institutions, teachers or learners), the fact that pioneering ecological experiments may be implemented, or the fact that these experiments turn out to be positive in one way or another (e.g., that they improved learners' motivation). Whether the system "is used" is the killing argument.

This example illustrates that the techno-pushed dimension of the field is to be analyzed taking into consideration the *raison d'être* of systems and their complexity, which lead to different educational/technical interplays. Moreover, the socio-technical dimensions of the field also play an important role (see discussion in Chap. 3, Sect. 3.2).

Many ICT-based systems are as techno-centered as the first uses of CS in education. The difference lies in the fact that the nature of what the technology is about (communication) and the fact that adaptation is easy creates a context that facilitates the process of going from the techno-centered idea to efficient educational software. This process is not always managed, and many systems are just techno-centered innovations. However, this appears less salient than for other types of systems, which is related to the nature of their role and the loose notion of "success" for this type of system.

De facto, the technology-pushed approach (as opposed to software elaborated as responses to previously defined problems) often addresses users' interests rather than users' needs. These notions are, however, dynamic: the fact that technology opens some new possibilities creates a context within which new needs may appear.

2.2 TEL as a Field Where Some CS Problems Arise

Educational software may be approached by computer scientists as a field that generates CS problems to be solved. Within such an approach, emphasis is on elaborating CS abstractions or implementing models and processes from TEL specifications. This corresponds to addressing CS issues taking their origins in TEL concerns, but disentangled from these.

2.2.1 Disentangling CS Dimensions from Their TEL Origins

When considering educational software design and implementation, at a certain level of granularity, problems are disentangled from their original context and turned into purely technical issues. As a matter of fact, programs always end as series of 0s and 1s.

As we have mentioned it Chap. 2, Sect. 3.2 (analysis of SPR/CBPS relationships), the process of going from educational descriptions to a program is not a simple translation from something expressed at a level n to something expressed at a less abstract level $n-1$. There is not a kind of line separating educational concerns and CS concerns. Rather than a line, it is a large zone within which occurs the education/CS interplay, which includes conceptualizing issues, defining pertinent notions, designing artifacts, iteratively testing ideas and artifacts, etc. This zone and the level at which educational software issues become pure CS issues is very dependent on the project and the actor's perspective.

Acting in the education/CS interplay zone may take place at different phases: when imagining how educational ideas or concerns may be implemented; when attempting to turn precise educational ideas or requirements into technical specifications; when analyzing software usage.

A. Newell has powerfully shown, in the case of knowledge based systems,[5] the fact that going from a model defined at the knowledge level to an operational model is generally associated with semantic losses. Analyzing level $n-1$ does generally not allow reconstruction of level n: the CS level is related to educational dimensions that have impacted the preceding levels, that of conceptualizing what is to be done and designing the system, but only part of these elements is reified in the system, and only partly reified. This is why maintaining models that allow this connection to be clearly maintained is an absolute requirement for linking usage or learning outcomes to the design (see Chap. 8, Sect. 2).

---

[5]Newell, A. (1982). The Knowledge Level. *Artificial Intelligence*, 18(1), 87–127.

2.2.2 Addressing CS Issues

Addressing CS issues as such requires precise specifications, and results are to be analyzed consistently with these specifications.

Let us consider the construction of a piece of software whose objective is, given a chat tool, to categorize learners' interactions as questions, ideas, arguments or counterarguments. This may be decomposed into two sub-problems. First, elaborate the required educational abstractions (e.g., the categories, their characteristics, and the categorization criteria). This problem is both an educational problem (elaborate the meaningful categories) and a TEL problem (elaborating the categorization criteria), taking place in the education/CS interplay zone. Second, elaborate and implement the algorithms applying these criteria and producing the output (the messages classified by categories) from the input (the learners' messages). This second problem is a purely CS matter, which may be addressed independently from its pedagogical rationale, and whose solving leads to some advancement in TEL.

With respect to the piece of software, what is addressed is not "does categorizing sentences helps to scaffold learners?" or a similar educational issue, but "is categorization as here defined implementable" or "what categorization ratio can be obtained?" Such a work may allow results such as "algorithm A allows 82% of messages to be correctly categorized" or "technique B improves categorization by a factor of 0.3". Sticking to the CS dimension does not allow, for instance, comparison of two systems categorizing learners' interactions according to different categories.

Conversely, when the overall project includes a sub-project that consists of a CS issue, such work is not to be evaluated with respect to educational outcomes, but with respect to the technical specifications. The CS work may be perfectly successful from the point of view of the addressed CS objective, independently of whether the underlying learning hypothesis makes sense, the software is used as expected or has the targeted impact. The success of the CS work can be distinguished from the success of the project it is part of.

2.3 *TEL as a Proper Field*

Finally, educational software may be approached by computer scientists as a proper field, to be addressed as such. Within such an approach, emphasis is on elaborating the abstractions required to understand, design and implement educational software in a way that transcends disciplinary boundaries (transdisciplinarity).

Adopting such a view does not mean that all educational software issues are to be addressed in this way. Rather, it may be developed by acknowledging that some issues are purely educational issues, some others are purely CS issues, but the education/CS interplay zone cannot be addressed by translating or projecting educational issues onto a technical plan: there is not a pedagogical idea on the one side and CS work on the other, but co-constructions.

Within this view, the specific skill of TEL-oriented computer scientists (or, in other words, TEL-specialists with a background in CS) is the capacity to pertinently address the conceptual zone within which occur the education/CS interplays. In the case of innovation, it consists of the capacity of interpreting and analyzing in terms of CBPSs the new possibilities opened by technological advancement. In the case of TEL problems from which CS problems are derived, it consists of the capacity to manage the difficulty of going from a problem expressed at a CBPS level to a problem expressed at a technical level. In this second case, more particularly, this includes participating in the transdisciplinary work of conceptualizing issues and defining pertinent notions, the ability not to fall into naïve interpretations of pedagogical issues and, for instance, a reductive projection of complex issues onto technology. In both cases, it requires the capacity to understand and manage the pedagogical and technical complexity and dynamics, and maintain the correspondence and the traceability between the CBPS-level models and the computable models (see Chap. 8, Sect. 2).

These characteristics typically denote issues that may powerfully be addressed in the light of an engineering view of the field (see Chap. 6).

3 Conclusions

In this section, different roles that may be played by CS and the different approaches within which computer scientists may address the TEL field and these roles have been disentangled. These roles and views are not orthogonal to each other and usually co-exist as different dimensions of effective work. They must not be seen as categories to be chosen, but rather as analytical distinctions that may help in making clear and understanding what underlines projects, actions or discourses. Considering such questions is likely to make clearer these features only if, however, it is not conducted in a way that leads to opposing disciplines and addressing in a disciplinary way issues which are intrinsically multidisciplinary.

Concluding this CS analysis of the field, it might be worth pointing out that the disciplinary dimension is both a matter of content and of institutions. Indeed, it is interesting to reflect on the nature of knowledge or theories concerned in the elaboration of a notion or the implementation of a project, what implicit or explicit points of views or representations underlie a given position, etc. However, disciplines are also institutional constructions. Positioning with respect to such dimensions is sometimes related, to a greater or lesser extent, to individual needs to be recognized as a member of a discipline. This of course creates noise and disturbances. As a matter of fact, it is not unusual that researchers focusing on educational software define themselves as such (e.g., "TEL researchers") and not as "computer scientists concerned in TEL" or "psychologists concerned in TEL". This is, however, more often the case at a stage of the academic career that does not require, for instance, an institutional position to be obtained.

Chapter 6
Educational Software Engineering

Abstract This chapter clarifies the concept of engineering as a vector for addressing (and elaborating knowledge related to) complex artifacts design, and how this may be applied to educational software. In the conclusion, the relationships between TEL and CS research are questioned again, in the light of this analysis.

We have mentioned in Chap. 1 that capitalizing knowledge related to educational software design issues may be powerfully addressed via the design and analysis of systems if, however, considerations, issues, hypotheses, alternatives, means (etc.) are made explicit. In this chapter, we come back to this point and study it in more detail in the light of the *Sciences of the Artificial* way of considering engineering. We first recall the notion of engineering (Sect. 1), and define educational software engineering within this perspective (Sect. 2). Analyzing the implications of such a view will allow us to make more precise the rationale for the issues and contributions considered in this book. In Sect. 3 we reconsider the CS-TEL relation (first addressed in Chap. 5) with respect to this engineering approach to the field.

1 Engineering and Research

Engineering is generally referred to as what is required for designing and implementing artifacts that meet a desired objective. As a consequence, engineering is often contrasted with research: research considers the understanding of phenomena, while engineering considers the use of this understanding and the organizing of know-how in order to tackle development projects.

As an example of the research/engineering dichotomy in TEL, part of research in educational psychology considers the elaboration of knowledge related to human learning. It considers an external problem (how subjects learn) and attempts to provide answers. It is clearly different from "engineering" in the sense of "elaborating solutions", e.g., elaborating a solution to the problem of teaching a given topic to a given set of learners in a given setting. In such a context, engineering consists of searching in knowledge elaborated by science for solutions to the considered problem (or, rather, elements of solutions that can be pragmatically articulated).

Work in line with Simon's perspective[1] have, however, popularized the notion of Sciences of the Artificial. Within this perspective, designing complex artificial objects cannot be considered as the simple application of knowledge defined elsewhere. While natural sciences consider things as they are, within the Sciences of the Artificial one considers things as they may be, possible objectives and means to address them. In other words, while basic sciences are driven by the objective of understanding things that already exist (e.g., understanding how people learn), design-oriented sciences are driven by the objective of solving problems through building artifacts (e.g., software). Researchers and practitioners concerned with such areas consider as scientific objects, and within scientific processes, both the objects they build and the design processes they elaborate to build these objects.

Designing complex artifacts that meet their requirements cannot be achieved by applying a collection of lessons learned: it is not intuitive and it is not easy. It not only requires theoretical work and knowledge elaborated in "academic sciences", but also proper knowledge. Such a view thus promotes transdisciplinary approaches and fruitful synergies of theoretical and technical work.

2 Educational Software Engineering as a Scientific Field

2.1 Educational Software as Complex Artificial Objects

CBPSs and educational software are artificial objects. They are created by humans, for humans: they are not "natural". They create settings that do not exist prior to the creation of the artifact. They are contingent on the purposes and context for which they have been created.

CBPSs and educational software are complex due, in particular, to their intrinsic nature: they are socio-technical objects. Design of educational software cannot be thought of without considering a wider context including the CBPS and teaching setting levels. It requires cycles consistently articulating *a priori* analyses (pedagogical dimensions, epistemological dimensions, expected usage, expected impact, etc.), technical implementation, usage analysis and evaluation.

Problems related to educational software design are thus not limited to engineering issues in the traditional sense, i.e., building a solution from preexisting knowledge from one or another discipline. Learning, cognitive, teaching or software engineering theories only provide more or less relevant and useful perspectives, analysis

---

[1]Simon, H. (1969 and following editions). The Sciences of the Artificial. Cambridge: MIT Press.

frameworks or notions. There is no comprehensive set of ready-to-use notions or techniques to be used, and the history of the field has shown that building systems on the simple basis of knowledge and processes elaborated in other contexts (e.g., psychology on the one hand, CS on the other) rarely leads to satisfactory results.

As mentioned in Chap. 5, considering TEL as a field that poses complex issues, for which specific TEL constructions might be necessary, leads to consideration of TEL as a proper field, to be addressed within a transdisciplinary approach.

Both (1) work related to complex systems in general and (2) Software Engineering advances[2] suggest addressing complexity by building multiple viewpoints, i.e., interpretations from different perspectives that allow different dimensions to be captured. Adopting a given viewpoint does not consist of breaking a complex problem into separate simple sub-problems and, in particular, into separate disciplinary views. Rather, it consists of disentangling what may be disentangled with no loss as a means to make a given dimension addressable. While some of these viewpoints may be separated from one another, the essence of complexity is that some others are not independent. Considering the overall problem from the different viewpoints is a means to address complexity in a tractable way.

For instance, designing an ITS such as *JavIT* requires consideration of different viewpoints related to different dimensions: the domain (object-oriented design and programming); the way the domain may be conceptualized for teaching issues; the issue of interpreting learners' outputs; relationships with the CBPS and the teaching setting; the socio-technical dimensions related to these artifacts; etc. Most of these views and underlying models are interrelated with others. Difficulties lie in identifying what models are necessary to capture what is needed, elaborating these models while not falling into simplification, managing the different models' articulation and coherency, and implementing them in a way that allows their traceability.

2.2 Definition and Matters of Concern

Taking an engineering perspective (in the sense defined in Sect. 1), educational software engineering may be defined as:

> *Educational software engineering* is the scientific field the objective of which is to study the issues related to educational software design and implementation. It is concerned with the notions, methods, theories, techniques, technologies or lessons learned that may facilitate the design, implementation, evaluation or diffusion of CBPSs, educational software and pedagogical-setting support software in a way that allows more than just *ad hoc* treatment of issues and problems.

---

[2]See for example approaches such as UML (Unified Modeling Language; http://www.uml.org; retrieved November 11, 2010) or MDA (Model Driven Architecture; http://www.omg.org/mda/; retrieved November 11, 2010).

Educational software engineering requires articulation of the CS dimensions of design and implementation (concepts, principles, processes, methods, techniques, technologies) and the Human and Social Sciences dimensions that must be considered at design time due to the pedagogical purpose of the constructed artifact and to the fact that it is used by humans (specific learning, teaching or usage phenomena; relationships between educational software and CBPSs or, when pertinent, teaching settings; relationships between design processes and usage or impact dimensions; etc.). The way these dimensions are articulated defines the nature of X when stating that design is an X-disciplinary work (see Chap. 3, Sect. 5).

Efforts dedicated to educational software engineering may correspond to:

1. Transversal efforts, whose objective is to clarify issues, define concepts, contrast possible approaches, etc. This is the perspective adopted in this book.
2. Specific efforts, whose objective is to build engineering methodologies.

We more precisely define these two options (which are disentangled here, but which may cohabit) and the conditions for effective projects to allow knowledge development in the following sections.

2.3 Transversal Efforts to Clarify Issues

In the preceding chapters, we have highlighted that the educational discourse in the light of which software dimensions are to be addressed often leaves open many options. This may be related to an array of reasons: differences in matters of concern; differences of perspective, for instance with respect to the importance of software properties as influencing factors; unawareness of the level of precision required by software design; unawareness of difficulties; etc.

This issue may be thought of as something educationalists should solve, i.e., one may consider that educationalists should be helped to produce sufficiently precise specifications for computer scientists to act as computer scientists only, i.e., elaborate the required CS abstractions and/or enable the specified models and processes to be run on computers (see Chap. 5, Sect. 1). This is consistent with the view that a kind of line separates educational work and CS work.

In direct contrast, taking an engineering perspective (in the sense defined in Sect. 1) leads one to consider that an intrinsic dimension of educational software design is the existence of a zone within which occurs an education/CS interplay, and this zone must be addressed within a transdisciplinary approach.

Conducting such work requires the different actors to share some understanding of the *raison d'être*, rationale, objectives, specifications, models, descriptions, analyses (etc.) underlying the notions and artifacts at stake. As illustrated by the preceding chapters, this is of particular difficulty in the TEL area given the variety of perspectives that may co-exist with respect to what "educational software" is, what "designing educational software" may refer to (both in terms of design and technical dimensions), what important notions such as "impact" or "activity" may refer to, the different roles of CS-dimensions in the process, etc.

Within this perspective, a central issue of educational software engineering is to identify these difficulties and provide conceptual means to support their addressing. This is what this book is about, and the rationale for its contributions:

1. A general conceptualization oriented towards educational software engineering, introducing definitions that are of interest for disentangling issues and specific notions such as software pedagogical rationale (Chap. 2).
2. A highlight of the importance of understanding differences of perspective and an analysis of a set of issues that may lead to misunderstandings (Chap. 3).
3. Examples which may provide insights (Chap. 4).
4. An analysis of CS roles – and computer scientists' possible views – whose explicitation may, here again, contribute to understanding engagements and actions (Chap. 5).
5. An analysis of educational software engineering (this chapter).
6. A list of analysis axes and characterizing dimensions for educational software engineering work (Chap. 7).
7. General methodological considerations (Chap. 8).
8. A perspective on the way to push the field forward (Chap. 9).

Such transversal efforts serve both conceptual and pragmatic goals as they tend in the direction of:

1. Contributing to a general understanding of the field. TEL, as a complex field, requires description of the complexity and elaboration of different conceptualizations denoting different perspectives. Educational-software-engineering is one such perspective.
2. Defining intermediation objects (or elements to build intermediation objects) for actors acting from different perspectives, in both research and development projects.
3. Providing a consistent basis for elaborating knowledge (see Sect. 2.5).

2.4 Specific Efforts to Build Engineering Methodologies

Elaborating an educational software engineering methodology consists of describing a more or less precise process of how to build such software, i.e., (1) a sequence of actions described at a given level of detail and, possibly, (2) tools facilitating the implementation of this process (e.g., a modeling language or a dedicated software engineering framework). Compiling lessons learned serves similar goals.

Educational software denotes too large a variety of artifacts, considered settings or matters of concern to allow a useful engineering methodology to be elaborated. Indeed, this would result in considering issues at a level that is common to all settings, which would lead to only very general principles.

By contrast, it makes sense to consider engineering methodologies related to a precise type of object x, taking into account what this x is and what considered matters of concern, notions or issues are. For instance:

- For $x =$ "on-line learning setting defined as a setting within which learners are provided with a set of on-line documents and a scenario stating how to go through these resources", what can be considered is, for example, a list of tasks to be tackled in order to identify and elaborate the resources: what are the pedagogical objectives? How may these pedagogical objectives be broken down? How do the pieces of knowledge relate to each other (prerequisites, etc.)? What resources and tasks may be related to these pieces of knowledge? How should these tasks be scheduled? etc. This may be based on, for example, instructional design approaches.
- For $x =$ "collaborative learning setting", it is possible, for instance, to list notions of importance when attempting to build scenarios and technical settings that enhance the chances that learners collaborate, such as the definition of roles, the way learners should be grouped or the issues to be considered.[3]
- For $x =$ "computer-based simulation", what may be considered is concepts, issues or lessons learned related to such simulations: how learners usually behave when confronted with a simulation, the issues that learners encounter to transfer what has been practiced within a simulation to an effective setting, etc. The addressed level leads to consideration of general notions that take specific importance and meaning in this context (e.g., the notion of *representation*). The analysis is implicitly positioned at a level that is independent of the taught domain.
- For $x =$ "simulation-based inquiry learning", what may be considered is the learning mechanisms related to inquiry and the simulation dimensions as related to these learning mechanisms: the positioning and, thus, the considered concepts and issues are different.
- For $x =$ "dynamic geometry", what may be considered is related to the specific studied domain (geometry), its properties, specific knowledge related to learners' issues with respect to geometry, how geometrical notions may be directly manipulated on the screen or the synergies that may be gained from using different representation registers. For a more precise x, e.g., $x =$ "dynamic geometry seen within the perspective of Brousseau's theory of didactical situations",[4] an engineering methodology may build on the basis of the notions introduced by the theory such as *situation*, *didactical transposition* or *didactical contract* (these different terms having precise meanings defined by the theory).

If engineering approaches may build from theories such as instructional design, domain-specific teaching theories or cognitive theories, the level of the considered

---

[3]See for example Tchounikine, P. (2008). Operationalizing macro-scripts in CSCL technological settings. *International Journal of Computer-Supported Collaborative Learning*, 3(2), 193–233.

[4]Brousseau, G. (1997). Theory of Didactical Situations in Mathematics. Dordrecht: Kluwer.

teaching setting and its organization may also be a matter of concern; see the way institutions such as Universities may divide up tasks between different services.

Efforts may also address specific types of systems (e.g., a methodology that allows building of ITSs), addressing the ITS notion in general or within a particular perspective and specific matters of concern (see how very different concerns may be considered with the presentation of *JavIT* in Chap. 4).

2.5 Conducting Projects as Vectors for Knowledge Development

Following the view of engineering introduced in Sect. 1, building systems is a core vector for elaborating knowledge. When addressing design and implementation of educational software, there is not, on the one hand, a "scientific" activity consisting of the understanding of some "fundamental" issues and, on the other hand, a "technical" activity consisting of building systems: both dimensions are intrinsically meshed. Knowledge (theories if any, models, techniques, methods or lessons learned) may be addressed via the efforts to identify, understand and describe issues, to elaborate and analyze possible solutions, to capitalize lessons learned or to consider generalization issues.

In the case of research projects, cases studies can be defined according to the considered issue (a tailorability mechanism, an algorithm to build learners' models, a strategy to make learners argue, an innovative type of interface, etc.). Typically, this may consist of identifying the system or series of systems whose construction requires the research question to be addressed, and conducting the project in a way that considers abstract constructions and knowledge (as opposed to an *ad hoc* solution), the spectrum of validity or interest of these constructions, etc. Within such a process, the constructed system is both the resource and the objective of the scientific work. If the constructed system turns out to be pedagogically useful one may of course consider dissemination.

In the context of development projects, knowledge may be elaborated by making specific explicitation and capitalization efforts, in addition to the objective of implementing the system (see also Chap. 9). Analyzing how basic software is used by learners and teachers is also a resource.

As we have mentioned it in Chap. 3, addressing design of educational software as an important dimension is related to the hypothesis that the fact that a system presents some features and/or some properties rather than others may make – or contribute to – a difference (notion of *impact of a given system*, to be considered within the general perspective explained in the preceding chapters and not repeated here). In order to be productive of knowledge, work conducted in the context of particular projects must thus address the level of the general software functions and that of the detailed properties, which is one of the levels where design alternatives are to be considered, and decisions made. Building on the example of communication tools, considering in the same way chat tools presenting different properties (e.g. chronological presentation of freely typed sentences, presence of sentence-openers or graphical representation) is very unproductive.

As we have mentioned it, many dimensions related to software usage are subject to complexity and uncertainties. Considerations related to software properties must be examined at the level where they make sense. For instance, the impact of *Biosim*'s cognitive tools' properties on learners' inquiry processes may be rendered contingent by other factors (e.g., the way this CBPS is introduced to learners, pre- and post-sequences or institutional dimensions). It is thus of core importance to disentangle issues and matters of concern. Considering how software properties may be used to influence learners' activity is a precise and limited topic, which addresses only one dimension of a more general issue but, nevertheless, may be regarded as such. This may be contrasted with approaches whose explicit objective is to define methodologies aiming to improve practices (and develop knowledge)[5]: although, when studying software properties, improving practices may be an underlying objective, entry points, matters of concern, objects to be considered or methodologies are different.

3 Reconsidering the CS-TEL Relationship

3.1 Educational Software Engineering and Research

In this chapter, we have said that engineering and research should not be treated as contradictory. Although the motivations, control, validation or diffusion processes are different than when just considering the objective of obtaining a usable system, differentiating engineering and research work is difficult since different dimensions and matters of concern are often entangled. A research project may require one to engage in purely programming work as a requirement to experiment with ideas. Conversely, the basic objective of obtaining a usable system may require one to produce innovative techniques and interesting lessons learned: design and implementation of systems often acts as a generator of problems, which may be disciplinary problems (e.g., psychology, pedagogy or CS) or TEL problems (e.g., perception and understanding of learners' activity or elaboration of learners' models). However, researchers should be able, at any time, to explain the research dimension.

Part of the misunderstanding related to the relationship between engineering and research stems from the fact that many of the disciplines addressing the TEL field have developed more common approaches to research and knowledge elaboration. For instance, when using empirical evaluation and statistical analysis in

---
[5]See for example Wang, F. & Hannafin, M.J. (2005). Design-based research and Technology-Enhanced Learning Environments. *Educational Technology Research and Development*, 53(4), 5–23.

psychology, the methodology and how a hypothesis may be turned into knowledge is crystal clear. In CS, the evaluation issue varies considerably depending on the type of work. For instance, a project related to the building of an algorithm may be examined by means of both qualitative and quantitative evaluations: the algorithm works or does not (given some input, it provides the expected output or does not); a proof can be exhibited (formal properties of an algorithm are demonstrated, using mathematical or logical foundations); the algorithm can be analyzed with respect to some metrics (e.g., given a benchmark, it produces the output in less time, or with more precision, than a comparative algorithm). However, benchmarks or proofs are rather rare in the TEL field. Evaluating a model, a process or a method is much more difficult. For instance, given a model or a method that is supposed to help in the design of computer-based systems, it is just not possible to create experimental conditions such as a set of modeling teams (not to say companies) that solve the same problem and for which the support provided by the model or method is the only impacting factor.

Within research communities, discussions related to methodologies are also often more or less implicitly underlined by the "research" status of the considered work. For instance, in the educational field, many discussions address differences separating empirical approaches ("code and count"), ethno-methodological approaches ("explore and understand"), design-based research or, now, neuroimaging. In CS, many misunderstandings separate people focusing on mathematical proofs of the properties of a given algorithm from the ones focusing on (for example) participative software-engineering methodologies. The educational software engineering field is not defined by a given methodology, but by the questions and issues it raises.

3.2 Educational Software Engineering and CS Research

Considering educational software engineering as a scientific field makes it possible to re-question the relationships between TEL and CS and, in particular, CS research. We explore hereafter the relationship of TEL with three different visions of CS: (1) a vision focusing on the theoretical foundations of data processing, (2) a technical or technological vision focusing on artifacts and (3) a socio-technical vision, and come back to computer scientists' engagement and specific skills.

3.2.1 TEL and the Theoretical Dimensions of CS

When considering CS as the field studying the theoretical foundations of data processing by computers, TEL is basically a potential application domain for the technological applications of CS.

3.2.2 TEL and the Technological Dimensions of CS

When considering a technical or technological vision of CS, focusing on artifacts and their design processes, TEL is, like various other fields (e.g., information systems, HCI or knowledge engineering), a domain that allows the study of a variety of general CS issues: model-driven engineering, knowledge modeling, problem solving, interaction analysis, software adaptability, etc. Designing and implementing educational software leads to the addressing of issues that may, at a certain degree of granularity, be disentangled from their initial context and addressed as such.

Within this view, the general interest of TEL is (similarly to some other application fields) to create a context in which techniques and methods (in AI, software engineering, HCI, networking, etc.) may be analyzed and improved with respect to externally defined explicit constraints. This makes it possible not to consider these issues within "toy" artificial problems. Such work may lead to advances related to the TEL field and/or which find a wider application scope.

As an example of how TEL creates interesting instances of general CS issues and provides an interesting context in which to address them, let us consider tailorability, i.e., the fact that a system may provide its users with integrated support for modifying it in the context of its use. For educational software, tailorability appears to be a potential means to combine the two objectives of (1) providing learners with software designed to guide and support them, this design being based on pedagogical decisions, while (2) providing learners with built-in flexibility features to adapt software to their emergent activity and needs, in context. Introduction of tailorability in educational software, however, raises major issues: tailorability for learners ought to be studied with respect to the intention underlying the system, and if the system is designed to reify some pedagogic principles, its potential flexibility must be studied with respect to these principles and constraints. Furthermore, tailoring must be technically easy to carry out. Finally, tailoring is, with respect to the learners' activity as related to the learning scenario, another activity; therefore, the risk of generating a breakdown in the activity flow should be taken into account. TEL defines a context where a classical CS issue is a core issue, has a particular instantiation, and is subject to specific constraints.

When considering this technical or technological vision of CS, the specific interest of TEL is the importance of human and social dimensions, the multiplicity and complexity of the levels to be taken into account (sociological and psychological; individual and collective; etc.) and the evolutionary character of users.[6] The major drawback may be the difficulty of evaluation.

---

[6]By definition, educational software's objective is that users' (learners') activities and knowledge evolve.

3.2.3 TEL and the Socio-technical Dimensions of CS

Within a socio-technical vision of CS, CS is concerned with the functional dimension of software and with all the dimensions that may influence its effective usage.

Works related to TEL are of particular interest for CS in this respect. In addition to the technical dimensions (see *supra*), it provides a particularly productive field for studying socio-technical issues such as understanding the features that may influence stakeholders' activities and how to take them into account at the design stage and/or by providing software with run-time adaptation features as a way to contextually adapt to actors' effective activity. In other words, TEL is a means of addressing one of the fundamental issues of CS: understanding what *designing software to support human activity* means, and how to address this issue.[7] Here again, TEL may be used to elaborate knowledge that has a wider application scope.

3.2.4 Engagement of Computer Scientists

Putting emphasis on the engineering dimension raises the particular importance of elaborating pertinent abstractions in a way that transcend the boundaries of conventional academic disciplines, i.e., in a transdisciplinary way. This allows to be made more precise the different types of actions that computer scientists engaged in educational software design may be concerned with:

- Participating in the understanding of TEL issues, the elaboration of TEL-specific notions (e.g., learners' models) or processes (e.g., specific methodology) and, more generally, in the overall definition and understanding of the field.
- Elaborating and defining the CS dimensions of TEL projects.
- Solving the CS issues of TEL projects, building CS abstractions and implementing them.
- And, on another dimension: finding and exploring clever educational applications of CS technical advancements.

As mentioned in Chap. 5, Sect. 2.3, the specific skill of TEL-oriented computer scientists (or, in other words, TEL specialists with a background in CS) is the capacity to pertinently address the conceptual zone within which occur the education/CS interplays. TEL requires actors (researchers, engineers) with computational and TEL expertise allowing them to understand TEL concerns when managing the initial design, going from general issues to design decisions and participating in the interpretation of usage with respect to design issues. Methodological skills (not specific to TEL) such as technology-driven design, participatory design (involving future users in design), empirically-based design (prototyping with user testing), theory-based design (basing a design on a theory or conceptual framework originating outside of the technology domain) or evolutionary (incremental) design

---

[7] A provocative way to highlight this dimension is to suggest that some dimensions of CS may be viewed as part of the Human and Social Sciences.

are also of interest for conducting projects, as well as the CS skills allowing the management of the CS issues disentangled from their educational context.

4 Conclusions

In this chapter, we have re-examined a certain number of considerations related to educational software design issues that were first addressed in Chap. 1, and anchored them in a theoretical perspective. These considerations define the rationale for this book: addressing the problem of making explicit matters of concern and work, within the intrinsic difficulties and limits of this exercise. Without going again through the argumentation developed in Chap. 1, in summary, drawing attention to this issue and proposing means to address it serves objectives such as: facing the issues related to developing some shared understanding in a multidisciplinary team; reutilizing or adapting preceding work; refining or reconsidering design decisions; enhancing the chances that work is understood; identifying results and how they should be evaluated; avoiding re-inventing or re-building things that already exist, wasting time in work that does not produce any progress or falling into well-known methodological traps; capitalizing lessons learned or developing methodological guidelines; contributing to whether educational software is based on scientific knowledge and is not only subject to inventiveness or, less positively, technological push and the latest trends.

Addressing issues within a transdisciplinary perspective does not contradict the fact that some issues are disciplinary from the start, and that some others may become disciplinary at some level of granularity. Similarly, for computer scientists, TEL may be addressed both as a transdisciplinary field, within which they act as TEL specialists, and as an application field for different CS domains (e.g., Software Engineering, HCI or AI).

Finally, we have disentangled the objectives of understanding the issues related to educational software engineering and that of building an engineering methodology. This is a classic approach in software engineering. For instance, in object-oriented design, emphasizing the importance of disentangling static and dynamic views of classes or exploring the issues posed by identifying classes (etc.) is different from listing phases to be addressed when designing software and, for each of these phases, the tasks to be addressed and how they should be realized.

Chapter 7
Characterizing the Design Context and the Software Artifact

Abstract This chapter introduces a list of analysis axes and characterizing dimensions for educational software engineering work. This list is meant to suggest questions whose answers may help to clarify *raison d'être*, matters of concern or objectives of work, in particular when addressing the zone within which occurs the education/CS interplay.

In the preceding chapters we have highlighted the importance of making explicit what is considered and how when designing and implementing educational software,[1] as an important requirement for (1) helping multidisciplinary teams to work together and (2) capitalizing knowledge. We have also highlighted why such a clarification is necessary and may be difficult: variety of possible matters of concern and levels at which issues may be regarded; actors' disciplinary backgrounds, views of the field or of their roles; entanglement of objectives and the fact that they may be addressed by the software design and/or the setting; variety of approaches such as building on technical innovation or solving an educational issue or, in the technical dimension, building new software from scratch or adapting existing components; variety of perspectives on core notions such as impact or the task/activity duality and ways of taking this into account.

As mentioned in Chap. 1, making something explicit is difficult for different reasons. One of these is that what should be addressed (what features should be made explicit as important dimensions in which lack of clarity or misunderstandings would be an issue) is not necessarily obvious.

Actors usually present their work according to the work's dynamics as they see it. An external list of possible considerations may allow, in addition, analyzing this work in a new and different way.

---

[1] In order to keep the text fluid we will stick to the *educational software* notion and term. Most of the issues addressed in this chapter do, however, also apply, *mutatis mutandis*, to pedagogical-setting support software as defined in Chap. 2.

In this chapter,[2] we introduce a list of analysis axes and characterizing dimensions for educational software engineering work. First, in Sect. 1, we introduce the content and the general structure. In Sect. 2 we list the elements suggested for characterizing the design context (i.e., mainly, some CBPS dimensions) and, in Sect. 3, the elements suggested for characterizing the software as a computer-based system (i.e., mainly, the implemented processes). In Sect. 4, we illustrate the use of these characteristics on two examples.

1 Introduction

Content

The suggested analysis axes and characterizing dimensions related to the context of the educational software design are:

- Nature of the work (research project, development project)
- Theoretical background
- Nature of the targeted outcome
- Rationale for designing software
- How software is considered within the CBPS
- Design approach
- Actors concerned
- Context and historical dimensions of the project.

The suggested analysis axes and characterizing dimensions related to educational software as computer-based systems are:

- Level of analysis of software properties
- Actions considered at the level of software
- Reification of the pedagogical intention in software
- Nature of the CS treatments
- Level of achievement

For each analysis axis a list of possible prototypical values is introduced, as a way to clarify the axis and provide a possible resource.

---

[2]Part of this chapter takes its origins from research work conducted with Baker, M., Balacheff, N., Baron, M., Derycke, A., Guin, D., Nicaud, J.-F. & Rabardel, P. and disseminated as: Tchounikine, P. et al. (2004). Platon-1: quelques dimensions pour l'analyse des travaux de recherche en conception d'EIAH (in French). Public report (département STIC du CNRS).

1 Introduction

Objective

The proposed lists are meant to suggest consideration of questions whose answers may help to clarify what is at stake when designing educational software. Scaling a project on these different dimensions may act as an eye-opener and help to address the zone within which the education/CS interplay occurs by providing support for:

1. Clarifying concerns and objectives, and avoiding misunderstandings
2. Considering verification and validation issues[3]
3. Describing the considered problem and the considered solution and, thus, the advance, if any

As an example, considering whether a CBPS is thought of *in reference to non-computer-based settings*, and, in this case, what the *type of reference* is (e.g., a construction whose general structure is inspired by a non-computer-based setting or a precise transposition which requires a list of properties to be preserved) may help to clarify and order objectives and constraints. For instance, if one considers as a reference a group of learners collaboratively solving a problem in a classroom, the way this reference is addressed when designing an on-line setting may lead to very different concerns, stemming from very general considerations (should one introduce a forum and/or a chat tool?) to very precise ones (how should one transpose the non-verbal awareness dimensions related to expressing approbations or doubts with respect to a peer's proposal?).

As another example, considering the *added value expected from the educational software* may help to reveal that some actors consider that software is meant to *improve learning outcomes with respect to the non-computer-based reference settings*, while what some others have in mind is to allow creation of CBPSs that are *alternatives* or *complements*, which changes the rationale, the evaluation and many other dimensions (e.g., the issue of consistency with other dimensions of the teaching setting).

As other examples: clarifying whether software properties are considered to be the constitutive elements defining a specific epistemic *milieu* informs the importance that must be given to whether learners use the software or not, and thus the design decision to be taken with respect to this dimension; clarifying the learners' actions that are effectively considered at the level of software (as opposed to the CBPS level) or the nature of the considered analysis and interpretation processes helps in specifying software requirements and comparing systems; etc.

---

[3]*Verification* consists of evaluating whether software functioning is correct; *validation* consists of evaluating whether software meets requirements.

Nature

The axes listed in Sects. 2 and 3 are introduced as a resource for analysis from different viewpoints, within the engineering perspective developed in Chap. 6. As a consequence:

1. The list is not meant to be exhaustive, but to suggest the value of making explicit such issues and to provide a basis. It may be usefully extended.
2. For a given project, only some of these axes may appear pertinent, and some others (or rephrasing some of these) appear necessary. This is consistent with the acknowledgement of the variety of projects and contexts that may be conducted in TEL, and the fact that matters of concern may vary.
3. The introduced axes are partially redundant, which means that some dimension of a project may be addressed within several axes. This is consistent with the acknowledgement of the fact that complexity must not be addressed by defining and using perspectives that are independent of each other. On the contrary, complexity leads to consideration of views that place emphasis on different issues and thus may partially intersect each other.

General Structure

In order to provide a general view, Tables 7.1 and 7.2 synthesize the proposed analysis axes, the major underlying issues and examples of impacted dimensions.

The different lists and sub-lists are structured to simplify their use. However, the adopted structure is only one possible structure. Although considering the highlighted features may have a heuristic value for conducting projects, the objective is not to suggest a design methodology.

2 Characterizing the Design Context

2.1 Research/Development Nature of the Work

A first dimension to be made clear is whether design of educational software is addressed as a development project only (i.e., the objective is to allow some given CBPS to be implemented in some given effective setting), a research project (i.e., the *raison d'être* of the CBPS and/or software design is to obtain the means required for studying some considered research issues) or a mixed project, and what is the research dimension about, if any.

2 Characterizing the Design Context

Table 7.1 Characterizing the design context

Analysis axis	Main underlying issues	Examples of impacted elements
Nature of the work (research/development)	What are the reasons for considering the design of educational software?	Type of targeted outcome
Theoretical background	What is the focus (the central object) of the study? What is the theoretical substratum? What is the type of reference to the knowledge at stake?	Conceptual and methodological context of the work and related issues (approach, considered objects, considered constraints, etc.) Genericity and reusable dimensions of the outcome
Nature of the targeted outcome	What are the matters of concern? (to be examined at different levels of granularity)	Constraints on the design and subsequent decision criteria Evaluation criteria
Rationale for designing software	What is the overall objective?	Level of achievement of software
How software is considered within the CBPS	What expectations are placed on the software design? What is the reference for defining the targeted properties of the software?	Design process Software specification Hypotheses and issues related to usage Evaluation criteria
Design approach	What is the design process entry-point? What are the properties of the design process?	Considered objects
Actors concerned	Which actors are concerned in the specification, design, implementation and usage of the software?	Nature of work Type of targeted outcomes Design process
Context and historical dimensions	What is the project's present and past life?	Nature of work Type of targeted outcomes

Research issues may be associated with various fields (e.g., TEL as such, education, psychology or CS) and address different issues, for example:

- The adequacy, transposability or informative character of a theory for designing CBPSs and/or a given type of educational software.
- A model (e.g., an interaction model).
- A software component (e.g., a problem-solving component).
- A hypothesis (e.g., a psychological hypothesis) that requires a given CBPS or educational software for experimentations.
- A CS issue (e.g., problem-solving control, tailorability or conversational agents) for which the design of educational software provides a pertinent context.
- A methodological engineering or re-engineering process.
- Etc.

Table 7.2 Characterizing the computer-based system

Analysis axis	Main underlying issues	Examples of impacted elements
Level of analysis of software properties	To what levels of detail are the software features and interfaces considered?	Considered objects Design process Evaluation criteria
Actions considered at the level of software	To what levels of details are the learners' actions considered?	Considered objects Design process
Reification of the pedagogical intention in software	What pedagogical properties are embedded in the software?	Considered objects Design process
Nature of the CS treatments	What are the natures of the implemented CS processes?	Software architecture Reuse of existing components Genericity and reusable dimensions of the designed components
Level of achievement	What is the purpose and (if pertinent) the usage context of the software?	Software architecture Type of evaluation

Clarifying the research/development dimensions of the work is of particular importance for TEL projects as many misunderstandings may appear, in particular in relation to the nature of the CS dimensions.

More generally, research projects often consider several more or less related objectives that may be disentangled. For instance, designing a system may be both a way to demonstrate that a given model can be made computable and a way to implement some innovative CBPSs, and implementing these CBPSs in effective settings may be both an objective as such and a means for studying how such innovations may impact practices. Projects may also mix development and research dimensions that can be disentangled in some places (e.g., the basic construction of a piece of code) and not in others (e.g., the addressing of the design dimensions, or when the adopted methodology intrinsically intertwines development and research dimensions such as in the design-based research approach[4]).

2.2 *Theoretical Background*

Design may refer, in different ways, to some theoretical background(s). Clarifying this dimension not only requires this theoretical background to be stated but,

---

[4]Wang, F. & Hannafin, M. J. (2005). Design-based research and technology-enhanced learning environments. *Educational Technology Research and Development*, 53(4), 5–23.

importantly, the dimensions it addresses or allows one to address and how it is used. This may lead one to consider[5]:

- The focus of the stated theoretical background (different focuses related to different levels of granularity may coexist, and hybridizations are possible), for instance:
  - Focus on learning phenomena.
  - Focus on the activity notion.
  - Focus on usage phenomena.
  - Focus on technical dimensions.
  - Etc.
- The stated theory (or family of theories) and its nature (articulations, interactions or hybridizations of theories are possible), for instance:
  - A learning theory.
  - A cognitive theory.
  - A teaching theory.
  - A domain theory.
  - A domain-specific teaching theory.
  - An interaction or communication theory.
  - A human development theory.
  - A CS theory.
  - Etc.
- The correspondence between the stated theory and the effective work, for instance:
  - How the adequacy of the theory to the considered issues is made evident.
  - The description of the hypotheses or of the conceptual transformations allowing use of the theory.
  - Etc.
- How the theory is used, for instance:
  - As a general reference denoting the adopted view on (for instance) learning or teaching.
  - As a general reference underlying the conceptualization within which is considered the teaching setting, the CBPS or the educational software.
  - As a reference defining elements (notions, axes, principles, etc.) for identifying the targeted educational software properties.
  - Etc.
- The reference to the learning domain, if any. The relationships to the domain may be envisaged in a variety of ways (which may differ according to the considered level of granularity) such as:
  - Approach considering the domain knowledge at stake and the knowledge-specific construction processes (e.g., founding design on mathematical education work).

---

[5]The theoretical background related to the design process is addressed in Sect. 2.6.

- Approach considering dimensions related to the type or structure of the domain (e.g., common issues related to the experimental nature of some scientific domains).
- Approach independent of the domain and the knowledge at stake, completely generic.

2.3 Nature of the Targeted Outcome

It has been mentioned in Chap. 2 that educational software projects may consider different types of objectives, intertwined objectives and/or series of objectives ($objective_1$ is considered as a means for $objective_2$), and these objectives may be of different levels of granularity. Disentangling and making explicit the expected (and effective) outcomes of a project (and different subprojects, if any) is a productive way to clarify this dimension, and specify evaluation processes.

For instance, a project may produce as an outcome the fact that a given piece of software presents a given property, although the elaborated system turns out not to allow the implementation of the targeted CBPS. Similarly, the outcome may be that the designed software allows implementation of the CBPS but this CBPS does not lead to the expected learners' activity, this activity does not lead to the expected learning outcomes, or the CBPS does not allow the transformation of the teaching setting as expected. As another type of example, a project may fail in constructing the expected software but contribute to the understanding of an issue, or allow elaboration of innovative CBPSs whilst the specific software that was supposed to be its basis is no longer considered.

Projects involving design of educational software may target different outcomes such as:

- The construction of an object, a product or a service, for instance,
  - Constructing a CBPS.
  - Constructing a scenario.
  - Constructing a pedagogical resource.
  - Constructing a model of the knowledge to be taught.
  - Constructing a model of some dimension transversal to different domains.
  - Constructing a piece of software (see *infra*).
  - Providing learners with a question/answer service.
  - Providing teachers with supervising tools.
  - Etc.
- The addressing of a pedagogical objective, for instance,
  - Whether learners have applied themselves to a problem, a setting or a resource.
  - Whether learners have practiced some skills.
  - Whether learners have developed some knowledge or skill.

2 Characterizing the Design Context

- Whether some teachers' tasks have been facilitated or supported.
- Whether a teaching setting or type of teaching setting has been made more accessible, had its organization or efficiency improved, etc.
- Etc.

- The transformation of a setting, for instance,

  - Transformation of how a given domain is taught (as an example, dynamic geometry software has dramatically changed geometry teaching).
  - Transformation of actors' interplay within a teaching setting (as an example, networked learning settings).
  - Etc.

- The elaboration of a theory, i.e., knowledge explaining a given phenomenon.
- The elaboration of some understanding[6] of a phenomenon or an object, e.g., of how some given properties of some given software may impact learners' activity.
- The elaboration of some statement or lesson learned, i.e., elaborate or (in) validate some knowledge, e.g., knowledge stipulating that under certain circumstances it is preferable to provide immediate feedback.
- The elaboration of a model, i.e., an abstraction that denotes important features of an object or a setting with respect to a given objective. In the context of educational software, models may address different (non-exclusive) objectives such as:

  - Model as a support for thinking.
  - Model as a support for analysis.
  - Model as a support for human-human communication.
  - Model as a prediction tool.
  - Model as a simulation tool.
  - Model as a CS design or specification tool.
  - Model as an intermediate structure in between two objects (other models, software components, etc.).
  - Model as a run-time control or configuration tool for a process (interface adaptation, data flow control, feedback and support control, etc.).
  - Etc.

- The elaboration of a process or some methodological considerations, i.e., concepts, knowledge, techniques (etc.) useful for tackling a problem, for instance:

  - A description of issues.
  - A general approach to some issue.
  - A method.

---

[6]Elaborating an understanding is a very broad category that subsumes all others, but may be useful for denoting some projects at some level of granularity (elsewhere this is broken down into more precise categories) and/or at some period of a project's history.

- An engineering or re-engineering process.
- A benchmark.
- A lesson learned.
- Etc.

- The elaboration of a conceptualization, i.e., a set of concepts proposed as a substratum for thinking about or for elaborating a model or a theory.
- The implementation of some software or some software component, i.e., building a program defined by a set of CS descriptions (general architecture, functional signatures and axiomatic definitions, interface descriptions, etc.), for instance,
  - Implement a solver that can build the solution to a given type of problem or exercise.
  - Implement a logic formula manipulation engine that presents properties useful for representing and managing learners' profiles.
  - Implement a visualization tool that allows a particular data presentation.
  - Implement an innovative mobile object.
  - Implement a diagnostic or categorization algorithm.
  - Etc.

- The definition of a problem, i.e., identifying and conceptualizing the obstacles to addressing a given objective, and formulating them as a problem or an issue. For instance, considering a teaching issue related to how to support learners in developing problem-solving skills may lead to identification of issues to be addressed such as "elaborate a method for identifying meta-knowledge used by teachers when presenting solutions in classrooms".

2.4 Rationale for Designing Software

The rationale underlying the design of educational software may be, very directly, to obtain the targeted outcome, e.g.

- Implement a CBPS or a type of CBPSs.
- Address a pedagogical objective.
- Transform a setting.
- Etc.

However, targeted outcomes may find their rationale in larger considerations. Disentangling local outcomes from the overall intention may help to make explicit that what is an outcome for one actor is a means for another actor (or at a different period of time), or clarifying otherwise implicit constraints and issues. For instance, design and implementation of a piece of software may find its rationale in whether one wants to obtain data related to learners' usage in order to elaborate some understanding of something, to obtain an experimental setting that allows testing of a hypothesis or a model, to allow understanding of whether some construction can be made computable (operationalization of a model or process, interoperability means, etc.), to allow exploration of an idea, etc.

2.5 How Software Is Considered Within the CBPS

Educational software is intrinsically related to CBPSs or types of CBPSs. As a consequence, clarifying the software design-context not only requires a description of the considered CBPSs but, importantly, the way the CBPS/educational software relationship is thought of and addressed. This may require consideration of different dimensions such as:

- The type of reference to non-computer-based settings, if any. For instance:
  - The CBPS may be envisaged as a construction whose general structure is inspired by a non-computer-based setting.
  - The CBPS may be envisaged as a transposition of a non-computer-based setting, which is considered as a reference whose detailed properties are to be preserved in the computer-based version.
  - The CBPS may be envisaged as a novel type of pedagogical setting, not making any significant reference to non-computer-based settings.

Analysis of the relationships between the CBPS and the reference non-computer-based setting (if any) makes sense at a given level of granularity, and for precise objects. For instance, at the teaching setting level, matters of concern may be limited to whether learners engage in problem-solving exercises, which may lead one to consider in the same way whether they solve problems via an ITS or in a classic paper-pencil in-classroom way. Similarly, the two approaches may be compared at the CBPS structural level (the scenario, how the problem is introduced, what type of activity is expected from learners, etc.). However, this no longer holds when, for instance, considering an epistemic analysis of the actions allowed within the software interface, which has no correspondence with any dimension of the classroom setting. As another example, a given chat may be seen as a communication tool that, at a certain level of abstraction and from a certain point of view, allows a transposition for on-line learners of how in-presence learners may interact in a classroom. However, taken at another level and from another point of view, typing a text on a keyboard or perceiving interlocutors' communication-related issues via icons is rather different from the face-to-face setting considered (at another level) as a reference.

- The added value expected from the educational software. For instance:
  - The expected added value is to allow creation of CBPSs that present improved learning outcomes with respect to the non-computer-based reference settings. Such an expectation may be directly related to the system (e.g., expectations related to the fact that the interactions between the learner and the system lead to better learning outcomes than the interactions between the

learner and a teacher) or indirectly related (e.g., the interactions between the learner and the system, completed by the interactions with the teacher – at the same time, before or afterwards – lead to better learning outcomes than with the teacher only; as another example: within a CBPS involving a teacher and several learners, the fact that teachers do not have to perform the basic tasks which are handled by the system allows them to focus on the more important ones which leads, *in fine*, to better learning outcomes).
  - The expected added value is to allow creation of CBPSs that are alternatives to the non-computer-based reference settings, or to complement them. For instance, the issue may be to overcome limitations (e.g., creating ITSs or on-line learning platforms as a way to solve issues related to a lack of human teachers, geographical constraints, synchronization constraints or financial constraints), or to provide learners and/or teachers with types of resources other than those that may be handled without software.

- The role of software in the CBPS. This role may be viewed in different ways, for instance the two opposite extremes:
  - Software is considered to have an impact on the activity that learners will develop in relation to the task they have been assigned. It is designed with the objective that this impact contributes to the fact that their activity presents the expected pedagogical properties.
  - Educational software is considered to be merely a resource.

The role of software is to be put in relation with the importance given to whether learners use the system. In the first case, whether learners use the system (and how) is of great importance, and software may be introduced in a way that suggests, strongly suggests or makes it mandatory for learners to use it. In the second case, its effective usage by learners may be contingent, the fact that they do not use it, or not as expected, not being an important matter of concern.

- The constraints applying to the design or implementation processes. Constraints and issues may be of different natures (in relation to the overall rationale in particular), for instance,
  - Obtaining educational software that is usable (i.e., software whose usability may be shown or argued).
  - Obtaining educational software that is used (if nothing else, by a limited group).
  - Obtaining educational software that is widespread. This may be considered from an economic perspective (software that is bought and/or downloaded), from an ecological-usage perspective (software used in effective settings, within a certain period of time) or in the sense of software integrated into common practices.
  - Obtaining educational software that may be used as a support for reflection (e.g., for elaborating models).

2 Characterizing the Design Context 135

- Obtaining educational software that may be used to test hypotheses in limited controlled settings.
- Etc.

- The expected usage and relation to objectives. Design of educational software, just like any software, is associated with hypotheses related to how users will use it. In the case of educational software, it is not only required to clarify what this expected usage is but, also, and of major importance, the relationships between this usage and the pedagogical objectives, for instance,

  - The fact that a given usage is considered as denoting that a pedagogical objective is being or has been addressed (e.g., that of making learners consider some issue).
  - The fact that a given usage is considered as denoting that learners are practicing some given skills.
  - The fact that usage differs from expectations is potentially a symptom of the fact that learners' activity is not in line with the targeted objectives.
  - Etc.

- The hypotheses underlying the expected usage, i.e., why it is expected that learners will use software in this way. For instance, it may be expected that software will be used in a particular way:

  - Because this usage is explicitly introduced as a constraint mentioned in the scenario (e.g., "build a model using the *Phys-edit* software") or by the teacher.
  - Because institutional constraints or habits allow this usage to be hypothesized.
  - Because this is the only way to tackle the task that learners are presented with.
  - Because this is suggested or encouraged by teachers.
  - Because this evidently facilitates the achievement of the task and there is no doubt (for the designers) that learners will be aware of this.
  - Etc.

2.6 Design Approach

Clarifying the way design is addressed not only requires consideration of the design model (e.g., highlighting that an iterative process is used) but, importantly, the dimensions that underlie or influence the design. This may lead one to consider dimensions such as:

- The design entry point, which may be for instance (there may be articulations, interactions or hybridizations):

  - An innovative idea.
  - A CBPS that defines specifications for the software to be designed.
  - A technology (e.g., the hyperlink notion, the capacity to implement a given type of reasoning process, network allowing distant access to resources, mobile

devices or virtual reality techniques) which it is hypothesized allows new possibilities and, in particular, creation of innovative and/or more efficient CBPSs.
- A technological framework within which software is to be constructed and/or a set of components that may be aggregated (i.e., what can be done is constrained from the start, e.g., it is to be implemented within a specific LMS and as a mash-up of its components, for economic and/or institutional reasons).
- An engineering process (or part of an engineering process), norms and standards related to TEL (e.g., IMS-LD,[7] SCORM,[8] LOM[9] or LTSA[10]) and/or to Software Engineering (e.g., MDA[11]).
- A Human and Social Sciences model or theory (e.g., learning theory, cognitive theory, teaching theory or activity theory) considered as a basis for designing CBPSs and associated educational software.
- An analysis of knowledge to be learned, i.e., a disciplinary analysis (and/or traditional pedagogical practices analysis) highlighting the knowledge's properties and characteristics of its acquisition, and the conditions within which non-computer-based learning settings may be transposed to computer-based settings in a way that preserves the characteristics identified as favorable to the knowledge construction processes.
- An analysis of some teacher's (tutor's, etc.) tasks to be supported.
- The identification of an anomaly to be reduced (e.g., an analysis of learners' usage of some technology revealing that activity is subject to breakdowns or does not meet the targeted pedagogical characteristics).
- A compilation of empirical results allowing elaboration of design guidelines (e.g., how information should be visualized or how best to use animations), which do not correspond to any particular theoretical model.
- Etc.

- What the theoretical background (if any) is used for, for instance,
    - As a way to denote a general approach (e.g., "takes place within a constructivist approach" or "integrates a social dimension").
    - As a framework that provides directive axes.
    - As a framework that provides guidelines for design (e.g., how to react to learners' errors).

---

[7]IMS Learning Design (http://www.imsglobal.org/learningdesign/index.html; retrieved November 11, 2010).

[8]ADL Sharable Content Object Reference Model (http://www.adlnet.gov; retrieved November 11, 2010).

[9]IEEE Standard for Learning Object Metadata (http://ieeeltsc.org; retrieved November 11, 2010).

[10]IEEE Standard for Learning Technology Systems Architecture (http://ieeeltsc.org; retrieved November 11, 2010).

[11]Model Driven Architecture (http://www.omg.org/mda; retrieved November 11, 2010).

2 Characterizing the Design Context

- As a framework that provides concepts that may be used in design (e.g., implementation or transposition of the notion of *proximal zone of development* to software).

- How the stated theoretical background (if any) is used, which may be for instance:

  - In a direct way.
  - Via some transposition.
  - Embedded (or partially embedded) in software (e.g., in control mechanisms).

- The design model, which may be for instance:

  - Linear design (elaborating precise specifications and then building software).
  - Iterative design (testing incrementally different versions).
  - User-centered design (placing users at the center of design).
  - Participative design (involving future users in design).
  - Design continued in usage (upgrading of software during effective use and not only out-of-context tests).

- How users are concerned in design, for instance,

  - The part of design that is left to users.
  - The conditions under which users are involved (by whom, at what time, what to do, etc.).

2.7 Actors Concerned

Actors concerned in educational software design may be multiple and may be concerned in different interactions. This may be clarified by stating and analyzing:

- The types of actors concerned (or the roles with which actors engage), for instance,

  - Researcher.
  - Designer.
  - Engineer.
  - Expert providing knowledge or a model.
  - Teacher.
  - Learner.
  - Institution representative.
  - Prescriber.
  - Sponsor.
  - User from a community of practice.
  - Etc.

- The forms of interaction between actors, for instance,
  - Service offered by actors from discipline$_1$ to discipline$_2$.
  - Service offered by type-of-actors$_1$ to type-of-actors$_2$ (e.g., by user to researcher or by researcher to engineer).
  - Co-construction of models, methodologies, etc.
  - Etc.

It may also be pertinent to keep track of the evolution of these actors and their roles or relationships.

2.8 Context and Historical Dimensions of the Project

The rationale for constructing software, considering some issues or taking some decisions may be related to dimensions that evolve during design and/or software use. Clarifying the project's evolution may lead one to address dimensions such as:

- The elements forming the original context of software design, which may be for instance:
  - An identified learning or teaching issue.
  - A technology.
  - Some existing basic software.
  - A model or a theory.
  - An innovative idea.
  - A call for projects, a demand.
  - An opportunity (e.g., the existence of domain-specific teaching theory or the accessibility of a teaching context for experiments[12]).
  - Etc.
- The general context and the history of the project, for instance,
  - The project lifecycle.
  - The history and/or evolution of the project.
  - The history and/or evolution of the actors concerned.
  - The reasons why the project was launched.
  - The reasons why the project lasted or did not last.
  - The impact of the context (e.g., the political, social or economical context) of the project and its evolution.
  - Etc.

---

[12]As an example, within a research project focusing on (for example) how to implement a particular feedback mechanism, the choice of the application domain may be contingent, and governed by the available experimental setting. This is a frequent cause of misunderstandings between actors who are focusing on general mechanisms (e.g., feedback or diagnosis) and actors who are interested in the domain *per se*.

3 Characterizing the Software Artifact

3.1 Level of Analysis of Software Properties

For educational software as for any software, the objects presented to users via interfaces, and the way these objects may be used or manipulated, carry meanings. However, this dimension and the software properties may be thought of in different ways, for instance:

- Software is not considered more precisely than at the level of general features. For instance, considering a collaborative setting, the communication dimension is addressed in terms of "synchronous communication means", without going into further details. At this level of granularity, the fact that the chat tool in question presents some particularities is not a matter of concern. Replacing it by another chat tool would be a contingent issue: the way the setting is considered is unchanged, as both tools satisfy in the same way the general specification.
- Software is considered at the level of the objects and features detailed properties. For instance, considering synchronous communication means, features such as how interactions are visualized, how interactions are structured by patterns or turn-taking constraints or the embedded objects (interaction thread, sentence openers, etc.) will be considered as distinguishing systems from one another, and changing some of the CBPS's characteristics. To give another example, a problem solver is not considered only from the point of view of its capacity to produce a solution but, in addition, giving importance to the fact that its process is controlled by explicit meta-knowledge or the knowledge-representation used.
- Software is considered as a constitutive element of the epistemic *milieu* to be offered to learners.

3.2 Actions Considered at the Level of Software

Within CBPSs, educational support and constraints may be implemented by both the setting structure and the software properties. As described by the SPR notion, only some of the CBPS considerations may influence design, and this influence may not be straightforward. As a consequence, clarifying what is considered at the software level is an issue of crucial importance.

Let us consider design of software with respect to the general objective of supporting learners to elaborate a common definition for a given set of notions. What types of actions will be considered at the level of software? A first analysis may envisage providing learners with (1) a set of prescriptions and hints (e.g., general approach to be followed, risks to be avoided or success criteria to be checked), (2) a set of means for exchanging documents and (3) communication means (e.g., chat tool and forum). Within such an analysis, the actions considered at the software level are *uploading a document*, *downloading a document* or *engaging in synchronous communication*. Another analysis may lead one to consider at the software level actions such as *refining the shared description of a concept*, *making arguments explicit* or *building on a peer's proposition*: this is very different. As another example, *solving problem P_1* may be addressed in a way that considers the problem-solving process details (supporting the various actions to be performed at every step of the process) or just at the level of editing of the final result via a predefined form that does not affect any dimension of the reasoning process. In other words, a general description may lead to very different matters of concern at the level of software. See also Chap. 3, Sect. 2.

Clarifying what the matters of concern are at the software level is a core dimension of the SPR definition. It may require disentangling and analyzing:

- The learners' actions considered at the level of the CBPS analysis.
- The learners' actions considered at the level of the software analysis.
- The hypothesis or relations linking these two analyses.

3.3 Reification of the Pedagogical Intention in Software

As mentioned when addressing the educational software notion, educational considerations may impact only the analysis within which software is thought of or, in addition, be reified in one way or another in the system. This is another important dimension to be clarified. A variety of cases may occur, for instance:

- Software presents features based on specific pedagogical notions reified in the system, for instance,
    - Learners' profile management capabilities.
    - Model of evolution of learners' conceptions and misconceptions.
    - Etc.
- Software presents features that can be distinguished (by their object, by their properties) from those that would have been designed without consideration of pedagogical considerations, or from those presented by basic software, for instance,
    - Model-editing features based on a domain-specific analysis of the knowledge at stake, how this knowledge may be developed or the modeling context.
    - Synchronous communication means proposing support and constraints (speech acts, turn-taking structures, domain-related sentence openers, visualization tools designed to facilitate the overall structure of interactions, etc.) linked to pedagogical considerations.
    - Problem-solving features allowing control of the reasoning process according to the type of learner.
    - Etc.

- Software presents basic features but integrates them or articulates them in a way that creates a specific activity-framework, for instance,

  - Collaborative-learning framework articulating different basic tools (communication means, resource exchanges, dataflow, etc.) in a way that implements a given scenario.
  - Inquiry-learning framework articulating a set of simulation components and modeling editors.
  - Etc.

3.4 Nature of the CS Treatments

Educational software is firstly described by its features and properties. However, clarifying the precise CS treatments may help in understanding matters of concern and, in any case, is mandatory for implementation, evaluation and capitalization.

Systems or components usually mix a variety of treatments. As examples of the nature of these treatments:

- Acquire data, for instance,

  - Acquire the computational events (logs) generated by learners' actions when using software (used features, accessed resources, etc.).
  - Acquire learners' output (answer to a question, etc.).
  - Etc.

- Analyze and interpret data,[13] i.e., allow the system or a human actor to structure, synthesize and/or associate a meaning with data related to software. Such an analysis may be processed during the CBPS enactment (e.g., to implement feedback) or afterwards (e.g., for re-engineering processes). Such a piece of software may be designed as a component, to be used by others (e.g., as part of an ITS architecture) or as a standalone tool dedicated to teachers or human analysts. It may address different objectives. As examples:

  - Associating a meaning with a statement that is expressed in a particular syntax or in Natural Language.
  - Associating a meaning with actions captured at the software interface (e.g., analyzing logs associated with the tools used by learners with respect to the prescribed scenario).
  - Etc.

---

[13]*Data analysis and interpretation* are here dissociated from *data elaboration*, although they may be considered as particular cases.

- Elaborate data (numerical data, text, reasoning process, etc.) that is useful for other software components or for a human actor in the CBPS. As examples:
  - Elaborate a solution to the problem that is presented to learners, or to the problems presented by learners.
  - Elaborate a reasoning process to be presented to learners or to be used as a reference for feedback issues.
  - Elaborate (in a reactive or proactive way) a text corresponding to a hint or recommendation.
  - Elaborate or reorganize the structure of a hypermedia system according to a constraint or event.
  - Elaborate an abstract model from rough logs.
  - Elaborate a model of a learner.
  - Elaborate the pertinent actions to be enacted by an ITS as a teaching plan.
  - Etc.

- Visualize data,[14] i.e., present a particular visualization of data produced by a software component or a human actor of the CBPS. As examples:
  - Communication-tool interface following a particular structure for interactions (e.g., highlighting threads, arguments/counter-arguments or social dimensions).
  - Simulation interface highlighting a particular dimension of an experiment.
  - Supervision tool presenting to tutors a synthetic presentation of learners' itineraries within the proposed on-line resources.
  - Etc.

- Manage access to data or features, i.e., decide what data (elaborated by a software component or a human actor of the CBPS), what functions,[15] what interfaces (etc.) will be provided (to whom, under what conditions, etc.). As examples:
  - Manage hyperlink accessibility in a hypermedia document.
  - Manage itineraries within a set of on-line resources delivered by a LMS.
  - Manage how learners involved in a microworld will be given access to different features according to their profile or to the microworld state.
  - Etc.

- Handle a complex task,[16] i.e., manage tasks requiring articulation of different features. As examples:
  - Conduct a diagnostic of the setting enactment (which may imply: acquiring the required data and interpreting it).

---

[14]*Data visualization* is here dissociated from *task achievement*, although it may be considered as a particular case.

[15]The issue here is to solve the problem consisting of deciding what features will be made available at the software interface and how they may be presented or articulated, which is a different problem from that of designing the corresponding pieces of software.

[16]What is meant here is a task of a different nature from those (*elaboration of data* or *managing access*) dissociated above.

- Determine the nature and/or the content of the feedback to be presented (which may imply: diagnosing learners' activity, determining the pertinent intervention, and then elaborating a textual hint to be presented, modifying the scenario or transforming the interface).
- Manage an interactive dialogue with a learner.
- Manage the coherence or the evolution of a virtual world.
- Elaborate or maintain learners' profiles.
- Build classes of learners (clusters) on the basis of the analysis of their outputs.
- Etc.

3.5 Level of Achievement

According to objectives or purposes, the required completeness or robustness of software may vary. For instance, testing a hypothesis may only require a prototype to be used in a controlled setting or, on the contrary, robust software to be used in ecological settings. As another example, in an effective setting, the fact that a system is not stable may be more or less acceptable.

Technically, designing and implementing robust software may raise specific issues, and impact design decisions. Clarifying the targeted level of achievement may thus be of importance. Different levels of achievement may be considered, for instance,

- Early prototype demonstrating general principles (e.g., interfaces).
- Prototype implementing main functions.
- Robust software that can be used in the ecological contexts it has been designed for.
- Stabilized software basically used in effective settings.

4 Examples

In this section, we present an example of application of these different characteristics to two of the systems introduced in Chap. 4: *GeLMS-4* and *JavIT* (as very different cases). As these systems do not exist, not all items are explored, and the analysis is kept to its minimum form, i.e., indicating the general idea and not going into details or justifications. The objective here is to show how such an application draws attention to different features. The text is re-engineered and not structured sub-item by sub-item in order to be kept more fluid.

4.1 GeLMS-4, *the Generic Learning Management System*

GeLMS is a development project. The *raison d'être* of the targeted system is to be used in effective settings.

Within this project, there is no reference to any particular theory. The focus of the study is on resource organization and on on-line learners' needs as empirically anticipated and then *a posteriori* experienced. There is no reference to the targeted knowledge: the work is conducted at a domain-independent level.

The targeted outcomes are (1) an implemented architecture (a Web platform that meets a set of requirements), (2) the fact that learners and teachers are offered different services (to be listed) and (3) at a more general level, the transformation of a teaching setting (on-line learning) and actors' interplay.

The overall rationale for designing *GeLMS* is, very directly, to obtain the considered outcomes and, in particular, to change the state of on-line learning at an organizational level.

With respect to CBPSs, *GeLMS* is a platform that focuses on courses rather than on the CBPS notion as such. Different features may however be highlighted:

- The expected added value of the targeted software is to allow alternatives to in-presence settings and paper-based distant-learning.
- The role of software may be viewed in different ways. The platform is thought of as something that (1) impacts the way learners conceptualize on-line teaching and (2) supports their actions. However, these actions are not really studied as such (e.g., there is no reference to the task/activity duality or to any cognitive dimension).
- The major constraint applying to design and implementation is to obtain usable and scalable software.
- The expected usage is that learners will have a general behavioral activity consistent with the proposed agenda and institutional messages, achieving the tasks indicated for the courses (accessing resources, considering the proposed exercises, etc.) using the platform services (communication tools, file transfer facilities, advancement declarations, etc.).
- The reasons why they should develop this usage are that it is expected that they have acknowledged the principles of what is an on-line course delivered by such a platform and that they are supposed to conform to the institutional demand.
- The relationship between the expected usage and the targeted objectives is that the fact learners access resources (or not) and their declaration of advancement via the specific tool denotes the way in which learners enact the teachers' instructions indicated in the course description.

With respect to the design approach:

- The entry point is a given technology (Web platforms). There are, however, other influences: a norm (LOM), analysis of teachers' tasks (supervision and support), identification of anomalies to be reduced (issues of accessing pedagogical resources; learners' difficulties in understanding expectations; learners' lack

of autonomy) and compilation of empirical results (lessons learned from other platforms and successive *GeLMS* versions).
- The design model is iterative, testing incrementally different versions.
- The involved actors are designers, engineers, institution representatives and users from a community of practice (which developed after *GeLMS-1*).
- The interactions among these actors is that the general specification has been defined by the institution representatives and, later on, designers and engineers have interacted on the basis of feedback and ideas collected from the community of practice.
- The original context of the project was the development of a teaching platform from an open-source information system, as a CS Masters student application project. The platform was first informally used by some teachers as a way to put some resources on-line. It was later decided by the University U_x to launch a set of on-line courses using this platform, and the platform was re-engineered according to the institutional specifications. The platform has been disseminated, and a community of practice has emerged, which provided input for iterative improvements.

The level of analysis of software properties is that of a basic functional analysis. General features related to resource access or platform communication means have been specified at a general level (e.g., "providing synchronous communication means", without going into further details). By contrast, the advancement tool interfaces have been analyzed in detail: considering lessons learned from learners' difficulty in understanding what is expected from them and how to analyze their work, a variety of interfaces have been tested via ergonomic studies. It may be noticed that, more or less implicitly, the general structure of the Web platform is also considered as carrying meanings and structuring learners' perception of what the different institutional structures are (e.g., programs or courses).

The actions considered at software level are the basic learners' usage of the software functions such as *learner L#14 is accessing resource R#12, dropping file F#4 into the exchange zone* or *declaring task T#11 has been achieved at 80%*.

The platform exhibits two features based on specific pedagogical notions reified in the system, *advancement* (since *GeLMS-3*) and *scenario* (*GeLMS-4*). The other general features have been designed without taking account of particular pedagogical considerations: they are standard Web-platform features articulated in a way that is thought of as creating a kind of activity framework, this notion referring here to processes such as *keeping aware of the general agenda, accessing resources related to a course* or *sending homework to teachers*.

The platform interoperates a variety of features involving different types of CS processing. Fundamentally, the processes concerned are (1) management of access to data and functions and (2) management of visualization issues. The advancement function, however, also requires acquisition of learners' outputs and the computational events generated by learners' actions when using software and, to a limited extent, analysis and interpretation of them.

The level of achievement is stabilized software, basically used in effective settings.

4.2 JavIT, *the Java Programming Intelligent Tutoring System*

JavIT is a research project. The *raison d'être* of the targeted system is to be a means for studying issues related to design and implementation of epistemic-feedback components. We will focus here on *JavIT-E*, which builds on a domain-specific analysis of the difficulties learners encounter when considering object-oriented notions.

The project's theoretical-background focus is on teaching. At a general level, the project is anchored in constructivist theories. At a more precise level, it builds on the hybridization of a domain-specific teaching theory, a domain theory (object-oriented modeling) and a cognitive theory. The project takes into account the specifics of the knowledge at stake and this knowledge construction process, e.g., the different views of inheritance that may be developed.[17]

The targeted outcomes are (1) an understanding of whether and how considered theories help the construction of epistemic feedback components that improve learning outcomes, (2) lessons learned related to the feedback issue and (3) useful models and reusable software components, if possible.

The rationale for software design is to (1) develop understanding of issues and solutions while constructing the system and (2) obtain means to evaluate the impact of the provided feedback and test learning outcomes.

With respect to the way software is considered within the CBPS:

- The expected added value of the targeted software is to allow creation of CBPSs that are alternatives to the non-computer-based reference settings, or may complement them.
- The CBPS is envisaged as a transposition of a non-computer-based setting considered as a reference, the identified learning properties of which are to be respected.
- The software is considered to have an expected impact on the cognitive activity that learners will develop in relation to the task they have been assigned (building programs and practicing object-oriented design and programming). The software is introduced in a way that makes it mandatory for learners to use it.
- The constraint applying to software design and implementation is to obtain a system that can be used to test hypotheses.
- The expected usage of the system is that learners follow the instructions and hints.

---

[17]If an effective system were to be considered, analysis of the *theoretical background* should be conducted in more detail, making explicit the involved theories and notions, how these theories are hybridized, the justification of the use of these theories for the considered setting, etc.

- The reasons why learners should follow the instructions and hints is that they are considered as under the control of the system, which is pro-active.
- The relationship between the expected usage and the targeted objectives is that usage differing from expectations may denote a conflict between the pedagogical intention embedded in the system and learners' activity and, possibly, the fact that the system is not efficient.

With respect to the design approach:

- The entry point is a set of theories and an analysis of knowledge to be learned.
- The theoretical background is used for different purposes. The constructivist approach is used as a general reference for the targeted CBPS's design (learning by doing via problem solving). The teaching and domain theories provide directive axes and guidelines for the elaboration of the problems that learners are presented with (these problems are elaborated so as to destabilize learners' conceptions and misconceptions). The specific cognitive theory provides concepts and directive axes for the feedback model (e.g., when to provide immediate or delayed feedback). The domain, teaching and cognitive theories provide bases for learners' model management.
- The theoretical background is used both in a direct way (the cognitive theory) and via transposition (the teaching theory). Part of the cognitive theory (the feedback-related features) is reified in the system.

The design model is linear (specifications are based on the theory; experience-based evolutions only relate to marginal ergonomic changes). No users are involved in design.

The actors concerned are researchers (who specify the system) and CS engineers (who implement the system).

The original context of the project was the existence of a teaching theory and the research issue "can this theory serve as a basis to design and implement ITSs?" Addressing this issue led to looking for an instantiation of this theory in a particular domain, which resulted in selecting object-oriented design and considering a theory of this domain. Attempting to implement feedback led to the conclusion that it should be epistemic, which in turn led to looking for a cognitive theory providing bases for managing learners' epistemic models and epistemic feedback.

The level of analysis of software properties is extremely detailed: software properties are considered as constitutive elements defining a specific epistemic *milieu*. The *epistemic milieu* notion refers here to a domain-specific construction carrying meanings studied as elements that impact learners' cognitive activity and act as teaching vectors.

The actions considered at the software level are the learners' usage of the software functions such as *drawing an inheritance relation between C_1 and C_2* or *introducing an intermediate abstract class* with the programming editor. These actions are considered to denote cognitive processes such as *generalizing a hierarchy* and/or to correspond to particular views such as a *logical* or *structural* perspective on the inheritance notion.

The system reifies some specific human analysts' and human teachers' constructions (learners' model, domain theory, etc.) and processes (learners' output analysis, elaboration of pertinent feedback, etc.).

The system is based on the articulation of different components implementing different complex tasks and involving different types of CS processing: diagnosing learners' constructions, which implies acquiring the learners' outputs (the class diagram, the Java program, etc.) and the logs denoting their use of the system, and interpreting this data in terms of object-oriented design and conceptions/misconceptions of the related notions and skills; solving the problem that consists of determining the nature and/or the content of the epistemic feedback to be provided (which implies conducting a reasoning process based on pedagogical knowledge to determine the pertinent action to be taken and then elaborating the textual hint to be presented); maintaining learners' profiles; etc.

The level of achievement is a prototype that may be used in a laboratory for experimental studies.

5 Conclusions

Educational software design work is often introduced by featuring the CBPSs that the considered system allows to be implemented, and its specific interest with respect to these CBPSs. Using, in addition, an external list of characteristics draws attention to other dimensions and questions, which may have remained unaddressed or unclear. More generally, it suggests the importance of clarifying matters of concern and approaches.

The set of characteristics introduced in this chapter is only a resource. Keeping axes non-articulated makes it possible to add items and values easily, which would be much more difficult if items and values were related to each other. Similarly, suggesting different views that may, in some cases, be redundant, is a more robust approach than attempting to build partitions: what is redundant for some projects and/or in some settings may highlight different features in other cases.

A first version of these analysis axes (very similar to the one presented here) has been experimented. Designers of different types of systems (microworld, ITS, etc.) were asked to characterize their design work according to these axes, and the result was discussed with a multidisciplinary audience. It has also been used by various PhD students as a way to analyze their research work. Although limited, these experiences, in addition to having helped to refine and clarify the analysis axes, suggest different considerations.

First, the exercise causes both interest and frustration. Interest, as it develops an unusual perspective on one's work, different from the way in which it is spontaneously presented. Indeed, it results in one confronting some questions that were never considered, or not in this way. Frustration, as this is not the way in which designers usually want to present their work (this, however, is not an issue: the point here is not to present work, but to analyze it[18]).

Second, the exercise may appear difficult. When analysis is conducted in detail, the proposed characteristics may lead one to consider unexpected dimensions and difficult questions. Moreover, within this process, some of the proposed characteristics may fit perfectly, while others may appear unclear in the context of the project, or not well adapted. This highlights the intrinsic difficulty of explicitation processes and constructions (see Chap. 1, Sect. 4.4).

Finally, and this attenuates the second point, the process introduces a dynamic that tends to lead designers, when characteristics appear meaningless or unclear, to rephrase them and/or propose alternatives or, in other words, to comply with the overall clarification objective.

As a conclusion, lets us recall that if using an external resource improves clarification of matters of concern, approaches or implicit hypotheses, this does not mean that it results in a state where everything is "explicit" and understood in the same way by all actors (see the theoretical issues related to explicitness in Chap. 1). The result of such a process is that a resource that is likely to be pertinent for developing a shared understanding is made available, and a dynamic is engaged. Moreover, such lists of characteristics must be seen as a resource and a support for reflection, and not as a normalizing structure. At this level, keeping characteristics disentangled is an important dimension.

---

[18] The way such an external list of characteristics leads to another analysis of work is only illustrated to a very limited extent by the examples developed in Sect. 4 as we had already used these systems to illustrate different ideas. Moreover, such analyses only make sense when considering effective systems: conducted at an abstract level (which considering imaginary systems may lead to) the analysis may easily fall into a kind of categorization process, which is indeed not the objective.

Chapter 8
Methodological Considerations

Abstract This chapter explores some transversal methodological dimensions.

In this chapter, we explore various methodological considerations related to educational software design and, more precisely, considerations in line with the engineering perspective developed in Chap. 6. The addressed items are:

1. Clarifying concerns
2. Dealing with complexity and models
3. Making the SPR explicit
4. Considering activity and indirect design
5. Developing knowledge

1 Clarifying Concerns

We have emphasized in Chap. 1 and throughout the other chapters the importance of clarifying matters of concern, both in development and research projects. When thinking about, designing or testing educational software or CBPSs, there are humans in the loop and so there is place for complexity, uncertainty, misunderstandings and non-scientific dimensions. Effective collaboration between actors from different disciplines, as well as from the same discipline, requires sharing views and understandings or, at least, acknowledging each other's perspective. TEL's intrinsic nature imposes, as in all scientific fields but with even greater importance, the need for clear definitions and explicitation of work.

The analysis conducted in the preceding chapters suggests giving particular importance to:

- The definition of the considered general context (teaching setting).
- The definition and characterization of the targeted (type of) CBPSs.
- The definition and disentanglement of the pedagogical objectives.

- The definition of the SPR.
- The definition and characterization of the targeted software properties.
- The adoption of an iterative process.
- And, as a transversal task, from the very start of the project, listing the different notions used when addressing the CBPS, SPR or software, and making explicit the different actors' views on these notions and, more generally, when useful, on the project or the field.

Precisely defining and characterizing work is of particular importance for software-related dimensions due to the natural tendency, and ease, of a factual description. In particular, a statement such as "work addressed design and implementation of software whose features are …" is scant information if the different dimensions within which this design is addressed and makes sense (considered CPBSs, software roles, considered notions, theoretical background, etc.) are not precisely defined. The sometimes implicit premise that software may be envisaged in such a way that it is "pedagogically neutral" is not tenable.

From a research point of view, issues related to absence, incompleteness or superficiality of descriptions have been raised in the preceding chapters: major incomprehension, slow-down of the capitalization of knowledge and reuse of models or software components and, more generally, evolution of the field and practices based on research results and evidence.

2 Dealing with Complexity and Models

In Chap. 6, we have emphasized CBPSs and educational software are complex in nature, which gives particular importance to the modeling dimension.

2.1 Multiplicity of Models

Complex artifacts design and analysis require the articulation of multiple models denoting different views.

A specific feature of complex systems is that while some dimensions may be disentangled and studied separately, others cannot be reduced to a juxtaposition of problems and require several perspectives to be managed simultaneously.

As an example, educational software thought of as a *milieu* reacting to learners' actions may lead to consideration of: a model of the taught domain-knowledge (which may lead to dissociation of institutional "reference" knowledge, teachers' knowledge and learners' knowledge); a teaching scenario; a model of learners' possible actions within the framework; a model of the framework feedback and/or of mediated communications (communication between learners and software, learners and teacher or among learners); a model for capturing and interpreting learners' actions and/or learners' interactions; a model for controlling interactions; a model for managing learners' individual characteristics and/or learners' knowledge evolution; a model for evaluating learning outcomes.

The multiplicity and entanglement of models require particular attention when:

- Describing the models.
- Clarifying what these models model.
- Defining the nature and the objective of these models.
- Describing the way these models are articulated.

2.2 Foundations of Models

A model is an artifact. The elaboration of this artifact may be based on different foundations, for instance:

- A theory or a set of theories providing bases or guidelines for model elaboration.
- An original empirical proposition, inspired by some specific analysis.
- An adaptation or transformation of an already existing model.

TEL, by its nature, refers to Human and Social Sciences theories: behaviorism, constructivism, socio-constructivism, situated cognition, distributed cognition, activity theory, etc. One of the central issues of educational software engineering is the articulation between issues related to educational software and the theories used as references, in particular because:

1. The theories usually used as references have basically been proposed as means to interpret and explain settings and phenomena.
2. The theories usually used as references have not been elaborated in a way that takes into account the specifics of computer-based settings. This poses the problem of migration of these theories (and models) to such settings as, *de facto*, the fact that the setting involves a computer changes the socio-technical dimensions, see for instance the impact on the task/activity duality.

The fact that a theory that *explains* learning-related phenomena may also be used as a basis to *design* pedagogical settings, CBPSs or educational software, is not a given. Turning a model for understanding (e.g., a model allowing representation of learners' knowledge and prediction of its evolution) into a basis for design (e.g., to implement the diagnosis and feedback features of an ITS) is a recurrent pattern in TEL whose interest and pertinence must, however, be studied case by case. The fact that a model powerfully allows understanding of settings does not grant that it has any virtue for design.

It may be noticed that models used in TEL are not necessarily built from Human and Social Sciences theories or work. As in other domains concerned with AI, efficient implementations may be based on models that are by no means useful for understanding (e.g., diagnosis based on generic statistical mechanisms).

2.3 Traceability of Models

For an engineering field presenting a strong experimental dimension, it is of great importance to be able to study alternatives (different approaches, different designs, different properties, etc.). This requires interpretation of results (e.g., impact of a design decision) at an abstract level, that is, the level of the used models. This is a requirement for both conducting projects and capitalizing knowledge that may inform future design decisions.

For such a purpose, an important notion is that of *traceability*. We define traceability as the maintenance of a correspondence between (1) the theoretical elements used as foundations (if any), (2) the used models and (3) the pieces of code (components, architecture, etc.).

Traceability is of particular importance in addressing the complexity issues related to the fact that as CBPSs involve human and technical features, it is difficult to separate impact factors and attribute causality.

As an example, let us consider the *Colab-solver* system. The system's *raison d'être* is to make learners develop a certain type of interactions. The targeted settings are built on the basis of problem-solving exercises. Such a system may be designed by developing a first version integrating the tools that may be considered useful in such settings, and iteratively refining the system as needed. Within such a process, understanding what happens as a means to refine the design is completely empirical. Another approach is to explicitly build the system on the basis of, for example: (1) a model of collaborative interactions introducing abstract notions such as *common ground* or *regulation* and providing a certain understanding of how learners may interact; (2) a model of problem-solving providing a certain understanding of problem-solving's different phases, e.g., *understanding the problem* or *adopting a strategy*; (3) a model of organization providing a certain understanding of how learners may organize themselves, e.g., how they may *share goals* or *separate* them, *detect* and *solve conflicts* or *breakdowns*, etc. Founding design on these different models and their interplay not only provides rationale for design, but also for understanding the setting enactment in terms of the models, re-engineering design and capitalizing abstract knowledge.

In the case of educational software, managing traceability is difficult for different reasons, in particular:

1. Drawing relationships between computable models on the one hand and, on the other hand, theories, models or notions from non-CS (or non-mathematical) disciplines is not straightforward. In particular, as highlighted throughout this book, such a process may be subject to differences in perspectives and interpretations.
2. Considering educational software, models may be used in a variety of ways, e.g., to provide a general understanding of some phenomena or setting, as something that informs design models or that is to be embedded or reified in software.

These issues give particular importance to an accurate analysis and characterization of the relationships between theories and models (what the theoretical background is, what it is used for, how, etc.), the impacted elements (the CBPS structure, software dimensions, etc.) and what the impact is, the SPR, etc.; see Chap. 7.

Within this context, description of models is of particular importance. A model presented as a few boxes and arrows, the semantics of which are not clearly defined, provides scant information. Specific attention is thus required with respect to how models are presented and described, clarifying what the model models, why, and for whom. This may lead one to consider dimensions such as:

- Whether the model is informative or computable.
- The nature of the representation language used to describe the model, in particular,
  - The definition of the modeling primitives (objects, relationships) and the associated coherence and constraint rules.
  - The level of abstraction (e.g., Knowledge Level – as defined by Newell[1] – or symbolic level).
  - The level of formalization (e.g., Natural Language, semi-formal knowledge such as UML basic formalism, or formal languages).
- The coverage of the model, i.e., definition of what the model can model and what it cannot model.

3 Making the SPR Explicit

In Chap. 2, we have emphasized the notion of *Software Pedagogical Rationale* (SPR), which has been defined as the part of the CBPS (and, possibly, teaching setting) objectives and related considerations which has a tangible impact on the software design. Various examples have been given. In line with this notion, we have emphasized in Chap. 7 that considering with particular attention the dimensions of learners' activity that are effectively considered at the level of software is a key issue.

Making explicit the SPR is a key dimension for conducting design. It is a difficult issue, for various reasons including the considerations related to models addressed in Sect. 2 and the fact that it is a topic on which educationalists' and computer scientists' matters of concern and understandings may diverge.

As a way to illustrate this specific point and highlight that differences are not only related to the nature of CBPSs but also to how CBPSs are addressed, let us consider one of the possible perspectives that may be used when analyzing

---

[1]Newell, A. (1982). The Knowledge Level. *Artificial Intelligence*, 18(1), 87–127.

CBPSs: the dichotomy between *resource accessibility* and *performance*.[2] The former denotes consideration of the problem of providing learners with resources according to pedagogical considerations and criteria. This is very common in approaches such as the one underlying LMSs, but also in smarter systems such as adaptive hypermedia. The latter denotes consideration of the problem of making learners carry out a task, this task and the way it is suggested, allowed, supported or permitted to be carried out being studied according to pedagogical considerations. A typical example is ITSs.

Let us now consider two CBPSs broadly defined as follows:

1. S_1 is a setting within which learners are presented with (a) a text visualized on the screen and (b) the task that consists of reading this text, understanding it and producing a synthesis.
2. S_2 is a setting within which learners are presented with (a) the task of solving a physics problem, e.g., building a prescriptive model of how various solid bodies may interact after one of these objects is given some initial movement, (b) a piece of software implementing a visual simulation of the phenomena to be understood in order to solve the problem, and (c) a specific model editor that provides constructions corresponding to the domain-specific notions to be used in solving this problem (e.g., *Phys-edit*).

Analysis of S_1

If one considers the software dimensions, S_1 is introduced in terms of accessibility: the way the relationship between learners' activity and software is introduced leads to consideration, at the software level, of the following problems: (1) make the text accessible on the screen; (2) allow learners to edit a text (the synthesis).

The software's role is to present the instructions (an explanation of what is to be done), retrieve the text to be read by learners (this may be basic or complex, e.g., dynamically retrieving one text or another from a database according to the learners' profile and the text characteristics as denoted by meta-data, or constructing the text on the fly), present the text on the screen, and provide an editor for typing the synthesis.

Within this view, the dimensions and issues related to the task "understand the text" such as the identification of the notions and ideas that appear in the text and their conceptual relations, or the arguments and counter-arguments that may be associated with some statements (etc.), are not addressed at the software level. In other words, these dimensions and the underlying objects or mechanisms are not matters of concern; they are not part of the SPR.

---

[2]Murray, T. (1999). Authoring Intelligent Tutoring Systems: An Analysis of the State of the Art. *International Journal of Artificial Intelligence in Education*, 10, 98–129.

Analysis of S_2

If one considers the software dimensions, S_2 is introduced in terms of performance: the way the relationship between learners' activity and the software is introduced leads to consideration, at the software level, of the following problems: (1) present learners with precise conceptual notions and associated constraints (e.g., the type of relationship that may be drawn between two objects according to their types); (2) suggest and support their usage.

As for S_1, one of the software roles is to present the instructions and retrieve the pertinent resources (the problem presentation; here again, this problem may be selected from a database and/or customized on the fly according to a variety of considerations).

However, in this case, the major role of the software, which is its *raison d'être* and will guide design, is that software is supposed to act as an epistemic *milieu* that allows achievement of the task in a way that will influence learners' activity and learning outcomes: the nature of the learners' expected processes and the way in which the software may lead learners to conceptualize the setting and achieve the proposed task are carefully studied so as to suggest, scaffold and accompany the targeted activity and learning.

Comparison

The way in which software is considered with respect to its relation to learners' expected activity (matters of concern, impact on learners' activity, etc.) is very different in S_1 and S_2.

As a first consequence, when considering software design (and analysis, and evaluation), the issues considered vary considerably. In the S_1 case, matters of concern are related to resource management (if considering canned documents in a database, this is similar to basic Information Systems issues). In the S_2 case, matters of concern include the way the physics knowledge may be constructed by learners, identification of the epistemic primitives to be offered, simulation properties that can act as learning vectors, pedagogical constraints that should govern the use of the editor to best support learners' knowledge-construction processes, etc.

There are various other consequences. For instance, the hypothesis underlying S_2 is that if learners elaborate their model via the proposed tool, this will influence their conceptualization and their learning. This gives particular importance to the effective usage of the software, why it may be expected that learners will develop such usage, how to react if they develop another usage, etc.

However, the difference highlighted here in terms of what is considered at software level is not related to the intrinsic natures of S_1 and S_2, but to the way they are introduced and considered. In both cases, learners are presented with a task and are supposed to be active: in S_1, learners are supposed to read, think, identify ideas, notions and arguments, etc.; in S_2, learners are supposed to read, manipulate, elaborate, etc.

In fact, both S_1 and S_2 may be considered in terms of accessibility or performance. S_2 could be addressed by presenting learners with a basic simulation and/or editor, e.g., a graphical tool that allows learners to edit their solution but does not provide any epistemic support. Similarly, S_1 could be addressed by identifying the specific issues encountered by learners when synthesizing texts, providing a conceptual-graph editor as a way to support the identification and analysis of notions and ideas, etc.

Conclusions

What elements are taken into account at the software level (the SPR) does not directly relate to the nature of the considered CBPS. Settings based on constructivists' views may perfectly well be implemented with software considered in terms of resource accessibility. Similarly, settings based on software considered in terms of performance and providing functions that allow learners to build artifacts with the provided tools may be inaccurate representations of constructivists' principles.

Moreover, a given type of software may be envisaged in very different ways. Typically, ITSs, microworlds, simulation-based environments or structured collaborative frameworks are considered in terms of performance. However, the nature of the software used may vary according to the issues considered (very general pedagogical approach or domain-specific analysis; framework designed to support problem-solving elaboration or just for editing the problem-solving result; etc.). For instance, a platform designed to support scenario-based collaboration may be based on accessibility considerations (introducing the scenario, presenting learners with resources according to their role in the scenario and providing communication tools) and/or in terms of performance (conceptualizing the activity framework to be presented to learners so as to enhance some types of interactions, support their collective organization or perceive other learners' actions).

Describing CBPSs, the general approach or what type of system is considered is thus not sufficient. A specific effort to clarify how the software is considered, matters of concern and, in particular, the SPR, is necessary.

4 Considering Activity and Indirect Design

In Chaps. 2 and 3, we have emphasized the importance of the activity notion and the fact that this dimension may be more or less acknowledged and, when acknowledged, differently taken into account in design.

4 Considering Activity and Indirect Design

Considering and taking into account activity is of particular importance for software thought of as an epistemic *milieu* or an activity framework in performance-oriented settings.

Within this view, designing artifacts (CBPSs, software) in order for learners to develop an activity that is favorable to the addressing of the considered objectives requires an indirection issue to be addressed.

Basically, the different CBPS features define or impact some of the modalities within which learners are confronted with the task. What is to be considered is the activity in relation to the task that is developed by learners, and whether it is favorable to the addressing of the considered pedagogical objectives. The term *activity in relation to the task* is here used to emphasize the fact that assimilating learners' activity to *achieving the task* or *using software* is misleading. The activity developed by learners in relation to the task is part of a more general activity system, involving activities of different levels and of different natures. As raised in Chap. 3, activities in relation to the task may be associated with different motivations such as responding to an explicit institutional demand or constraint (or to personal representations or beliefs about the demands or constraints), achieving the task, "playing the game" of the CBPS and/or software, exploring the software features, collaborating with peers or demonstrating one's qualities. The nature or focus of these motivations may also be reevaluated and change. They influence and are influenced by the more general activity system of which they are part.

Software, as such, is only one of the dimensions defining the modalities within which learners are confronted with the task, and is only a mediator of learners' activity. It is a proposition, which will be *perceived* by each learner in some way, who will transform it into something that makes sense to him/her and appropriate it to him/herself. These perception, transformation and appropriation processes are related to different features such as the concerned artifacts (the task, scenario or software properties and presentation), the general context (teaching setting, etc.), individual characteristics (representations, motivations, objectives, knowledge, experiences, etc.) or group phenomena, and to the way these features interact with each other (see for example notions such as affordances or instrumental genesis in Chap. 3).

In other words, how learners will perceive the prescriptions and the technological setting cannot be defined, but must be thought of as something that will dynamically emerge and evolve from the prescriptions (the CBPS and, more generally, the teaching setting), the educational software properties and presentation, and learners' activity itself.

Such an analysis leads one to consider *indirect design*[3] approaches, not focusing on the artifacts but on their usage or enaction. In some sense, at an abstract level,

---

[3] To explore the notion of indirect design in the context of CSCL see Jones, C., Dirckinck-Holmfeld L. & Lindström, B. (2006). A relational, indirect, meso-level approach to CSCL design in the next decade. *International Journal of Computer-Supported Collaborative Learning*, 1(1), 35–56.

CBPSs and educational software are not what designers have designed but what learners make of these propositions.

Such a view is consistent with iterative, participative or continued-in-usage design approaches. It requires articulation, within consistent cycles, of *a priori* analyses, technical implementation, usage and emergent phenomena analyses, and evaluation of outcomes. Traceability (see Sect. 2) is an important dimension. Technically, it requires robust prototypes allowing ecological experimentations, and suggests the introduction of flexibility and tailorability features allowing software to be adapted, in context, to the emergent effective activity.

5 Developing Knowledge

Knowledge related to educational software may be produced via an array of means, both theoretical and empirical, within disciplinary or multidisciplinary research work. As emphasized in Chap. 6, one of these is to capitalize knowledge in the context of particular projects, which may be conducted in both research and development projects.

There are some specific dimensions to a knowledge-production activity: (1) a precise definition of the considered issue (a problem for which a solution is necessary, a question, etc.), (2) a precise description of the proposed solution or result and (3) an evaluation process providing evidence or argumentation for this solution or result, as opposed to a simple belief.

Capitalizing knowledge requires being precise and, in particular, going further than surface analyses such as stating that an experiment or a piece of software is interesting. "Interesting" is not a scientific term: anybody may have a personal point of view and, as a matter of fact, everybody has a personal point of view on teaching or learning.[4] Something "interesting" may be more productively analyzed as an innovation from which one may get some inspiration (and stating what the innovation is, what makes a difference, etc.), as a lesson learned (and stating what the lesson is, when it may be applied or what evidence it relies on) or some other type of result.

5.1 Definition of Issues

5.1.1 Clarifying What Is Considered

The implication of acknowledging educational software engineering complexity is that problems cannot be broken down into a partition of independent sub-problems

---

[4]An issue in TEL is the noise created by simplifications, misconceptions and false ideas related to the fact that it may be addressed, and is often addressed, on the basis of uninformed idiosyncratic views, typically related to personal experiences or anecdotes.

(see Sect. 2). This does not mean that sub-problems cannot be identified, but that there is an additional issue related to their interactions.

Problems defined at a high level often denote rather general considerations, e.g., how to promote on-line collaboration. Such an abstract level leaves open many interpretations, and considerations may range from sharing resources on Web-platforms to cognitive processes: effective work, what may be considered as a result and how this may be evaluated can be very different. This issue is emphasized by the fact that there might be important differences between the matters of concern at the CBPS level and the implications at the software level. From a knowledge-capitalization perspective, an important requirement is to consider issues and results defined at the same abstraction level, using the same notions and/or notions whose connection (transposition, etc.) is made explicit. The characterization features introduced in Chap. 7 may support such a process.

5.1.2 Clarifying What the Difficulty Is

In particular because of the multidisciplinary character of the field (Chap. 3, Sect. 5), a non-trivial dimension is to describe precisely the difficulty of the considered problem and why it requires the elaboration of some new knowledge, going further than the general idea according to which TEL projects are difficult because they are multidisciplinary.

A variety of issues may appear to be difficult, for instance:

- Identifying and describing functions or properties the software should present, which may be difficult for different reasons such as the fact that the understanding of the CBPS or actors' activity, how to relate these elements to software properties or how supporting activity is to be thought of is difficult.
- Designing or implementing a given piece of software, for instance because it requires models, algorithms, techniques, interfaces (etc.) the elaboration of which is difficult.
- Evaluating software usage or impact.
- Elaborating or proposing a contribution to methodological elements (process, method, standard, etc.), e.g., design methodology for some type of software or CBPS, or processes related to evaluation, usage analysis or re-engineering.
- Elaborating or proposing a contribution to the elaboration of some reference framework (theory, conceptualization, model, etc.) which is descriptive, explicative and/or predictive of some phenomena related to educational software or CBPSs.

As a matter of fact, if one considers systems that are effectively designed, mixing research efforts and development projects, difficulties are often more related to the specification dimensions (i.e., understanding issues to be taken into account and their impact on specifications and design) than to the technical difficulties in implementing these specifications. This partly explains why research projects are little subject to direct technology transfers in industry or teaching institutions: often their underlying idea may easily be implemented (see for example evolution of networked learning environments). However, there are noticeable exceptions such as learners' modeling or interaction analysis issues.

5.2 Definition of Results

Work related to educational software design may lead to claims related to different dimensions such as:

- The artifact (software, CBPS) that has been designed, for instance the fact that software presents some properties.
- The actors' (learners' or teachers') software usage.
- The learners' activity (for instance the fact that they engage in some behavioral and/or cognitive processes) and its relation to the software properties.
- The learning-related phenomena (for instance the fact learners develop some domain knowledge or skills) and their relation to the software properties.
- Some CBPS-related phenomena (more generally), for instance the fact that learners (or teachers) open up their minds, develop some interest or some motivation, familiarize themselves with something (e.g., a type of setting, a type of task or a type of software), change their perception or change their way of acting; the development of social links; the development of a dynamic; etc.
- The satisfaction of the actors (learners, teachers, tutors, institutional representatives, etc.).
- The integration into practices, the development of communities of practice, the transformation of teaching settings, etc.
- The fact that a method, a model, a theory or a technology appears to be a base for, guides, allows or facilitates design of educational software, pedagogical-setting support software or CBPSs.
- Etc.

As TEL projects are usually iterative projects, and difficulties may appear or change during the project life, an *a posteriori* analysis of the relationships between the work undertaken and the obtained results may be interesting. This may lead one to consider, for example:

- The overall contribution of the work.
- The differences between the objectives and the results.
- The description of the various problems that emerged.
- The description of the various problems that are still to be addressed.
- The description of what was anticipated to be difficult and what was effectively difficult.
- The social, economical, scientific or institutional impact.
- Etc.

Produced knowledge may be both disciplinary (a psychological or educational lesson learned, a CS technique for controlling problem-solving processes or analyzing rough data, etc.) or transdisciplinary (how a given theory can be transposed and used powerfully to guide the design and implementation of a kind of CBPS, a model and pieces of software used to elaborate and manage learners' epistemic models, etc.).

5.3 Evaluation of Results

In relation to the type of result considered, the elements put forward as evidence to state that a proposition is a result may assume a variety of forms, for instance:

- Evidence of properties. For instance, given an objective formulated as a set of CS specifications (e.g., the fact that the software will produce x as an output if it is given y as an input, presents a specific interface or provides user-adaptation features), evaluation may consist of presenting a piece of code and how it corresponds to these objectives. This type of analysis may be based on different processes: formal proof, test, benchmark, description, etc.
- Empirical evaluation. For instance, given an objective formulated as a hypothesis (e.g., software property p_1 has impact i_1 on learners' activity), evaluation may consist of an empirical study based on experimentation methodologies (e.g., experimenting with different software versions presenting and not presenting p_1), which may be conducted according to quantitative and/or qualitative approaches.
- Argumentation. For instance, given an objective formulated as a phenomenon or a process to be understood (e.g., how users use some software or how a problem or an approach may be conceptualized), evaluation may consist of analyzing the proposal and the arguments *pro* and *con* related to how and why the analysis is adequate to denote and understand the considered objects or phenomena, its explicative or predictive character or its usefulness.

Evaluation dimensions often intersect. For instance, evaluation of issues related to long periods of time and large scales (e.g., integration of software into basic practices or adaptation to institutional structures) may require a combination of empirical evaluations and argumentations.

As mentioned in Chap. 6, Sect. 3.1, evaluation is addressed in very different ways according to disciplines, nature of results and context. Empirical evaluation as used in psychology (definition of the hypothesis, identification of the variables, construction of a setting that allows the targeted variable to be studied, experimentation with test groups and control groups, and statistical analysis) is rigorous and powerful. However, it may not be applicable in some contexts due to the complexity of the setting (multiplicity of variables and interrelations, ecological constraints, duration of the CBPS, external stakeholders, etc.). Other methods attempt to address such constraints, such as design-based research approaches. When considering software design processes or approaches, it is possible to argue about their respective advantages. However, whether one approach guides designers more efficiently than the other (or some other considerations such as whether it helps designers save time, requires less staff, is more reliable or leads to artifacts exhibiting better qualities) is unlikely to allow empirical evaluation given the number of variables and the context-dependent issues such as the actors involved in design, the skills and experience of these actors, the issues to be considered for the considered design or other external factors. Considering such issues, evidence is more likely to accrue via usage experiences and knowledge capitalization processes.

Chapter 9
Conclusions

Abstract This chapter provides an analysis of issues for the development of the TEL field, and considers how to push forward educational software engineering.

In the different chapters of this book, we have studied various issues related to educational software engineering, and introduced a certain number of conceptual means that may help to address these issues (they have been listed in Chaps. 1 and 6). Rather than a hazardous exploration of what future systems may be, we explore in this final chapter how educational software engineering (as a scientific area) may develop. First, in Sect. 1, we argue that technological evolution does not change the need to consider design issues, although what design refers to does evolve. In Sect. 2, we study why research-oriented work and knowledge capitalization have little impact on effectively used systems. In Sect. 3, we analyze how knowledge capitalization may be pushed forward, and the particular interest of focusing on *learners' activity*.

1 Educational Software Design and Evolution of Technologies

Educational software evolution is closely related to that of technologies, both in terms of the nature of the systems that may be considered and in terms of how software may be thought of.

Technological advances (basic algorithms, AI techniques, graphical simulation, network communications, mobile technologies, haptic interfaces, etc.) impact the nature of the systems and CBPSs that may be thought of, and implemented. They raise new possibilities and thus open new questions. For instance, mobile technologies create settings within which appear *intermittent interactions*; the dissemination of technology that may be used in different places and/or be interconnected synchronously or asynchronously allows reconsideration of issues such as the *articulation of formal/informal learning settings*, *expected/unexpected learning* or *implicit/explicit learning*, and how to support this; open settings raise the issue of *software flexibility* and/or tailorability; etc.

Technological advances also lead one to reconsider the very notion of software. We have highlighted in Chap. 1 that educational software may be addressed by designing and implementing new software (defining specifications and implementing them) or articulating software components to meet educational needs. Here again, this raises specific issues such as *interoperation of software components*, and how this may be addressed *at design time* and *on the fly*.

ICT is an example of technology that has dramatically changed the TEL field by changing both what may be thought of and what software design is. For a long period of time, using software for educational purposes required the development of new systems by computer scientists. Existing basic software was not very flexible, which made it frequently inadequate for pedagogical settings. Moreover, the emphasis was on software that played an important role within CBPSs (typically, ITS). Software Engineering developments such as building software on the basis of existing components have simplified complex software construction. However, this was an example of evolution. By contrast, ICT is a real change: it pushes forward possibilities (communication, resource sharing, collaboration, etc.) of particular interest for education; a large technological choice is available, part of which is freely available (platforms for sharing contents, communication tools, etc.); the technology is easy to use and to custom to specific settings or needs, and this customization often requires little CS, if any; practitioners (teachers, learning technologists) can easily implement ICT-based CBPSs and, in particular, innovative settings; innovation also stems from learners' new practices and demands, and teacher-learner synergies.

Such a revolution may lead one to question the very notion of educational software design, i.e., designing software *for* educational settings. It may lead one to consider that TEL is about using available technologies smartly and innovating.[1]

However, if one examines the ICT example, building on directly available technologies does not avoid design issues: it leads to a particular form of design, based on interpreting, analyzing, choosing, customizing and articulating software components according to the setting and to the considered educational objectives and constraints (see Chap. 1, Sect. 3). This does not change the nature of the central difficulty to be addressed, that of putting into relation pedagogical considerations and software properties. It only highlights the preeminence of this difficulty over the technical issues, and changes the level of granularity of the related concerns and processes (from both technical and cognitive points of view, defining specifications and then building artifacts is very different from selecting artifacts by "interpreting" their affordances with respect to needs and then adapting them).

---

[1] It may be noticed that another consequence of ICT is that, in many cases, the pattern of "running after the last emerging technology" (wikis, Web 2.0, etc.) remains unchanged, although who runs after the technology has changed: the fact that computer scientists were running after new technologies to build so-called innovative educational software is now often replaced (or completed) by educationalists making use of front-end technological innovations.

Similarly, thinking about services and articulations that may support the articulation of formal/informal learning settings or expected/unexpected learning is educational software design.

In other words, technological evolution does not change the need to consider the issues denoted by the "for" of "software designed for educational settings", although what design (and implementation) refers to does evolve.

It may also be noticed that viewing TEL as "what is allowed by using the available technology smartly" would mean, paradoxically, returning to a kind of technology-centered view, i.e., considering educational software as what may be built from existing technology rather than what is to be built to solve educational problems.[2] As a matter of fact, if one considers ICT, it only allows a limited type of software to be implemented and does not address many other types of systems including, in particular, ITS-like systems (i.e., systems that teach). More generally, advanced systems based on direct manipulations (simulation, microworlds, etc.) or enhancement features (e.g., CSCL software providing intelligent hints or tutoring) go beyond ICT's basic possibilities.

2 Lack of Knowledge Capitalization

TEL is a field for which there is very little knowledge capitalization. Although it is not a new field and, for instance, techno-centrism issues have been acknowledged for many decades, many things seem to be reconsidered at every new wave of technology (i.e., often), leading to more or less the same bunch of high expectations, disappointments and errors.

More generally, research work has rather limited impact on educational software usage in effective settings. Although some integrated-in-practices systems do originate from research-oriented work, they remain exceptions. This is consistent with the fact that, in many cases, difficulties are more conceptual than technical, lying in understanding what is to be done, and how, rather than in doing it.

However, it might be thought that, although few systems originate from research-oriented work, research results influence educational software engineering practices. Unfortunately, this is not much the case. Projects are rarely based on a theoretical background and, more surprisingly, rarely based on knowledge capitalized from in-lab or in-effective-settings projects.

Indeed, with respect to education, innovation in context and adaptation of ideas, systems or practices are key dimensions. Capitalizing (abstract) knowledge, however, is not in opposition to innovation.

---

[2]It may be noticed that, paradoxically, ICT gives a new dynamics to the perspective according to which emphasis should be on building a technological choice: it is more or less explicitly considered that, although such an approach did not lead to very positive results in the past, the fact that ICT is "naturally" useful for education, and technologies may be adapted or interoperated in different ways, now allows this approach to be productive.

The fact that, within a field that has a clear engineering dimension, a large proportion of basic development projects makes little reference to past work and existing knowledge is an issue. Not addressing this issue would mean acknowledging that educational software design should follow *generate-and-test* non-informed processes, i.e., considering some target CBPS, design and implement software that presents a functional response to the identified needs, test what happens and empirically adapt.

If one compares with other CS application fields (banking, medical care, transportation, etc.), TEL does not benefit from very large budgets. This is of course another part of the story. While keeping this in mind, we explore hereafter other reasons that may explain the small impact of research-oriented work and capitalization.

Difficulty of Evaluating Educational Software

Due to its socio-technical dimensions in particular, as soon as evaluation targets more than laboratory experiments (e.g., classrooms, on-line learning Universities or vocational training centers), evaluating educational software is an issue. Why educational software is used or not, and how, is related to a multiplicity of factors other than software properties (technologies' availability, involvement of teachers, goodness of fit with the setting, etc.). Another difficulty is that of time: adoption and use of software requires long periods.

One of the consequences of the difficulty of evaluation in basic settings is that of non-reduction of ambient noise: it leaves open a large space for efficiency to be addressed in terms of beliefs and argumentation rather than in terms of evidence. Similarly, pertinence is often addressed in terms of teachers' adoption of a system or a technology, which is an interesting dimension, but not the only interesting one. A multitude of ideas, principles, systems, approaches (etc.) are proposed and co-exist, in both scientific places and teaching settings, whose respective qualities are not clearly identified.

Non-necessary Multidisciplinary Character of Achievements

The fact that educational software projects should be addressed within multidisciplinary approaches has been emphasized in the literature for decades. However, this is technically not necessary and, as a matter of fact, is often not the case.

For instance, technically, a large part of ICT-based educational software does not need multidisciplinary work and does not require a particular expertise. Virtually anyone familiar with ICT may engage in the design and implementation of some educational software, on the basis of a more or less explicit and more or less meaningful idea of what teaching or learning consists of. Such processes may be conducted by teachers developing smart applications, companies selling their technical solutions (information system, workflow, etc.) on the educational market, and of course computer scientists (who will not be technically limited to ICT). And, because of the evaluation difficulty and the ambient noise, meaningless propositions are not necessarily detected.

This issue is emphasized by the fact that many studies address educational software usage and more generally TEL issues at a high level of abstraction, typically considering "software used in education" as a consistent notion, with poor consideration of software properties. Paradoxically, work related to design and to usage may coexist with little articulation, and this is what happens to a large extent.

High Volatility of the Field

Production of knowledge relative to TEL is related to the learning/technology/usage triptych. This triptych is rendered highly unstable due to the evolution of technologies and to how researchers and practitioners react to this evolution.

The fact that new technologies appear and that the pedagogical opportunities they may open are explored is not an issue. However, what is an issue is the fact that scientific mainstream studies move from one technology-focus to another, not taking enough time to explore issues in depth. This is an obstacle to maturation, addressing issues that require long periods of time (usage in effective settings, how teachers or institutions adapt to educational software considered as basic means, etc.), and knowledge capitalization.

There are notable counter-examples to this such as hypermedia, for which durable studies have been carried out, knowledge capitalized, and surprising results obtained (see for example controversies related to cognitive load; this domain also illustrates how anchoring design principles in a theoretical background and conducting both theoretical and empirical studies over long periods of time is a pertinent process for knowledge development).

Practices and Economy May Develop Independently from Research Advances

TEL is a field within which practices (see for example how teachers develop pedagogical applications of ICT) and economy (see for example commercial on-line learning platforms) may develop independently from advances in research and, *de facto*, do so. As a consequence, work issued by practitioners, researchers and industry coexist, which here again creates noise and contributes to the fact that, unlike other domains, interest in innovations is not really articulated with progress in research.

The point raised here is not that of quality. The fact that some educational software is developed independently of research does not say anything about its pedagogical usefulness: very satisfactory solutions are developed by teachers (within communities of practice in particular), satisfy their users' requirements and are conductive to changing practices. However, the fact that most software used in effective settings is not related to principles, lessons learned or evaluation processes is an issue for the scientific development of the field: when work is not articulated with some research perspective, it may be a useful example for other practitioners, but its contribution to knowledge capitalization is minimal. Noticing that projects are "interesting" is not sufficient.

Software Usage and Practice Developments Comply with Complex Dynamics

As in many other domains, educational usage of software and development of practices comply with complex dynamics. Factors at the origin of usage or influencing usage are diverse: trends, inertia, pressure of dominant usage, prescribers' institutional or commercial pressure, software availability or ease of use, freeness, etc. Software quality is only one of these factors, and not the main one.[3] Here again, this contributes to ambient noise.

3 Pushing Forward Educational Software Engineering

Various theoretical and applied research work may be conducted in relation to educational software, both disciplinary and X-disciplinary. In this section, we come back to the approach suggested in Chap. 6: addressing educational software engineering as a proper scientific area; considering capitalization of knowledge related to (1) how to think and analyze settings, issues, possible approaches, etc. (see Chap. 6, Sect. 2.3) and (2) in the context of precisely defined areas and associated considerations, how to support design processes (issues to be considered, alternatives, knowledge that may help one to develop some reasonable anticipation of the possible effects of design decisions, etc.; see Chap. 6, Sect. 2.4); using construction of systems as a means for developing knowledge and reusable constructions (models, software components, etc.).

---

[3]Although rather surprising with respect to other types of artifacts, it is quite often the case that some software applications are massively bought and used while reliable free alternatives exist.

3.1 Conditions for Capitalizing Knowledge

3.1.1 Addressing Precise Objects

Designing educational software leads to consideration of goals and of the means to address these goals. Informing design decisions requires one to address levels of detail where these issues are raised.

General considerations such as "software should be adaptable by teachers" or "end-users should be involved in design" are useful, but not sufficient. It is also necessary to address the level of software properties, e.g., that of the principles underlying interfaces, data flow, data analysis and interpretation, etc. – or, in functional terms, feedback capabilities or adaptation features.

Elaborating knowledge related to means and goals or considering how some given design decisions change something requires one to (1) define precisely what is considered (e.g., software usage or learning outcomes), (2) define what object is analyzed, evaluated or measured – analyzed will be used as a generic term (e.g., the effects of some software usage) and (3) define the modalities of the analysis (process, limits, validity, etc.). Not disentangling objects and considerations (which is not to be confused with breaking complex problems into separate problems) is an obstacle to knowledge capitalization. In Sect. 3.2, we review various possible options.

3.1.2 Considering the Generality Dimension

When considering design issues (approaches, processes, models, algorithms, etc.), degree of generality is an important concern, in particular within a perspective of knowledge capitalization.

First, considering the degree of generality of constructions improves the definition and applicability of results: it puts to the fore dimensions such as abstraction, invariants, validity scope, reuse or conditions for reuse. An interesting issue is, for instance, what clusters may be considered. While clustering may be based on types of systems (e.g., ITSs, microworlds, etc.), it may also be based on or consider matters of concern (e.g., how the activity notion is addressed).

Second, addressing issues related to generality helps one to identify established knowledge and issues to be addressed. It distinguishes topics for which some knowhow exists and may be capitalized in some way from the ones for which this is not the case, and considers the reason for this: lack of work, insufficient conceptualization of issues, impossibility of elaborating knowledge that would have a sufficiently general scope to be pertinent, etc.

When considering generality, a classic issue is that of over-generalizing the significance of a construction. Therefore, precise and careful definitions and characterizations of work and obtained results are of key importance.

The character of generality or of genericity[4] of a methodological process may be clarified by specifying:

- The application scope of the methodological process.
- The precise data and/or problems classes this process addresses.

The character of generality or of genericity of a model may be clarified by specifying:

- What the model models, and what it does not model.
- The data and/or problem classes that can be modeled with this model.
- How the fact that the model models in an adequate way what it is meant to model is hypothesized, established or checked.

The character of generality or genericity of a CS implementation may be clarified by specifying:

- The implemented mechanisms and the problem classes they consider.
- The context in which the generic mechanisms apply and the nature of the data or processes they manipulate or rely on.
- How this genericity is hypothesized, established or checked.

3.1.3 Developing Evaluation Means

Within the variety of reasons that may explain the lack of impact of research work on educational software dissemination (see Sect. 1), one of the issues, which underlies several of the others, is the fact that the added value of educational software and CBPS built on scientific knowledge is either insufficient or insufficiently demonstrated (and this demonstration disseminated).

As we have mentioned it, whether some software is used, or contributes to overall positive outcomes, depends on many dimensions. Nevertheless, this does not diminish the interest of studying -and, possibly, capitalizing knowledge related to- the impact of software properties (in the sense explained in the preceding chapters and not repeated here): studying if, how and why the fact that a system is replaced by another one, which presents other properties, changes the setting on some dimension of interest given the considered objectives (here again, disentangling issues and considering precise objects is mandatory).

Within this perspective, development of adequate evaluation processes is indeed one of the central issues of the field. Many projects face the following dilemma: on the one hand, following up "interesting" innovative ideas, implementing CBPSs

---

[4]*Genericity* refers here to the fact that a construction may be defined in an abstract way and, in context, instantiated with a given type of data or process. Generic constructions are abstract but precise, in particular when using parameterization. As an example, generic programming languages allow direct implementation of computable algorithms defined with respect to the abstract properties of data or processes. Similar examples may be found in meta-modeling techniques.

Table 9.1 Review of possible focuses

	Considered object	What is analyzed
Static dimensions	Educational software as a computer-based system	Innovative character and/or specific properties of the considered computer-based system as software
	CBPS definition	Whether the considered system's properties contribute to the definition of innovative CBPSs and/or CBPSs presenting specific characteristics related to these properties
Dynamic dimensions	CBPS unfolding	Impact of software properties relative to the way the CBPS unfolds
	Activity developed by learners	Impact of software properties relative to the activity developed by learners and/or dimensions underlying this activity
	Learning outcomes	Impact of software properties relative to the learning outcomes

that are obviously "exciting and of interest", interest in which may be formulated and characterized (see Chap. 7), but for which rigorous evaluation processes cannot be implemented. On the other hand, conducting work because evaluation processes exist or, in other words, not conducting some types of work due to the lack of existing applicable evaluation processes.[5]

3.2 Review of Possible Focuses

In Sect. 3.1, we have raised the importance of considering precise objects. In general, CBPSs' targeted objectives are learning outcomes (or indirectly relate to learning outcomes, see Chap. 1). However, this level is often difficult to articulate with software properties in a way that allows knowledge capitalization. We may thus need to consider some other objects. Table 9.1 lists different options. Putting to the fore one or another object leads to different perspectives.

3.2.1 Educational Software as a Computer-Based System

A computer-based system, as such, can be described by the features it provides and its properties. It is thus possible to consider *educational software as a computer-based system* and consider whether the system represents a potential *innovation* and/or presents some *improved properties*, and if so, why.

---

[5]This idea is illustrated by the classic joke of the guy who has lost his keys on the road but is looking for them in the garden because "this is where the light is".

Analyzing innovation (e.g., a new type of system or innovative interfaces' affordances) requires putting to the fore what now exists that did not previously, or what is now possible that was not before.

Analyzing improvements requires comparison with preexisting systems or software components. Advances may be related to various features: algorithm efficiency (we have already illustrated this by the example of algorithms to categorize learners' messages, which may be compared using benchmarking), interface usability, etc.

3.2.2 CBPS Definition

Educational software's core dimension is not the specifics of the computer-based system, but rather that of the CBPSs it allows to be implemented. One may thus consider the *definition of the CBPSs*, and the contribution of the considered software to the *innovative character* or the *specific characteristics* of the defined CBPSs.

Software properties (interfaces, data flow, diagnosis or feedback capabilities, etc.) may allow innovative CBPSs to be defined, the innovation being related to the fact that the system is itself innovative and/or that it presents some particular properties. Software properties may also change some dimension of the setting such as the way tasks are presented to learners, the roles of the different actors, the support provided to learners and teachers or elements of context, and/or impact on the interplay of these features.

Analyzing innovation or differences requires a precise description of the system properties and of the CBPS characteristics related to software, which gives particular importance to the conceptualization and description of these dimensions (see Chap. 7).

3.2.3 The Way the CBPS Unfolds, Learners' Activity and Learning Outcomes

The fact that learners are presented with some CBPS and associated software does not define the use they will make of this provision, and what the outputs of this usage will be. As stated in Chap. 8, CBPSs and educational software design processes may thus be viewed within indirect design processes: the designed artifacts may be analyzed as such but, *in fine*, the important dimension is what happens during the learning session.

What may be considered is thus the *CBPS unfolding*, and the role or impact of software properties relative to the way the CBPS unfolds or, in other words, the way software contributes (and how, and why) to the fact that the setting unfolds differently from if the software properties were different. This difference may be observed via qualitative analyses of a limited number of cases and/or quantitative analyses. As stated previously, considering the software influence does not implicitly suggest that this dimension is independent of others.

When considering CBPS unfolding, a variety of dimensions may be considered: engagement of actors and motivation, duration of sequences, appearance of breakdowns, tasks considered by the actors, actors' satisfaction, particular usage of software (...) and, in particular, *learners' activity* and *learning outcomes*.

Learners' activity may be regarded in different ways and/or at different levels of granularity (see Chap. 2, Sect. 1.3). As examples: the fact that learners consider some issues, involve themselves in some tasks (e.g., problem solving), practice some skills or cognitive activities (e.g., elaborate hypotheses, refine an inheritance relation, synthesize or argue). What may be analyzed is not only learners' activity but also related issues such as the conceptualization underlying the way learners address some tasks.

Considered learning outcomes may be of different natures: understanding of a notion, conceptualization, improvement of some skill, transfer of acquired knowledge from one context to another, etc. A variety of evaluation methods have been elaborated and documented in the education and psychology literatures.

When considering dynamic dimensions, the description of the system's properties and the CBPS's characteristics related to software must be complemented by a precise description of the expectations and objectives, and the underlying considerations or hypotheses. It is thus of particular importance that descriptions and analyses are conducted within consistent conceptualizations or theoretical backgrounds, and at consistent levels of granularities. This gives particular importance to the development of characterizing means (see Chap. 7) and to the traceability dimension, i.e., maintaining a correspondence between models and artifacts that allows one to interpret the influence of software on the way settings unfold (see Chap. 8, Sect. 2).

Another important dimension is the acknowledgement of the consequences of the fact that TEL is to a large extent an experimental field. One of these is the importance of evaluating design decisions in the context of effective settings, and not only in laboratory experiments. Another is that what is considered may evolve during research. For instance, designing educational software for some given CBPS rarely consists of considering the CBPS as fully defined and fixed. Tests and experiments often allow a better understanding of what happens, what phenomena are at stake, or how issues interact with each another, which often leads to a refinement of the CBPS definitions and/or what unfolding should be targeted. This gives some importance to the description and maintenance of the historical dimension of projects (see Chap. 7, Sect. 2.8 and Chap. 8, Sect. 5).

The fact that objectives may be refined during work may appear to be questionable, but is intrinsic to the complex and experimental nature of the field. Clarifying what is considered, how and why it is addressed (etc.) is not to be done once and for all, but is permanently questioned. For example this is central in design-based research methods which "simultaneously pursue the goals of developing effective learning environments and using such environments as natural laboratories to study learning and teaching".[6]

3.3 Analysis of the Different Perspectives

Describing and characterizing educational software as a computer-based system is useful in general and, in particular, at intermediate stages of a wider project. It may be sufficient when the objective is to improve some precise aspect of software that has already demonstrated its interest for implementing some CBPSs. As a matter of fact, if there are a lot of innovation proposals, there is very little benchmarking of precise properties, i.e., within a given CBPS and teaching setting, testing different design hypotheses. Indeed, if benchmarking is generally not easy to implement in TEL, because of the complexity of the involved features, it is possible when comparing systems' properties. At this level, as already mentioned, the high volatility of the field is an issue.

Focusing on the CBPS definition (as opposed to its effective unfolding) may allow analysis or comparison of work with respect to what it presents learners (or teachers) with. This, however, is arguably less interesting than software description as CBPSs are much more complex artifacts, and focusing on this dimension is prone to lead to some rather adventurous claims related to the unfolding.

Considering whether the learning outcome objectives have been addressed (when such objectives are defined) is the natural evaluation level for TEL in general. However, it is not necessarily the best one for investigating the dimension of educational software design. First, as mentioned in Chaps. 1 and 2, educational software design does not necessarily target learning objectives. For instance, if software is designed to create positive conditions as a basis on which teachers may build (create interest, destabilize misconceptions, etc.), what is to be considered is whether design has succeeded in achieving these goals. Whether targeting the creation of these conditions was a productive strategy or the CBPS unfolding allows the expected learning outcomes to be achieved is another question. Second, with respect to learning outcomes, both the impact of software properties and the various setting features may themselves be impacted by other dimensions, diminished or made contingent by some other CBPS features or teaching setting dimensions.

Consideration of *the activity developed by learners* is arguably a more productive focus. A variety of arguments may be highlighted:

- Learners' activity is at the core of learning processes.
- Focusing on this dimension is consistent with consideration of educational software as an artifact mediating activity (see Chap. 8).

---

[6]Sandoval, W.A., & Bell, P. (2004). Design-based research methods for studying learning in context: introduction. *Educational Psychologist*, 39(4), 199–201.

- This level is less subject to indirection than learning, which is related to learners' activity, but may also be impacted by other dimensions.
- Activity may be analyzed at different levels, which allows one to address different types of settings and/or at different levels of granularity.

Focusing on how the activity developed by learners is influenced by software is particularly interesting when existing work has already demonstrated links between activity and learning. As an example already emphasized in Chap. 2, Sect. 3.1, the objective of making learners develop interactions such as explanation, argumentation or conflict resolution has its rationale in work that has shown the relation between this type of interactions and learning. The impact of (for instance) a particular design of communication tools or the way collaborative problem-solving is supported may thus be studied with respect to learning outcomes but, also, with respect to the fact that learners actually engage in such interactions, which may be less difficult to measure and less subject to biases. For instance, if the considered object is "the nature of learners' interactions", tools such as *Argue-chat* (the graphical argumentation chat tool) or *Colab-solver* (the collaborative problem-solving environment) may be evaluated by examining features such as the number of argumentative exchanges or the perception developed by learners of the argumentative nature of their peers' messages. In this case, benchmarking is made easier, and results may be capitalized and inform design decisions.

Here again, let us recall that disentangling issues is this way does not suggest avoiding the issues related to their consistency and interactions. Studying, on the one hand, how software may impact some precise dimensions of learners' activity and, on the other hand, the relationships between learners' activity and learning outcomes, is a means to advance on some issues, but does not exhaust the subject.

3.4 Conclusions

From a general point of view, research-oriented work related to educational software engineering may:

1. Produce innovation, i.e., software that allows implementation of CBPSs that could not be envisaged before. The pedagogical interest of the innovation must, however, be analyzed.
2. Elaborate results (concepts, models, knowledge, algorithms, processes, methods, pieces of software, etc.) that allow design and implementation of educational software for which it is possible to show that it has (within the context of some given CBPSs, and in relation to other elements) a positive impact relative to some pedagogical objectives.

Using engineering as a means to develop knowledge and push forward the field requires different issues to be addressed and, in particular:

1. Elaboration of sharable conceptualizations favoring a common understanding of dimensions and issues at stake, the articulation of research actions and knowledge capitalization.
2. Elaboration of processes allowing measurements of software's and CBPSs' impacts on the development of learners' activity and/or learning outcomes (evaluation methodological dimensions).
3. Analysis of how such work may best be implemented (organization of research).

To measure advancement, in addition to the elaboration of new knowledge (research dimension) and to the socio-economic impact (for instance, via the dissemination of systems or the elaboration of engineering handbooks), a classic evaluation criterion is: has some teachable knowledge been elaborated?

Index

A
Activity, 7, 14, 32, 35, 36, 39, 41, 58, 66, 69, 71, 73, 158, 174, 176
Activity framework, 145, 159
Activity theory, 73
Affordance, 12, 73
Anthropological perspective, 70
Argue-chat, 13, 14, 19, 87

B
Basic software, 4
Behavioral activity, 36
Bio-sim, 12, 15, 17, 19, 35, 36, 46, 71, 90
Biology inquiry learning CBPS, 9, 12, 71

C
Characterization grid, 123
Cognitive activity, 36, 69
Colab-edit, 16, 17, 19, 88
Colab-solver, 94
Communication tool, 42
Complexity, 24, 112, 126, 152
Computer science, 3, 99, 118
Computer science research, 103, 109, 118, 119
Computer scientist, 2, 103
Computer-based pedagogical settings (CBPSs)
    definition, 5, 40, 55
    example, 8, 60, 155
Computer-supported collaborative learning (CSCL), 13, 16, 42, 49, 50, 52, 60, 67, 87, 88, 94, 101, 116, 154, 177
Conception, 58, 61, 69, 92
Conceptualization, 3, 24, 31

D
Design continued in usage, 25, 137, 160
Design-based research, 128, 163, 175

Development project, 1
Diagnostic, 69
Didactics, 58
Drill and practice, 43

E
Education/computer science interplay, 2, 15, 17, 106, 121
Educational software
    definition, 1, 4, 41, 55
    design, 1, 15, 18, 165
    example, 11, 41, 83, 143
    implementation, 1
Educational software engineering, vii, 112, 119, 153, 165, 170
Educationalist, 2
Engineering, 111
Engineering methodology, 115
Environment (software environment), 59
Epistemic milieu, 59, 63, 89, 147, 157, 159
Evaluation, 49, 118, 163, 168, 172
Explicitation
    definition, 23
    difficulty, 23
    example, 19, 60, 143, 155
    interest, 22
    means, 123

F
Feedback, 69

G
GeLMS, 12, 13, 43, 144
Genericity, 172
Geo-world, 95

H

Human and social sciences, 2
Hypermedia learning environments, 41

I

Impact (of a system), 7, 18, 65, 77, 89, 117, 174
Indirect design, 158, 174
Informal learning, 5, 44, 165, 167
Inquiry learning, 9, 12, 15, 37, 45, 90, 116
Instrument, instrumentation, instrumentalization, 73
Intelligent tutoring system (ITS), 7, 11, 41, 67, 69, 91, 101, 105, 146
Interdisciplinarity, 76
Iterative design, 75, 137

J

Java programming CBPS, 9, 11, 33, 53
JavIT, 11, 19, 33, 34, 69, 91, 146

K

Knowledge capitalization, vi, 22, 53, 69, 167, 171, 173, 178

L

Learning management system (LMS), 7, 12, 14, 34, 43, 63, 66, 75, 83, 144
Learning objective, 48
Learning theories forum CBPS, 10, 16, 46

M

Microworld, 41, 95
Misconception, 58, 61, 69, 92
Mobile learning, 42
Model, modeling, 101, 107, 113, 119, 152, 172
Multidisciplinarity, 76, 78, 161, 168

N

Networked learning, 7, 10

O

On-line learning platform, 42

P

Participative design, 75, 137, 160
Pedagogical objective, 6, 37, 48

Pedagogical setting
 definition, 32
 design, 39
Pedagogical-setting support software, 45, 84, 93
Phys-edit, 86
Presentation program, 40

R

Recommendation software, 41, 45
Research project, 1

S

Scen-play, 93
Scenario, 39, 49
Scenario player, 93
Sciences of the artificial, 112
Simulation, 10, 12, 41, 90, 95, 116, 156
Socio-technical dimensions, 7, 18, 67, 112, 121, 168
Software as a service, 43
Software pedagogical rationale (SPR)
 addressing, 52, 139, 155
 definition, 45
 example, 45, 60, 83, 143, 155

T

Tailorability, 35, 120, 160, 166
Task, 35
Task/activity duality, 35, 37, 74
Teacher, 6
Teaching setting, 6, 33
Techno-centrism, 104, 167
Technology enhanced learning (TEL), 2, 47
TEL CS actors' specific skills, 109, 121
Traceability, 109, 113, 154, 160, 175
Transdisciplinarity, 76, 78, 79, 103, 109, 112–114, 121, 122, 163

U

User-centered design, 75, 137

V

Virtual reality pedagogical environment, 41